Government Guarantees

Government Guarantees
Allocating and Valuing Risk in Privately Financed Infrastructure Projects

Timothy C. Irwin

THE WORLD BANK
Washington, D.C.

©2007 The International Bank for Reconstruction and Development/The World Bank
1818 H Street NW
Washington, DC 20433
Telephone: 202-473-1000
Internet: www.worldbank.org
E-mail: feedback@worldbank.org

This volume is a product of the staff of the International Bank for Reconstruction and Development/The World Bank. The findings, interpretations, and conclusions expressed in this volume do not necessarily reflect the views of the Executive Directors of The World Bank or the governments they represent.

The World Bank does not guarantee the accuracy of the data included in this work. The boundaries, colors, denominations, and other information shown on any map in this work do not imply any judgement on the part of The World Bank concerning the legal status of any territory or the endorsement or acceptance of such boundaries.

DOI: 10.1596/978-0-8213-6858-9

Library of Congress Cataloging-in-Publication Data

Irwin, Timothy.
    Government guarantees: allocating and valuing risk in privately financed infrastructure projects/ Timothy C. Irwin.
        p. cm.— (Directions in development)
Includes bibliographical references and index.
ISBN-13: 978-0-8213-6858-9
ISBN-10: 0-8213-6858-3
ISBN-10: 0-8213-6859-1 (electronic)
    1. Infrastructure (Economics)—Management. 2. Risk management. 3. Public-private sector cooperation. I. Title.

HC79.C3177 2007
363.6068'1—dc22

                                                                    2006039472

Contents

Figures

Tables

Preface

Many governments want private firms to finance new infrastructure. The firms, in turn, often want the government to bear some of the risks. They might ask the government to compensate them if demand falls short of forecasts or to promise to repay their debts if they become insolvent. At the very least, they probably want the government to allow them to charge a certain price or else compensate them accordingly.

This book aims to help governments respond to such requests. As well as seeking to make precise the oft-invoked principle that risks should be allocated to those best placed to manage them, it explains how governments can value the guarantees they are thinking of granting and how they can modify aspects of public-sector management to improve the likely quality of their decisions about guarantees.

Although intended mainly for governments and those who advise them, this book may be of interest to others, since the problems of allocating and valuing exposure to risk are not specific to governments. For similar reasons, although the focus of this book is physical infrastructure, it may be of interest to people working on public-private partnerships in education, health care, and other social services.

Acknowledgments

The book has benefited from comments and other assistance from many people, including Glenn Boyle, Hana Brixi, Penelope Brook, Jeff Delmon, David Ehrhardt, Antonio Estache, Mary Fisk, Tony Gómez-Ibáñez, David Hawes, Monika Kosior, José Luis Irigoyen, John Irwin, Ellis Juan, Laszlo Lovei, Marvin Phaup, Bengt Pramborg, Hossein Razavi, Chris Shugart, Thaisa Tiglao and Alan Townsend. The author owes an indirect debt to many other colleagues in LECG, the International Monetary Fund, the World Bank, and the New Zealand Treasury and to officials in many countries, including Chile, Hungary, Indonesia, the Republic of Korea, Mexico, Poland, South Africa, Thailand, and Uruguay.

CHAPTER 1

Overview

The use of government guarantees[1] to help persuade private investors to finance new infrastructure is appealing because it can allow the government to get the infrastructure built without paying anything immediately and to benefit from the skill and enterprise of private firms. But it can cause problems.

In the 1990s, for example, the government of the Republic of Korea guaranteed 90 percent of a 20-year forecast of revenue for a privately financed road linking Seoul to a new airport at Incheon. The government didn't have to pay anything up front and would get to keep any revenue exceeding 110 percent of the forecast. When the road opened in 2000, however, traffic revenue turned out to be less than half the forecast. As a result, the government has had to pay tens of millions

---

1 *Guarantee* can refer to an agreement to pay another person's debt if that person fails to do so or to ensure the performance of some other obligation by another person. In this sense, a guarantee (or *guaranty or suretyship guarantee*) is always a secondary obligation (Goode 2004; O'Donovan and Phillips 2003). But the term is also used in a broader sense, to refer to something that assures a particular outcome. For our purposes, government guarantees may, but need not, be guarantees in the narrow sense; they may instead take the legal form of an indemnity, insurance policy, financial option, or other undertaking. For our purposes, they are agreements by which the government bears some or all of the downside risks of a project, other than as a shareholder, creditor, customer, or taxer of the project.

of dollars every year. How much it will have to pay over the life of the guarantee is uncertain; as a present value, it may be about $1.5 billion (Irwin 2004).

The government's guarantee may not have been wrong, but it does raise questions. Should the government really have borne demand risk in the project? Could it have estimated the cost of its guarantee before granting the guarantee? If so, should it have disclosed an estimate of the cost in its accounts? More generally, could the government have built the road more cheaply using public finance? Or would it have been better to use private finance without a revenue guarantee, if necessary giving the firm a straightforward subsidy?

These questions are hard to answer even though governments have been using guarantees to help finance infrastructure since the early 19th century. Argentina, for example, guaranteed railway investors returns of 6 or 7 percent on the capital they invested.[2] The guarantees helped Argentina attract investment from foreign capital markets and reflected a view that Argentina had to compete for such funds by offering incentives like those offered by other countries. Yet the government didn't always have enough money to meet its commitments, in part because of the difficulty of accurately budgeting for claims and in part because the government usually had to make larger payments just when its tax revenue was low. In time, the guarantees contributed to a fiscal crisis that may sound familiar:

> As the principal official obligation, railway guarantees . . . were largely responsible for the crisis of confidence which brought the whole fragile edifice of the Argentine economic miracle to ruin. . . . Many of the companies formed during this period were committed to long-term dependence upon the guarantee. Indeed . . . it might be argued that many were projected merely for the purpose of obtaining a guarantee. (Colin Lewis 1983, 86)

Guarantees do not always cause such problems. The Chilean government has given many revenue guarantees and a few exchange-rate guarantees to privately financed toll roads. The revenue guarantees typically ensure that the concessionaire gets revenue equal to 70 percent of the estimated present value of its costs, including the costs of investment, operations, and maintenance; the guaranteed revenue might be spread over 20 years, providing as much as 85 percent of forecast revenue in early years and less later on. So far, the government has

---

2 Argentina's 19th-century guarantees are discussed by Colin Lewis (1983) and Winthrop Wright (1974).

attracted a great deal of investment without having to pay much because of these guarantees.

Even in Chile, however, the guarantees raise questions. A recession would cause traffic to grow more slowly than expected, possibly triggering many guarantees just when tax revenue was weak. How serious is this risk? How can the government measure it? What is the value of the government's outstanding liability? And should the government be planning now for the possibility of future payments?

The questions raised by guarantees are most pressing in developing countries but are not unique to them. To take just one example, the state of New South Wales in Australia gave a revenue guarantee in the early 1990s to the Sydney Harbour Tunnel, a project developed as an alternative to the Sydney Harbour Bridge. Toll revenue was expected to be too low to cover the tunnel's costs, but by the terms of an "ensured revenue agreement," the government contracted to give the tunnel company a specified amount, less tolls on the tunnel. Thus, the government, not the company, bore demand risk. The auditor-general concluded that the project was more public than private and that, for accounting purposes, the tunnel and associated liabilities were the government's. It qualified its audit of the financial statements of the government agency promoting the road and argued that the agency had chosen nominally private but effectively public finance partly as a way of circumventing a cap on public borrowing (Government of New South Wales, Australia, Auditor-General's Office 1994).

It is difficult for governments to make good decisions about guarantees. To start with, there is no agreement among advisers about which risks governments should bear in privately financed projects. Should they bear demand risk in toll-road projects? Should they give exchange-rate guarantees when investors borrow in foreign currencies? Or should they shield investors from exchange-rate risk by increasing the price of the service when the local currency depreciates? Should they protect creditors from losses in the event that the project is terminated? Should they compensate investors for changes in government policy? All changes? Some changes but not others? No changes? Opinions on these subjects are plentiful, but there is no consensus.

The difficulty of knowing how best to allocate risks is compounded by other problems. First, politics can encourage governments to bear more risk than is in the public interest. Governments are buffeted on all sides by proposals for subsidies, but unless the beneficiaries are widely regarded as deserving, the most transparent of such proposals tend to fail. Successful proposals tend to have opaque costs and to come with a rationale explaining how they are good for the country and don't merely redistribute value. Proposals for guarantees can meet these criteria, especially when the government's accounting and budgeting fail to recognize their costs. They come with plausible rationales about risk sharing, and taxpayers are unlikely to understand the costs.

Second, government decisions would be difficult even in the absence of political pressures. Psychological research shows that people struggle to make accurate judgments about risks and then fail to make the best use of even their imperfect judgments. Most people, for example, are overconfident in their judgments and therefore think the world is more predictable than it is. Government decision makers may fall into the same trap, underestimating the risks to which they are exposing the public when they issue guarantees. They may also make decisions about guarantees that are irrational given their judgments. Research shows that people can switch from being risk averse to being risk seeking just because the framing of a choice changes. They can also be irrationally risk averse when they consider risks one by one, instead of thinking of their total portfolio of assets and liabilities. Sensitized to the risks created by government guarantees by stories such as those of Korea and 19th-century Argentina, governments may be needlessly timid about taking risks that are small in the scheme of things.

In sum, governments can easily make poor decisions about guarantees. There is no simple solution to this problem, but good decisions are more likely if three conditions are met:

1. The government's advisers and decision makers have a framework for judging when a guarantee is likely to be justified.
2. The government's advisers know how to estimate the cost of a guarantee.
3. The government's decision makers follow rules that encourage careful consideration of a guarantee's costs and benefits.

Helping governments fulfill these three conditions is the aim of this book.

Allocation

To judge when governments should bear risk, we need a framework for deciding the more general question of how risk should be allocated. And to set out such a framework, we need to clarify what we mean by risk.

As we will use the term, *risk* is unpredictable variation in value. It includes the possibility of unexpectedly good, as well as unexpectedly bad, outcomes. The *risk of a project* is unpredictable variation in the total value of the project, taking account not only of the value of the project company but also of the value accruing to customers, the government, and other stakeholders. A *stakeholder's risk* in a project is unpredictable variation in the value of the stakeholder's interest in the project.

Particular risks can also be defined. *Demand risk* is unpredictable variation in value arising from unpredictable variation in demand. *Construction-cost risk* is unpredictable variation in value arising from unpredictable variation in construction costs. Thus, we use *risk* to refer both to the total risk of the project and to the components of such risk. We describe the sources of risk as *risk factors*.

How should risks be allocated? The conventional answer is that each risk should be allocated to the party best able to manage it. The answer looks right, but it is too vague to be very helpful by itself. The following principle tries to clarify it: each risk should be allocated, along with rights to make related decisions, so as to maximize total project value, taking account of each party's ability to

1. Influence the corresponding risk factor.
2. Influence the sensitivity of total project value to the corresponding risk factor—for example, by anticipating or responding to the risk factor.
3. Absorb the risk.

The principle refers to three ways in which a risk can be managed. First, there are times when someone can influence the risk factor—that is, can take action to improve or worsen the risky outcome. For example, a construction company can change construction costs by its choice of materials and techniques and by the way it pays and manages its workers. If no one else can manage construction-cost risk, the principle says that the risk should be allocated to the construction company. Such an allocation doesn't eliminate the risk; the construction company's profits are uncertain. But compared with other allocations, it will tend to lower the cost of construction and increase the total value of the project.

Second, there are times when someone can influence the sensitivity of the value of the project to the risk factor. For example, no one can influence whether an earthquake occurs, but by carefully choosing the site of a project, the firm or the government may be able to reduce the loss that an earthquake would cause. If the risk is thus anticipated, the value of the project is made less sensitive to the risk factor. Someone may also be able to respond to variation in a risk factor. A firm may be able to switch between inputs as their relative price changes, mitigating downside risk in the price of one input and exploiting upside risk in the price of the other. The principle says that, other things being equal, the party that can best anticipate or respond to the risk factor should bear the risk.

Third, there are times when no one can influence, anticipate, or respond to a risk factor in a way that changes the project's value. At such times, the risk should be allocated to the party that can absorb the risk most easily or, in other words, bear the immutable risk at the lowest cost. Customers, for example, may be able to absorb the risk of inflation in the price of a service because their incomes increase with inflation. The firm or the government may be able to absorb a risk because it can buy derivatives or insurance to protect it from the risk. And the shareholders who ultimately bear risk allocated to the firm may be able to absorb a risk simply because they have well-diversified portfolios.

Applying the principle of risk allocation to a particular government's decision to bear a particular risk in a particular project can be hard. The details of the government, the risk, and the project matter. Thus, trying to give definitive general advice on whether governments should bear particular risks is futile. Without trying to be definitive, however, subsequent chapters argue that governments should be inclined to bear project-specific risks that they control or strongly influence, such as risks related to prices and quality standards that they set. One way governments can do so is to contract with the firm to set prices or quality standards in a particular way and hence assume an obligation to compensate the firm if they change their mind. Governments sometimes strongly influence other risk factors, such as the demand for a road when that demand depends heavily on the construction of competing and complementary roads in a government-planned network. In such a case, it may make sense for the government to bear demand risk—by giving a revenue guarantee, by financing the road itself, or by promising payments independent of demand to a company financing an untolled road.

The subsequent chapters also argue that governments should be disinclined to bear exchange-rate and other economywide risks. Although governments can often influence such risks, they shouldn't usually shape economywide policy to suit the interests of a particular project. Moreover, although the firm and its creditors cannot influence economywide risk factors, they can often influence the sensitivity of the project's value to the risk factor. Their choice of the extent of borrowing in foreign currency, for example, influences how sensitive the value of the project is to the exchange rate. For similar reasons, governments shouldn't usually bear the risk of the firm's insolvency by giving unconditional guarantees of the firm's debt.

The principle also says that the risks a government should bear depend on the way it allocates rights to make related decisions. The more rights it devolves, the more risk it can reasonably transfer. Conversely, the rights a government should retain depend on the risks it chooses to bear. If a government offers an exchange-rate guarantee, for example, it should not give the firm the right to choose how much to borrow in foreign currency.

Valuation

An understanding of when guarantees are justified won't ensure good decisions. Politics and psychology will still get in the way. To buttress the benefits of understanding, governments can estimate the cost of the guarantees they are thinking of giving—or, to use a different expression, can value those guarantees. Valuation allows policy makers to supplement their own susceptible intuition with quantitative estimates, thereby reducing the temptation to bear risk when it is unlikely to increase total project value.

Although some of the details of valuation are technical, the main ideas are simple. The first step is to identify the risks the government is thinking of bearing. What are the government's financial rights and financial obligations in the project? And what are the risk factors (demand, construction costs, and so on) that will determine how much the government receives or pays as a result of those rights and obligations?

Given a model of those risk factors, the next step is to measure the government's exposure to risk—that is, to answer questions such as these: What is the most the government might lose? How much can it expect to lose? And what is the chance of its making certain large losses? To take a simple example, suppose the government tosses a coin four times and offers to pay the firm $1 every time the coin lands head up. The most it could lose is $4. The amount it can expect to lose—what it would lose on average if it played the game many times—is $2. And the probability of its losing, say, $4 is 1 in 16 ($1/2 \times 1/2 \times 1/2 \times 1/2$).

The third step is to estimate the cost of bearing the risk. To do that, one must adjust the expected payment to take account of time and risk. Adjusting for the timing of payments is the easier of the two tasks. A payment made in the future is less costly than a payment made now, so the future payment needs to be discounted at an interest rate reflecting the time value of money (the *riskless rate of interest*).

Adjusting for the risk of payments is harder, and dodging the problem is often justified in practice. But most guarantees are worth more than their expected value discounted at the riskless rate of interest. So a government that ignores the cost of bearing risk will issue too many guarantees. Fortunately, there are methods widely used in financial markets that can often generate a reasonable estimate of the cost of bearing risk.

Rules

Improvements in decisions about guarantees can be sought case by case; with better knowledge of the principles of risk allocation and the ability to value exposure to risk, governments can try to make better decisions in each case they encounter. Improvements can also be sought, however, in the rules that govern case-by-case decisions. In particular, governments can change those rules to try to ensure that decision makers have access to relevant information and have incentives to act in the public interest.

Accounting standards are crucial. Cash accounting encourages governments to ignore the costs of decisions that generate no immediate cash expenditures or revenues. Modern accrual accounting standards, however, require the immediate recognition of at least some obligations to make payments later. The best standards require recognition of the obligations created by some guarantees. And when modern accrual accounting standards don't require the recognition of an obligation, they often require the disclosure of relevant information in notes to the accounts.

Budget rules are also crucial. Good budget rules require governments to examine spending proposals simultaneously and therefore confront the tradeoffs inherent in them. Decisions about exposure to risk should be made in the same way. Budgets should give approval to incur noncash costs, as well as to disburse cash, and a dollar's cost incurred by guarantee should count as a dollar spent in cash. Budgeting with good accounting helps, but even the best accounting standards disregard the cost of some forms of exposure to risk, and most governments are still some way from reporting to the best standards.

Thus, stopgap measures that force the counting of guarantees may help. Some governments have used special funds to make up for weak accounting and to help manage the cash-flow risks of guarantees. When a ministry issues a guarantee, the government can require it to contribute the estimated cost of the guarantee to the special fund. The fund can then be used to meet—or to contribute toward—payments if the guarantee is called.

Governments can also change rules to enlist the help of outsiders. Laws requiring the disclosure of contracts and other documents—routinely or after requests made under freedom-of-information laws—give members of the public the opportunity to comment on and criticize the government's decisions. Irritating as it may be for governments, the possibility of external criticism probably improves the average decision. Governments can also require that some guarantees be issued only for a price—a device that, among other things, means that the recipient of the guarantee is part of the group deciding whether the guarantee will be issued, which may reduce the chance of a guarantee's being granted when its costs exceed its benefits.

These ideas are developed in the chapters that follow. Chapter 4 sets out a framework for allocating risks and, therefore, for deciding when to grant guarantees, using demand risk as an example. Chapter 5 applies the framework to three other risks: exchange-rate risk, insolvency risk, and policy risk. Chapter 6 develops the argument for changing higher-level rules to improve case-by-case decisions. Then, chapter 7, using demand risk as an example, sets out a framework for measuring and valuing exposure to risks, including those created by guarantees. Chapter 8 applies the framework to exchange-rate risk, insolvency risk, and policy risk. We start, however, by reviewing the history of government guarantees (chapter 2) and the cognitive and political obstacles that stand in the way of good decisions about their use (chapter 3).

Lessons of History

Government guarantees are old, and modern governments can draw several lessons from the experiences of their predecessors. One is that a government wanting to avoid giving guarantees should be prepared to give up some control over investment decisions—accepting, for example, that investments be made later than the government would like. If the government insists on control, it may have to give guarantees or finance the investments itself and thus bear risks in a different way. Other lessons are relevant to a government that has decided to give guarantees. Chief among them are that the government should

- Ensure that its guarantees preserve investors' incentives to manage risks they can best manage.
- Check that what it guarantees is what it wants.
- Manage the risks it assumes by giving guarantees.

Before elaborating on these lessons, we review the history of government guarantees.

Early Guarantees

The code of Hammurabi, written nearly 4,000 years ago, contains what may be the earliest evidence of a government guarantee in the sense used here: it specified that the a community should compensate the victims of unsolved thefts within its territory.[1] Government guarantees also appear in ancient Rome. A treaty made by Rome and Carthage around 509 or 508 BC provided for guarantees not unlike those the governments of emerging markets sometimes give today to foreign investors selling to local utilities: "Men coming [from Rome] to trade may conclude no business except in the presence of a herald or town-clerk, and the price of whatever is sold in the presence of such shall be secured to the vendor by the [Carthaginian] state, if the sale take place in Libya or Sardinia" (Polybius 1922, 55 and 57).

According to Livy, Rome used private finance with a government guarantee in 215 BC to supply troops in Spain at war with Carthage.[2] The army needed grain and clothes, but the government had no money, and the prospects for new taxes were bleak. The government thus sought bids from private contractors on the understanding that they "would be the first to be paid when there was money in the treasury." Three companies bid, but all required the government to bear the risks of enemy attacks and bad weather. The government agreed, and "state business was conducted with private funding." Livy at first approves of the arrangement: "The scrupulousness with which the contracts were fulfilled matched the magnanimity with which they were taken on, and the soldiers were as well provisioned in every respect as if their support came from a well-stocked Treasury." Later in the book he seems to change his mind:

> Because, in the case of goods shipped to the troops, risks from violent storms were assumed by the State, these two [contractors] had invented stories of shipwrecks, and even the real ones that they had reported had been due not to accident, but to their dishonesty. They would put small quantities of goods of little worth on old ships in poor repair. They would then sink the ships on the open seas, picking up the crews in boats kept ready for the purpose, and falsely report the cargoes

---

1 See laws 22 and 23 of the code, which is available online at many sites, and Morgan (1927, 154).

2 Livy (2006, 192–93). Suetonius (1914, section 18), another Roman historian, writes that Claudius, emperor from 41 to 54 AD, provided a similar guarantee: "He resorted to every possible means to bring grain to Rome, even in the winter season. To the merchants he held out the certainty of profit by assuming the expense of any loss that they might suffer from storms." See also Bezançon (2004) on "2,000 years of public-private partnerships."

to have been many times more valuable than they really were (Livy 2006, 255).

The Bridge of Bordeaux

In the early 19th century, there emerge the kinds of guarantees that are the focus of this book. One of the first was granted in France, when, in 1817, the government was turning its attention from a long series of wars to matters such as transport infrastructure. Among its first steps was to grant a concession to complete the bridge of Bordeaux.[3] The government would build and maintain the bridge; the concessionaire would clean it, light it at night, and, crucially, pay FF 2 million for the construction. In return, it got the right to tolls for 99 years. If annual revenue fell below FF 190,000, however, the government would make up half the shortfall, and if revenue exceeded FF 250,000, the government would get half the surplus.

The success of this concession and revenue guarantee inspired other proposals. At about the same time, Louis Becquey, the director-general of the bureau of bridges, roads, and mines, was urging the government to carry out an ambitious program of canal building (Geiger 1994). Becquey favored private enterprise but thought that government support of some form would be necessary to get at least some of the canals built. He noted in particular that "the precise estimation of toll revenue, whose real value can be known only long after the works are finished, presents one of the greatest difficulties in the negotiation of temporary or perpetual concessions"[4] and viewed the revenue guarantee used in the bridge of Bordeaux as a solution to this problem. As we shall see, however, his proposal to use this kind of guarantee proved unsuccessful.

U.S. Canals

The use of government guarantees for canals is reported in the United States at about the same time. In 1819, Pennsylvania guaranteed a 6 percent dividend to shareholders in the Union Canal Company, which wanted to connect Middletown on the Susquehanna to Reading on the Schuylkill.[5] Work on the canal had begun in 1792, but soon faltered. Then, in 1811,

---

3 See Reverdy (2004) and the "Loi qui autorise l'acceptation de l'offre faite par plusieurs négocians et capitalistes de prêter deux millions pour l'achèvement du pont de Bordeaux".

4 Becquey (1820, 12), my translation. See also Geiger (1994, 134).

5 See An Act Supplementary to an Act, Entitled "An Act to Incorporate the Union Canal Company of Pennsylvania," dated March 29, 1819.

a new company was established to take up the work, and the Pennsylvania legislature helped the company raise money by giving it a monopoly on lotteries in the state. Still no progress was made, and in January 1819, the company petitioned the legislature for direct investment (which was common in U.S. states at the time).[6] The legislature declined but authorized the company to issue more stock to the public. This attempt, too, failed—until, in March, the state agreed to guarantee the payment of the dividend, using the lottery proceeds to provide the necessary money. The guarantee worked. Construction began in 1821, and the canal was opened in 1827.

Early Railway Guarantees

The first railway guarantees seem to have been granted in the United States. As early as 1833, for example, Maryland authorized the Baltimore and Susquehanna Railroad to borrow $350,000 and "in order to enable the said . . . company, to negotiate said loan upon the most favorable terms" agreed to guarantee the payment of up to 5 percent interest for 40 years.[7] Thus began a tradition of debt guarantees for U.S. railways that continues today.[8]

Perhaps the first European guarantee was issued in 1838 by King William I of the Netherlands for a railway from Amsterdam to Arnhem (Veenendaal 1995, 189). Frustrated by the Dutch parliament's refusal to authorize public spending on the railway, the king personally guaranteed the borrowing of the investors who agreed to build the railway. The first European *government* to offer a guarantee to railway investors was that of Poland, then under the control of Russia. In 1838, it guaranteed dividends at a rate of 4 percent on a railway from Warsaw to the Austro-Hungarian border—a decision ratified by Tsar Nicholas I in 1839 (Haywood 1969, 195–97; Westwood 1964, 25). (Guaranteed actual returns could be higher than guaranteed nominal returns because the guaranteed securities might be sold below par.)

Diffusion of Railway Guarantees

France had contemplated railway guarantees as early as 1837 but gave its first guarantee in 1840. The guarantee, of a return of 4 percent, was

---

6 U.S. states had been supporting private infrastructure companies for many years. Holbrook (1947, 45) notes that, "since 1787, it had been the policy of Virginia to encourage transportation by subscribing to the stock of canal, turnpike, and toll-bridge concerns."

7 Section 2 of "A Further Supplement to an Act to Incorporate the Baltimore and Susquehanna Rail Road Company" passed March 14, 1833.

8 Today, the Federal Railroad Administration offers debt guarantees under a program of railroad rehabilitation and improvement (http://www.fra.dot.gov/us/content/177).

designed to ensure the completion of the Paris-Orléans railway, which was in trouble because of an "orgy of speculation," "corrupt practices," and an economic downturn (Doukas 1945, 20).[9] France's decision seems to have been influential,[10] and as governments sought to accelerate the building of railways, guarantees spread throughout the world. One can find mention of their use in such European countries as Austria-Hungary, Germany, Italy, Portugal, Spain, and Sweden; in French colonies such as Haiti, Indo-China, and Tunisia; in Brazil and former Spanish colonies such as Argentina, Peru, Uruguay, and Venezuela; in British colonies such as Australia, Canada, India, New Zealand, South Africa, and Sri Lanka; and in other countries that, though not colonized, were influenced by Western practice, such as Japan, Persia, and the Ottoman Empire.[11] In countries such as Australia and New Zealand, guarantees were the exception. In others, such as Argentina, Canada, and India, they were the rule.

The Popularity of Guarantees

Why were government guarantees so popular? In part, it was the high value accorded to new transport infrastructure. In France, Becquey argued that canals would slow the deterioration of roads, reduce transport costs, and speed economic growth, which would, in turn, bolster the government's revenues, foster private initiative, and help develop

---

9 See "Loi relative aux chemins de fer de Paris à Orléans . . .," (Duvergier 1840, vol. 40, 265–81). See also Thévenez with Manesse (1909, 8).

10 On the influence of French guarantees, see Haywood (1969, 196); MacPherson (1955, 180); Thorner (1977 [1950], 55); and Westwood (1964, 39).

11 See Birmingham (2003, 139) on Portugal; Dunlavy (1994) on Germany; Faith (1990, 74–75) on Austria-Hungary and Sweden; and Ville (1990, 134–38) on Italy and Spain. See Staley (1935, 132, 281, and 336) on Haiti, Indo-China, and Tunisia. See Summerhill (1998) on Brazil; W. Wright (1974) on Argentina; http://www.perutren.org/english/fcc-en.html on Peru; Burton (1994, 123) on Uruguay; and Staley (1935, 131) on Venezuela. For Australia, see Australian Heritage Commission (2003, chapter 5) and the Government of Tasmania's 1870 Act to Amend "The Main Line of Railway Act"; for Canada, see the 1849 Act to Provide for Affording the Guarantee of the Province to the Bonds of Rail-Way Companies on Certain Terms and Conditions and A. Currie (1957, chapter 1); for India, see Thorner (1977 [1950]); for New Zealand, see the District Railways Act of 1877 and Leitch (1972, 138–39); for South Africa, see Burton (1994, 191, 201); and for Sri Lanka, see Burton (1994, 166) and Thorner (1977 [1950], 125). For Persia, see Staley (1935, 127); for Japan, see Ericson (1996); and for the Ottoman Empire, see Karkar (1972). In most cases, what the author describes as a guarantee is clearly a guarantee in the sense used here. In some cases, what the author describes as a guarantee might be something else, such as an agreement by the government to pay a certain sum independent of the railway's returns.

capital markets (Geiger 1984, 331–32). In Canada, the first article of the Railway Guarantee Act of 1849 asserted that "the means of rapid and easy communication by Rail-way, between the chief centres of population and trade in any country and the more remote parts thereof, are become not merely advantageous, but essential to its advancement and prosperity." Better transport links could also aid politicians' plans to build nation-states and allow the quicker mobilization of troops in war.

There was also a widely held belief that canals and railways should be built with private money, partly on the grounds that private enterprise was more efficient and partly on the grounds that governments could not afford the cost. Thus, most governments turned to private investors. Yet in the absence of guarantees or other forms of aid, private investors often held back.

Investors' reluctance might have led officials and politicians to revise their estimate of the value of canals and railways. Instead, it caused them to advance arguments for government support that are remarkably similar to those heard today. Some politicians pointed to the insufficient development of local capital markets. The just-quoted first article of Canada's guarantee act, for example, goes on to refer to the scarcity of capital in "new" countries. (Laws against usury and the absence of an automatic limitation of shareholders' liability may also have impeded the raising of capital.) Other politicians argued that the public benefits of new transport links exceeded the benefits accruing to users and investors, so there would be too little investment in the absence of government support. Here is a U.S. congressman revealing, in 1818, a firm grasp of the ideas discussed today under the headings of externalities and transaction costs:

> [T]he aggregate benefit resulting to the whole society, from a public improvement [such as a road or a canal] may be such as to amply justify the investment of capital in its execution, and yet that benefit may be so distributed among different and distant persons as that they can never be got to act in concert. . . . I think it very possible that the capitalist, who should invest his money, in one of those objects, might not be reimbursed three per cent annually upon it. And yet society, in various forms, might actually reap fifteen or twenty per cent. The benefit resulting from a turnpike road, made by private associations, is divided between the capitalist who receives his tolls, the lands through which it passes, and which are augmented in their value, and the commodities whose value is

enhanced by the diminished expense of transportation. A combination . . .
of all these interests, to effect the improvement, is impracticable. And if
you await the arrival of the period when the tolls alone can produce a
competent dividend, it is evident that you will have to suspend its
execution until long after the general interests of society would have
authorized it.[12]

The argument for aid was stronger still when governments wanted
railways for military or nation-building reasons, since private investors
would take little account of these. When guarantees became widespread,
their proponents were also able to argue that they were necessary to
attract capital in a competitive global market (see Colin Lewis 1983, 11;
Thorner 1977 [1950], 125).

When politicians wavered in their support, railway promoters were
quick to lobby them and sometimes to bribe them.[13] In some cases, the
promoters had the press on their side. The *Times* of London, for example, complained of the "tedious caution" of the Indian government's initial
guarantee policy (Thorner 1977 [1950], 127), and the editor of the
Economist was instrumental in securing the guarantees (Thorner 1977
[1950], chapter 6).

Guarantees were of course controversial. In the Netherlands, they
were opposed because they made managers "less interested in economi-
cal management" (Veenendaal 1995, 191). In India, officials feared that
allocating risks to the government would distort investment decisions: it
was "not the wish or the interest of the Government to encourage any
project of this nature which does not hold out a fair prospect of moderate
profit without being dependent on the Government for its dividends"
(Thorner 1977 [1950], 88). And not everyone accepted the idea that
one country's guarantees justified another's. When shipping magnate
William Mackinnon sought a guarantee of £30,000 to £40,000 a year
from the British government for the Uganda Railway, the chancellor of the
exchequer responded, "You argue that the large subsidies given to foreign companies by foreign governments justify, or even require, the
British government to proceed on the same basis, but this is an argument
which has never been accepted, as far as I know, by any administration
on commercial or economic grounds" (Munro 1987, 228–29).

---

12 The *Annals of Congress*, 15th Congress, 1817–19, p. 1377.
13 Thorner (1977 [1950]) gives a detailed account of efforts of the promoters of Indian
   railways. Faith (1990), Westwood (1964), and W. Wright (1974) discuss bribes.

Yet the arguments for guarantees very often prevailed. The remainder of the first article of Canada's guarantee act seems to sum up the conclusion of many governments:

> [T]he assistance of the Government is necessary and may be safely afforded to the construction of lines of Rail-way of considerable extent; and ... such assistance is best given by extending to Companies engaged in constructing railways of a certain length, under Charter from, and consequently with the approval of the Legislature, the benefit of the guarantee of the Government ...

Most of the arguments for guarantees were arguments for government support in general, not for guarantees in particular. And, as well as guaranteeing revenues and returns, governments did lend money, buy shares, grant land, and subsidize construction. Ongoing, performance-based subsidies were often given to shipping companies and occasionally given to railways.[14] Just why governments chose guarantees when they did is not always clear.

The exposition accompanying France's first railway-guarantee law, however, explicitly compares the merits of loans, equity investments, lump-sum subsidies, and minimum-return guarantees (Duvergier 1840, vol. 40, 266–68). It notes that lump-sum subsidies expose the government to none of a railway's risk, and it says they are appropriate for small projects with predictable profits, but not for large projects with unpredictable profits. By comparison, guarantees offer just enough money to ensure the profitability of a railway, without running the risk of being unnecessarily generous. Guarantees also have the critical advantage of requiring no immediate expenditure. The exposition does refer to possible disadvantages of guarantees, including their tendency to encourage railways irrespective of public benefits and their effect on the government's ability to borrow. But it ultimately, if unconvincingly, dismisses objections to guarantees as unserious or vanishing on deeper examination (Duvergier 1840, vol. 40, 268). Discussion of the hypothesis that the guaranteed railway may return just 2 percent a year is prefaced with the words *par impossible*.

Often, it seems, decisions to give guarantees reflected the "dominance of pragmatism" (Fogel 1960, 39): transport infrastructure was valuable, it

---

14 In India, "20-year subsidies, but not guarantees, were granted to the Indian Branch Railway Company" in 1862 (Westwood 1974, 29). The French government gave a subsidy to a railway in Ethiopia (Staley 1935, 279).

needed government support, and whichever form of support was easiest to provide in the circumstances would do. If a government had little money at hand and no land to give away, it was likely to choose guarantees. The French government's discussion of its first railway guarantee perhaps expressed the approach of many. The law offered "no absolute solution": the government had wanted a "law of transaction, not of principle" (Duvergier 1840, vol. 40, 263, 268).

If You Insist on Something, Prepare to Bear the Risks

Determining whether guarantees were worth their costs is, given the number of confounding factors, perhaps impossible. Certainly, they were expensive. In India, the government eventually spent about £50 million on guarantee calls, compared with total British investment of some £150 million (Kerr 1995, 17–18). In Argentina, Russia, and several U.S. states, guarantee costs contributed to fiscal crises (Goodrich 1974 [1960]; Colin Lewis 1983; Westwood 1964). Yet guarantees also accelerated the building of enormously valuable infrastructure.

Though many studies have estimated the net contribution of railways to economic development, few consider whether guarantees were good policy. One partial exception is William Summerhill's work on Brazil, a country in which, after the failure of early efforts to encourage investment in railways, both the central and provincial governments offered guarantees.[15] Summerhill estimates the private and social profitability of six guaranteed railways and concludes that all six "generated large gains to the economy" and that at least some would have been privately unprofitable without guarantees (Summerhill 1998, 543). Thus, private finance with guarantees may have been better than purely private finance. Although careful and sophisticated, Summerhill's study doesn't consider whether guarantees were more efficient than other possible government interventions. Would Brazil have done better to use public finance, for example, or to offer private investors an annual or a per-passenger subsidy?

Even if we cannot discern from the historical evidence whether guarantees were good policy, we can draw lessons about their use and design. The most general of these lessons is that governments wanting to avoid

---

15 See Summerhill (1998, 2003). The first Brazilian railway to be constructed with a guarantee received a 7 percent guarantee, of which 5 percent came from the central government and 2 percent from the province of Rio de Janeiro (Summerhill 1998, 547). See also Fogel (1960) on guarantees for railways in the United States.

guarantees should be prepared to undertake the investments themselves (and thus bear risk in a different way) or to relinquish control of investment decisions. The lesson is well illustrated by the experience of France, where governments sought private finance for canals and railways but wanted to control the developments—a wish consistent with the French elite's belief in the value of a strong central government (Dobbin 1994).

French Canals

Becquey's initial plan for canals, financed with the help of only a partial revenue guarantee, attracted little interest from investors (Geiger 1994, chapter 5). Convinced of the need for a network of centrally planned canals, Becquey concluded that more generous government support was warranted. "Since the fear that capitalists experience of being mistaken in evaluating probable revenues is the principle cause of their withdrawal from enterprises of this nature," he wrote, "it is appropriate to reassure them on this matter by sheltering them from all risks" (Geiger 1994, 134).

And the government did indeed shelter them from all downside revenue risk and most other risks besides. It entered into contracts with special-purpose canal companies under which the companies lent the government money that was repaid using toll revenue.[16] If toll revenue was insufficient, however, the government had to make up the difference from its budget. Apart from the risk of the government not paying, the canal companies' only risk was on the upside: once the loans were repaid, the companies shared in the profits. Although the companies had a veto over changes in tolls, they didn't construct or operate the canals. The government's desire for control over investments thus led it to bear most of the risks of the investments—in an arrangement that might be described as essentially public finance, or as private finance with especially generous government guarantees.[17]

French Railways

The French government also sought private finance for railways and again insisted on control (and thus avoided the duplicate lines and mismatched gauges of Great Britain and the United States). Again, the

---

16 See, for example, the Loi relative à l'achèvement du canal Monsieur, which is reproduced in Duvergier (1821, vol. 23, 332–35). See also Geiger (1994).

17 The sharing of upside risk with investors meant the arrangement was not identical to public finance. Lenders' forecasts of future revenue may have influenced the interest rates they demanded and, hence, possibly which canals were built.

result was generous guarantees.[18] Recall that the government gave its first (4 percent) guarantee in 1840. In 1859, an economic crisis encouraged it to generalize the system of guarantees. It divided each of the major companies into an old network of lines that were operating or under construction by 1857 and a new network of lines that were planned but not yet under construction. And it guaranteed investors a return of 4.65 percent on the new network. Then, after another economic crisis in 1882, the government abolished the distinction between the old and new networks and guaranteed both a return of 5.75 percent. It further agreed that outstanding debts would bear no interest and that repayments would be reinvested in the companies as part of the government's contribution to the cost of new construction. It also introduced a sort of construction-cost guarantee: previously, the government had paid a lump-sum subsidy for construction costs, but the companies had paid the actual costs and, therefore, borne construction-cost risk; now the companies would pay a fixed amount for construction per kilometer, and the government would pay the actual costs and so bear the risk. Finally, the guarantee was extended from interest on bonds to dividends on shares as well. Increasingly generous guarantees seemed to be the price the government paid for ensuring the development of railways according to its plan and timetable.

Spanish Roads
A more recent example illustrates the consequences of insisting on control in a narrower domain. During the 1960s and early 1970s, the Spanish government gave exchange-rate guarantees to privately financed toll roads—at a cost by 1990 of Ptas 342 billion (Gómez-Ibáñez and Meyer 1993, 132). As Gómez-Ibáñez and Meyer (1993, 126) explain, the government's decision was a natural consequence of its desire to control the currency in which the firms borrowed:

> The Spanish government had required the early concessions to finance a large part of their costs from foreign debt in order to ease Spain's balance-of-payments problems and to avoid drawing away domestic savings from other projects. The 1972 law [on toll road concessions] set standards that at least 45 percent of construction costs be financed from foreign loans, at least 10 percent from equity, and no more than 45 percent from domestic loans. The early Spanish [highway] companies had trouble raising funds

---

18 For details, see Doukas (1945) and Thévenez with Manesse (1909).

from foreign capital markets, however, and in return the government agreed to guarantee some of these loans and to protect the companies from exchange rate fluctuations. The 1972 law specified that the government would guarantee up to 75 percent of the foreign loans; moreover, all foreign loans would be denominated in pesetas with the government assuming the full exchange rate risk.

British Exceptionialism

One notable exception to the rule of guarantees was Great Britain, the only European country where railway "finance came entirely from private sources" (Ville 1990, 131). The reasons for Great Britain's exceptionalism may be many. Its wealth and population density may have made the private benefits of railways larger than elsewhere. It may have had more entrepreneurs and a deeper capital market. Yet a difference in the government's desire for control also seems to have played a part—a difference that may have stemmed from a more general difference in view of the British elite about the appropriate role of government. If the 19th-century French elite stressed the importance of the central government, the British elite emphasized the central political role of individual landowners and the correspondingly limited role of the government.[19] When railways came on the scene, the government was thus more inclined to leave planning and development to investors, and it could more easily resist any pressure to guarantee returns.

Whether Great Britain's approach was better than France's is unclear. But it offers an example of how to avoid guarantees (or risk bearing in publicly financed projects): namely, to be willing to allow private investors to control investment decisions.

Try Not to Guarantee Risks Investors Can Manage

There are also lessons to be drawn for the design of guarantees. In particular, governments often got into trouble by guaranteeing risks that investors were better placed to manage. Instead of guaranteeing particular risks, governments typically guaranteed total *returns*. Investors benefiting from

---

19 See Dobbin (1994), who also discusses the intermediate case of the United States, where many of the elite were wary of federal government action but sympathetic to guarantees and other aid given by competing city and state governments—at least until concerns about losses and corruption led to a "revulsion" against government support and many states amended their constitutions to prohibit or restrict it (see also Goodrich 1950). That many British colonies gave guarantees suggests that differences in ideology were not conclusive.

guarantees therefore had little to gain by pressing managers to cut costs or boost revenues (that is, to influence cost and revenue risks). When most of a firm's investors benefited from guarantees, managers had little reason to manage the risks.[20]

Indian and Argentine Railways

In India, guarantees often ensured an attractive rate of return on most of the capital invested in a railway that had little prospect of earning more than the guaranteed return.[21] Investors in such railways had scant reason to trouble managers for lower costs or greater revenues. As the Indian finance minister said in 1872, "All the money came from the English capitalist, and so long as he was guaranteed 5 per cent on the revenues of India, it was immaterial to him whether the funds that he lent were thrown into the Hooghly or converted into brick and mortar" (Thorner 1977 [1950], 180). Or as an English investor said, "I care nothing about the line or what is done with the money . . . only that it is spent to secure 5 per cent to the shareholders" (MacPherson 1955, 181). In practice, it seems the companies did build railways at greater cost than necessary.[22]

Argentina, too, gave generous guarantees to railway investors, and those investors often relied on payments from the government rather than profits from the railways.[23] As a result, managers had weak incentives to cut costs or increase revenues. Recognizing the problem in the late 1870s, President Nicolás Avellaneda "refused to continue paying guarantees to companies that did not check their expenditures" (W. Wright 1974, 44). But the problems did not cease. A decade later, President Miguel Juárez warned that the government would withdraw its guarantee

---

20 Eichengreen (1996) emphasizes this problem.
21 See Thorner 1977 [1950], who describes the guarantee thus: "After deducting costs of operating, maintaining, and repairing the railway, and for establishing a 'reserve fund,' the remaining net receipts were to be used first for meeting the *current* 5 per cent interest charges (and thus 'to exonerate' the East India Company, if possible, from paying such interest). If any residue still remained, it was to be divided as follows: one-half was to go to the East India Company for repayment of any guaranteed interest it might have advanced in *previous* years; the other half was to go to the railway." (170–71; italics in the original)
22 Strong evidence is hard to come by, but see J. Johnson (1963, 11–13); Walker (1969, 112); and Westwood (1974, 26).
23 See Colin Lewis (1983) and W. Wright (1974). Argentina's first guarantee, in 1862, was for the Central Argentine Railway from Rosario to Córdoba. Its investors were guaranteed 7 percent a year on capital invested in the company up to £6,400 a mile. Subsequent guarantees had the same form.

from companies unless they "strained every nerve to increase traffic and earnings" (W. Wright 1974, 72). Some of the disputes between the government and the railways arose because the railways failed to comply with their contractual obligations; others may have reflected the government's attempt to escape its obligations. But the central problem, in India as in Argentina, was that the guarantees discouraged firms from managing risks they could have managed.

Guaranteeing Revenue Instead of Returns: Modern Toll-Road Guarantees

Many modern guarantees look better by comparison. Such guarantees, which are more often for toll roads than for railways, often protect investors only from revenue risk, something over which a toll road may have little influence. The Republic of Korea, for example, offers to guarantee infrastructure firms specified fractions of their forecast revenue.[24] Many other governments have given similar guarantees.[25] Whether or not revenue guarantees are good policy, they do have the advantage of preserving investors' interest in costs.

Modern revenue guarantees have many variants. Sometimes, for example, governments agree to extend the length of the concession if revenue falls short of expectations, an arrangement that reduces the

---

24 For the first five years of a solicited project, the fraction is 90 percent of forecast revenue; in the second five years, 80 percent; and in the third five years, 70 percent. In return, the government demands that it receive any revenue greater than 110, 120, and 130 percent of the forecast in, respectively, the first, second, and third five-year periods of the project. For unsolicited projects, the thresholds are 10 percentage points further away from the forecast; for example, in the first five years, the government guarantees 80 percent of the forecast and gets any revenue above 120 percent. In either case, the government pays nothing if revenue is less than 50 percent of the forecast. This last rule may be a response to the large losses on the Incheon highway mentioned in chapter 1. See Hahm (2003).

25 Other countries to have given revenue guarantees to toll roads are Chile (Gómez Lobo and Hinojosa 2000); Colombia (Christopher Lewis and Mody 1997); the Dominican Republic (Guasch 2004); Malaysia (Fishbein and Babbar 1996); South Africa (Government of South Africa, National Treasury 2002); and Spain (Gómez-Ibáñez and Meyer 1993, chapter 8, including 137 and n. 55). Revenue guarantees have also been used for airports in Chile and Colombia (Gómez Lobo and Hinojosa 2000; Juan 1996). Korea has guaranteed the revenue of a railway linking Incheon airport to Seoul (Project Finance Magazine 2004). And in Côte d'Ivoire, the private water company was at one point "guaranteed compensation if the amount of water actually consumed was less than forecast" (Kerf and others 1998, box 6.3, 97). Revenue guarantees are not unique to infrastructure: the United States, for example, gives farmers revenue guarantees for the sale of crops (Yin and Turvey 2003).

concessionaire's exposure to revenue risk.[26] If tolls will cease when the concession ends, this arrangement passes demand risks to future customers; if the government will maintain tolls, the arrangement is a form of government guarantee—though with much-delayed costs.

Ensuring There Are Unguaranteed Investors

The problems of Argentina and India were worse because the guarantees protected the majority of investors. If only a small fraction of investors had been protected, firms would have had stronger incentives to increase profits. Canada's Guarantee Act of 1849, which provided for guarantees of 6 percent interest on the debt of any railway half built and at least 75 miles long, was not an exceptionally prudent law.[27] Indeed, the act seemed to encourage railways to nowhere. (One guaranteed Canadian railway from a later era apparently ran initially "from nowhere to nowhere, neither passing through any major city nor interchanging with any other railway.")[28] But the act contained one important qualification: it effectively limited the guarantee to half the cost of the railway, thus ensuring that investors responsible for half the cost retained an interest in monitoring management.

Likewise, some modern revenue guarantees aim to keep some investors exposed to revenue risk. Mexico and South Africa have offered toll-road revenue guarantees under which payments are made only if debt-service payments are threatened, thus leaving equity investors exposed to revenue risk. Chilean revenue guarantees are intended to be

---

26 See Engel, Fischer, and Galetovic (1997, 2001). There are other variants as well. Two of Chile's early toll-road guarantees, for example, were of traffic rather than revenue. A public enterprise rather than the government may give the guarantee: Eurotunnel's revenue was guaranteed by the state-owned Société Nationale de Chemins de fer Français and the then-state-owned British Rail (Pratley and Pons 2004). Revenue guarantees are usually given to private firms, but Uruguay guaranteed the revenue of a state-owned firm with a "megaconcession" for a group of roads; this guarantee was higher than expected revenue, so the government bore most revenue risk (World Bank 2005). In Puerto Rico, the government agreed "to buy back the [San José lagoon toll bridge] at the concessionaire's request if traffic fell short of 80 percent of projections during the first three years and 100 percent of projections after nine years. In the event of a buy back, the government would reimburse the concessionaire for all project costs and pay it a 13 percent return on its investment" (Engel, Fischer, and Galetovic 1997, 93).

27 Before long, the Canadian government's British bankers worried that the unlimited scope of the guarantee was jeopardizing the government's credit and persuaded the government to restrict it to railways likely to form part of a trunk line (A. Currie 1957, chapter 1).

28 See the Wikipedia entry on the Pacific Great Eastern Railway in British Columbia at http://en.wikipedia.org/wiki/BC_Rail.

far enough below expected revenue to ensure that equity investors have a substantial stake in revenue.

Paying Only Some of the Losses

An alternative to ensuring the presence of unguaranteed investors is to expose even the guaranteed investors to some of the risks. Many 19th-century guarantees ensured that investors had an interest in returns *above* the threshold of the guarantee, even if there was some sharing of profits. Some guarantees also set a lower threshold below which investors were exposed to risk. Some of the Argentine, French, and Indian guarantees stipulated that the government would never pay more than the "guaranteed" return; for example, if the government guaranteed 5 percent on $100, it would never pay more than $5 a year. That meant that investors had an interest in costs and revenues if returns would have been negative in the absence of the guarantee.[29]

Better still are policies that give investors an interest in costs and revenues over the entire range of possible outcomes. Korea, to take a modern example, gives exchange-rate guarantees as well as revenue guarantees, but investors are required to bear all exchange losses up to a threshold and half the losses beyond that amount. Investors cannot influence the exchange rate, of course, but they can anticipate the risk in choosing the currency in which they borrow. In South Africa, there is a revenue guarantee that likewise compensates for only half of any revenue shortfall.

Making Loans, Not Grants

Another technique that preserves some of the guaranteed firm's incentive to manage risks partially assumed by the government is to make government payments under the guarantee loans to the firm, not grants. Many of the 19th-century railway guarantees, including those in Argentina, France, and India, had this form. More recently, Hungary and Mexico have offered toll-road firms subordinated loans to be disbursed when a firm's revenue falls below a threshold (European Commission 2004; Government of Mexico, Secretaría de Comunicaciones y Transportes and Banco Nacional de Obras y Servicios Públicos 2003).

None of these four techniques is foolproof; all leave the firm's investors less concerned about risks than they would be in the absence of the guarantee. And some may not work perfectly in practice. Canada's stipulation

---

29 For Argentina, see Colin Lewis (1983, 99); for France, see the 1840 railway law, section 2 reproduced in Duvergier (1841, 270); for India, see Westwood (1974, 13).

that it would guarantee returns on no more than half the cost of a railway may have been undermined by inflated estimates of cost; the effectiveness of making loans, not grants, may have been undermined by the expectation that loans would be forgiven—as they often were.[30] But each technique does something to preserve investors' incentives to manage risk.

Be Careful That What You Guarantee Is What You Want

When governments gave guarantees, they often got what they guaranteed. But what they guaranteed wasn't always what they wanted.

If Guarantees Are Not Performance Based

Sometimes the flaws in guarantee design must have been recognized at the time. In Russia, some guaranteed companies could collect guarantee payments even before they had opened their lines (Westwood 1964, 67–68). Likewise, in 1881, the Japanese government guaranteed investors an 8 percent rate of return on the Tokyo-Sendai-Aomori railway, to be paid "on subscribed capital while each section of the railroad was under construction" (Ericson 1996, 111). Investors with such guarantees could clearly afford to take things easy.

More often, governments were careful to pay only when services were provided. The New Zealand District Railways Act 1877, to take just one example, promised 7 percent interest to private railway investors but stipulated that payments could be made only when the railway was open for traffic. Moreover, to ensure local demand for the line, 5 percent had to come from a special tax levied on and approved by local taxpayers. (Such safeguards weren't enough to avoid problems. One of the lines thus financed was the Waimea Plains Railway, which opened in 1880. When the railway ran into financial trouble, local taxpayers refused to pay taxes for the guarantee, and the government refused to honor the guarantee. The company then refused to run further trains. In 1886, the government took over the railway at a "considerable loss to shareholders" [Leitch 1972, 138].)

If You Pay per Mile

Many railway guarantees offered investors a specified return per mile. Estimating the total costs of a line by multiplying its estimated distance by an estimate of the cost per mile was common and sensible, but

---

30 On Canada's guarantees, see A. Currie (1957, chapter 1). On loans in Russia, see Westwood (1964, 80): "It was hoped, and the hoped was justified, that when eventually the State acquired the private railways, their debts to the Government would be written off."

guaranteeing returns per mile encouraged companies to choose circuitous routes. The sultan of the Ottoman Empire offered investors "kilometric guarantees"[31] and, according to the journalist Henry Brailsford (1918 [1914]), got what he paid for:

> It seemed as though the line had laid itself across the countryside in the track of some writhing serpent. It curled in sinuous folds, it described enormous arcs, it bent and doubled so that a passing train resembled nothing so much as a kitten in pursuit of its own tail. Yet the country was a vast level plain. There were neither mountains nor rivers to avoid. Save for the obligation of serving towns in its course, most engineers in planning such a railway would simply have taken a ruler and drawn a straight line across the map. And oddly enough this railway did not seem to serve any visible town. Indeed, a plausible theory of its gyrations and its undulations might have been that it was desperately trying to dodge the towns. . . . The explanation was simple enough when one heard it. . . . [T]he concession included what is called a kilometric guarantee.

Brailsford took a dim view of the guarantees, also complaining that "the financiers extort a high rate of interest on the ground that Turkey is a disturbed and more or less insolvent country in which no investments are safe, and then contrive with the aid of diplomacy and the financial control to obtain for their enterprise a security which no investments possess in older countries."

If You Guarantee Some Lines but Not Others
Other problems occurred when governments guaranteed some railway lines but not others. In France, firms with both guaranteed and unguaranteed

---

31 H. Charles Woods (1917, 39–40) explains the Baghdad Railway Company's kilometric guarantee as follows: The guaranteed sum of 15,500 francs "is made up of two parts, the first being 11,000 francs per kilometer for construction provided by the Government, which hands over to the company the number of negotiable bonds (guaranteeing their interest at 4 per cent) necessary at that interest to bring 11,000 francs per kilometer per annum in addition to a small sum for redemption. The company then sells these bonds in order to raise the money necessary for construction. When the section in question is open and ready for traffic, the Government further provides 4,500 francs per year per kilometer for working expenses, or more correctly it supplies the difference between that sum and the actual gross receipts should they fall short of that amount. If the gross kilometric receipts of the line exceed 4,500 francs per annum but do not reach 10,000 francs per annum, then the surplus above the first amount belongs entirely to the Government. If the gross kilometric receipts exceed 10,000 francs per annum, then the surplus is divided so that the Government takes 60 per cent and the company 40 per cent of that surplus." Young (1906) contains copies of some of the concession contracts.

lines had an incentive to manipulate their accounts, suppressing the reported profits of the former, while inflating those of the latter (Howard 1918, 316). In Turkey, firms may have been able to divert traffic from guaranteed to unguaranteed lines. Wilhelm von Pressel, an engineer who helped build Turkey's railways, expressed his concerns thus:

> The companies will move heaven and earth to force the goods traffic to use these new routes for which there are no guarantees, and which, more important still, need never share their takings, whereas the other lines must pay part of their surplus to the government, once their gross revenue exceeds a certain amount. In consequence, the government will gain noth-ing . . . and the companies will make millions. (Pressel 1902, 7, translated in Luxemburg 1951, 442)

Turkey's guarantees were indeed much maligned. The Marxist political theorist Rosa Luxemburg (1951, chapter 30) described the part they played in the transfer of wealth from Turkish peasants to "the coffers" of Deutsche Bank by way of the Ottoman Public Debt Administration—a body controlled by foreign creditors that was created when Turkey default-ed on its debts and which collected taxes and administered the guarantees. Others implicated the guarantees in World War I. The biggest beneficiary of the guarantees was the Baghdad Railway, which was to link Constantinople to Baghdad and eventually Basra and the Persian Gulf. The railway was developed by German investors and backed by the German government, which hoped for "a continuous route from Hamburg to the Persian Gulf" and, hence, a "short cut" to India (Jastrow 2005 [1918], 97, 100). For thus bringing Germany into conflict with Great Britain and other powers that saw their own commercial and imperial ambitions threatened, the railway was once described as "the most significant single factor contributing to the outbreak of the long-foreseen war" (Jastrow 2005 [1918], 9).

To be fair to Turkey's guarantees, not all historians accord the Baghdad Railway such importance, and not all analysts conclude that the guaran-tees were unwarranted. Some argue that the Turkish government took a well-calculated risk and, far from being exploited, prospered from the investments (Earle 1923, 23; McMurray 2001, 50–51).

If You Guarantee Debt, but Not Equity
The design of guarantees also caused subtler problems. Usually guaran-tees applied to one kind of capital but not others and thus encouraged investment in one kind of capital at the expense of others. When guar-antees benefited debt investors but not shareholders or were more generous to debt investors, governments sometimes found that they had

encouraged very high leverage. For example, in 1880, bonds made up only 25 percent of railway capital in Great Britain, where there were no guarantees, but 80 percent of railway capital in France, which, at that time, was more generous in its guarantees of bonds than of shares (Caron 1983, 29). In Russia, before the revolution of 1917, the debt of private railways was generally guaranteed, while its equity was generally not, and railways' leverage reached 94 percent (Zhuravlyov 1983, 53–54).

Such high leverage increased the probability that railways would default on their debt and that governments' guarantees would be called. An analysis by Frank Lewis and Mary MacKinnon (1987, 194) of the Canadian Northern Railroad concludes that guarantees of debt encouraged the railway's promoters "to choose a debt-equity ratio which increased the likelihood of failure, because by doing so they increased the expected government transfer." The promoters did borrow heavily, and the railway did fail. Although protecting lenders but not shareholders may be part of a reasonable strategy to ensure that some investors retain an incentive to monitor management, it may misfire unless accompanied by limits on leverage.

Manage the Risks You Guarantee

When governments do bear risks that would normally be managed by the firm, they need to assume additional responsibilities. They need to direct the firm to contain costs, for example, and then monitor the firm to ensure that it does. In offering kilometric guarantees, the Turkish government needed to take responsibility for the choice of the railway's route to ensure it wasn't excessively long. When it guaranteed some lines but not others, it may have needed to control traffic.

Though not alone in having problems, Russia serves as an example (see Westwood 1964, 72–73). Its railway guarantees created three problems that could have been mitigated by better monitoring and control. First, the railways were able to inflate the estimate of costs per mile that the guarantees were based on. Then actual construction costs could be met solely through the sale of the government-guaranteed bonds. Second, investors could lower actual construction costs in ways that exploited the government. They could open a line early using cheap temporary bridges and other structures and then account for the completion of the work as operating expenses, which were covered by the guarantee. Third, the firm's managers could exploit the firm and the government by paying inflated prices to suppliers and construction companies that they owned or took bribes from. (Railway companies were not alone in Russia in using subterfuge to improve their position. In 1867, the government established a railway fund whose aim was partly "to camouflage the Government's enormous financial commitment to the railways and thus protect Russia's credit abroad" [Westwood 1964, 68–69].)

Governments with greater administrative capacity were more successful in monitoring guaranteed railways. In return for its guarantee to the East Indian Railway, one of the first in the country, the Indian colonial government had the rights to "determine the route, direction, and length of the lines"; see "virtually all the accounts, proceedings, minutes, papers, etc. of the Railway Company"; and appoint a member of the company's board with "a right of veto in all proceedings whatsoever" (Kerr 1995, 19). The government took its rights seriously and supervised the railways intensively. In France, too, a capable and powerful administration planned and supervised railway projects in great detail. Both the Indian and French governments have been criticized for exercising too much control and thwarting private initiative. According to one historian, for example, the French government wanted the private companies to provide money and to share in the risks without even "sharing in control" (Dunham 1941, 21). But, as we have seen, each government bore much of the risk associated with the railways, and thus had to take on responsibilities that would ordinarily fall to investors and their representatives.

Governments may, of course, have difficulty in effectively managing risks usually borne by firms. Officials may have little interest in the guaranteed firm's performance, or they may be bribed to ignore it. When governments have trouble managing the risks but still want to offer guarantees, they must rely more heavily on other mechanisms to mitigate the problems of guarantees—in particular, by ensuring that investors are still partially exposed to the risks and that the design of guarantees doesn't inadvertently create perverse incentives.

Progress?

Modern governments are in many ways better off than their predecessors. Appraising projects is easier because of advances in the theory of cost-benefit analysis. Valuing guarantees is easier because of advances in the theory of finance. Keeping track of liabilities is easier because of advances in accounting. Moreover, the pressure to give guarantees may have eased because of the growth of financial markets and the creation of development banks that give cheap loans to poor countries. Perhaps as a result, modern guarantees often seem better designed than those of the 19th century. Many protect firms only from risks over which investors have little influence, such as exchange-rate risk or a toll road's revenue risk. Many ensure a substantial presence of unguaranteed investors alongside the guaranteed ones.

But it is not hard to find examples of debt guarantees that protect investors from risks that they are probably best placed to manage.[32] Poland not long ago gave a debt guarantee to A2 motorway for a loan that was subordinated rather than senior to the claims of other lenders (Esty 2004, 317–18). Great Britain guaranteed several billion pounds of borrowing by Network Rail, the company that owns Great Britain's rail infrastructure.[33] Occasionally, governments protect firms specifically from cost risks. Chile gave a construction-cost guarantee to the El Melon tunnel that ended up costing it $10 million (Gómez Lobo and Hinojosa 2000, 21). Colombia gave one to the El Cortijo–El Vino toll road under which it would pay 100 percent of overruns of up to 30 percent on the cost of construction materials, 75 percent of overruns of between 30 and 50 percent, and 0 percent of overruns above 50 percent—at an expected cost in the mid-1990s of about $1 million (Christopher Lewis and Mody 1997, 136, 141).

Indeed, how many modern guarantees are better designed than that used for the bridge of Bordeaux in 1817, which kept investors exposed to cost risks while protecting them only partially from revenue risks? Today, as in Becquey's time, the desire to improve investors' incentives and to limit the government's losses is easily outweighed by the desire to attract private finance for projects the government nonetheless plans and controls.

And, today, as in Becquey's time, political pressure and cognitive problems in making decisions about risk still impede good choices about guarantees—the two topics to which we now turn.

---

32 Another example of a guarantee that may have protected the firm from cost risks comes from Catalonia, Spain, where in 1999 "the Autema concessionaire's operating surplus was guaranteed by the Catalonian government for the remainder of the concession term" (Macquarie Infrastructure Group 2001). The Philippines seemingly agreed to bear nearly all the risks in an urban rail project in Manila. In the build-lease-transfer agreement for the Metro Rail Transit III Phase I project, the government agreed to make rental payments that included a debt-service component that would ensure the project could repay its lenders "come hell or high water" and an equity-return component designed to give investors a 15 percent return on equity (National Economic Research Associates 2004).

33 See the National Accounts Classification Committee, U.K. Office for National Statistics (2004).

CHAPTER 3

Obstacles to Good Decisions

Deciding whether to bear a risk is hard because risk is complex. Fully understanding a risk requires knowing all the possible outcomes of the corresponding risk factor and, for each outcome, the effect of the risk factor on value. Research suggests that governments are likely to struggle to make accurate intuitive judgments about risks and good decisions about whether to bear them. In addition, the political struggle over public resources and the weaknesses of traditional government accounting conspire to encourage governments to subsidize firms not by giving them cash but by bearing some of the risks they face. This chapter explores these issues.

Cognitive Obstacles

To some, it may be obvious that people often choose badly when the outcomes of decisions are uncertain. Yet because so much economic and political analysis uses the simplifying assumption that people are rational, it's helpful to review the research of cognitive psychologists on human judgment and decision making.

Good decisions about bearing risk would have two components. First, they would be based on sound judgments about the risks to be borne.

When making a bet on the toss of a coin, an ideal decision maker would know what she stood to gain from each possible outcome and what the probabilities of the possible outcomes were (50–50, if the coin is fair). More generally, an ideal decision maker would know the value and probability of each possible state of the world under each possible course of action. An ideal government thinking of offering a revenue guarantee to a toll road, for example, would know the probability of the guarantee being triggered and the probability distribution of payments if the guarantee were called.

Second, good decisions would make good use of judgments. Ideal decisions would probably be described by expected-utility theory. That is, an ideal decision maker would evaluate the utility of each of the outcomes possibly created by a course of action, weigh each possible outcome by its estimated probability, and choose the option that created the greatest probability-weighted utility. If the decision maker were risk neutral, maximizing expected utility over monetary outcomes would amount to maximizing the expected monetary value of the outcome. Suppose, for example, that the decision maker had the option of having a fair coin tossed, getting $100 if it landed heads up, and losing $50 otherwise. The expected value of this option is $25 $((0.5 \times \$100) + (0.5 \times -\$50))$. The ideal risk-neutral decision maker would therefore be indifferent between this option and getting $25 for sure.

An ideal decision maker might reasonably be risk averse—as most of us seem to be. In the presence of risk aversion, maximizing expected utility differs from maximizing expected value. The utilities attached to the various outcomes—not the monetary values—must be considered and weighed by the probabilities of those outcomes. Otherwise, the approach remains the same. The ideal decision maker would know the utilities and probabilities of all possible outcomes under each possible action and choose the action that maximized expected utility.

The evidence shows that we have trouble with both aspects of decision making. We err predictably in judging risks, and when we choose, we misuse our imperfect judgments.

Problems with Decisions, Given Known Risks

Consider the evidence about how decisions are made when the risks are known. Expected-utility theory may accurately describe an ideal decision maker; a more promising theory of real decision makers is prospect theory (Kahneman and Tversky 1979; Tversky and Kahneman 1992).

Prospect theory—Like expected-utility theory, prospect theory considers simple gambles or "prospects"—or, in our terminology, simple decisions about bearing risk. It differs from expected-utility theory in three ways.

First, prospect theory says that the "carriers of utility" are not states of the world, but gains and losses relative to a reference point. It says that what determines choices about bearing risk are the amounts of money people stand to win or lose, not their resulting levels of wealth. Moreover, whether a change is viewed as a win or a loss can depend on how the choice is framed.

Second, prospect theory says that the function mapping monetary gains and losses to subjective value is like the S-shaped curve in figure 3.1. The curve is slightly concave in the domain of gains and slightly convex in the domain of losses. And it is steeper for losses than for gains.

Third, prospect theory posits that decision makers use decision weights that differ systematically from known probabilities (figure 3.2). Essentially, people are more sensitive to certain changes in probabilities than to others. An increase in the probability of an outcome from, say, 37 to 38 percent makes little difference to a typical decision, whereas an increase in the probability of an outcome from 0 to 1 percent makes a big difference, as does an increase from 99 to 100 percent. Guarantees that make investors certain of their returns might thus be highly valued.

Loss aversion—One implication of prospect theory is loss aversion. Because the slope of the value function in figure 3.1 is steeper in the domain of

Figure 3.1. A Typical Prospect-Theory Value Function

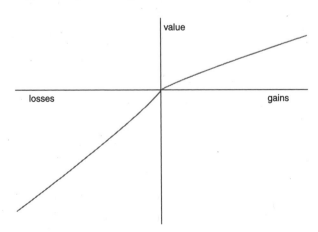

Source: Kahneman and Tversky 1979.

Figure 3.2. A Typical Prospect-Theory Decision-Weight Function

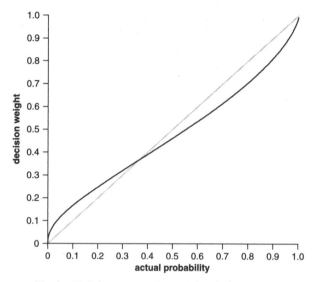

Source: Kahneman and Tversky 1979; Prelec 1998, as cited in Fox and Tversky 1998.
Note: The straight line at a 45 degree angle represents an ideal decision-weight function. The curved line represents actual decision weights according to prospect theory.

losses than in the domain of gains, losses loom larger than gains: we fear losses more than we desire gains of equal magnitude. Offered even chances of winning $100 and losing $100, most of us quickly decline. We prefer zero with certainty to a gamble with an expected value of zero (half of $100 plus half of –$100). Many of us decline such a gamble unless the possible positive outcome is twice as great as the possible negative outcome (Kahneman and Tversky 1995). Ordinary risk aversion seems at first a good explanation for the choice, but it turns out not to be (Rabin 2000).

The implications of loss aversion for government decisions about bearing risk are a matter of speculation; those decisions are complex in many ways not considered by the theory. But one might imagine that loss aversion would cause officials and ministers—at least those concerned about their government's fiscal position—to focus more on the downside risk created, say, by a revenue guarantee than on the upside risk created by an equally valuable revenue-sharing arrangement.

Risk aversion and risk seeking—Together, the value and decision-weight functions shown in figures 3.1 and 3.2 produce a complex pattern of risk aversion and risk seeking (table 3.1).

Table 3.1. The Fourfold Pattern of Risk Aversion and Risk Seeking: Certainty Equivalents for Four Risks

		Value	
		Gain ($100)	*Loss (–$100)*
Probability	Low (0.05)	Risk seeking ($14)	Risk aversion (–$8)
	High (0.95)	Risk aversion ($78)	Risk seeking (–$84)

Sources: Tversky and Fox 1995, based on Tversky and Kahneman 1992.
Note: The numbers in the cells of the table show the estimated certainty equivalent of a prospect offering the amount shown in the column heading with the probability shown in the row heading.

When considering gains with high probabilities, we tend to avoid risk. We might treat a 95 percent chance of gaining $100 as equivalent to getting $78 for sure (the lower-left cell in the table). Or—by extrapolation—we might require a risk premium to invest in stocks instead of riskless bonds. By contrast, when considering losses with high probabilities, we tend to seek risk. We might pay only $84 to avoid a 95 percent chance of losing $100. By extrapolation, someone faced with a probable loss, such as an unsuccessful trader in a bank, might prefer to double a bad bet than to realize a sure loss.

For low probabilities, typical preferences are reversed. Because we give unduly high weight to low-probability events, we seek risk when faced with low-probability gains. We might value a 5 percent chance of $100 at as much as $14—or, by extrapolation, buy a lottery ticket. Likewise, we tend to avoid risk when faced with a low-probability loss. We might pay $8 to avoid a 5 percent chance of losing $100—or, by extrapolation, buy insurance and guarantees.

Framing—Whether we frame a choice as being between possible gains or between possible losses is not fixed but depends on how the choice is described. Consider the following two problems (Kahneman and Tversky 1979, 27):

Problem 1. In addition to whatever you own, you have been given $1,000. You are now asked to choose between

A: $1,000 with a probability of 50 percent and
B: $500 with certainty.

Problem 2. In addition to whatever you own, you have been given $2,000. You are now asked to choose between

C: Losing $1,000 with a probability of 50 percent and
D: Losing $500 with certainty.

Most people confronted with problem 1 choose option B; they avoid risk. Most people confronted with problem 2 choose option C; they seek risk. Yet the only difference between the problems is the framing. In each, we are asked to choose between a certain gain of $1,500 and equally probable chances of gains of $1,000 and $2,000. Option A is the same as option C, and option B is the same as option D. We might consistently choose A and C or B and D, but not B and C. The reason we make the inconsistent choice is that problem 1 is formulated to make us think of gains, problem 2 to make us think of losses.

The implications for government decisions about guarantees are again a matter of speculation. We might imagine, however, that ministers thinking of giving guarantees against low-probability events would normally be risk averse. Yet ministers who framed their choices as being between losing options might seek risk. In a country facing a fiscal crisis, ministers might prefer a guarantee to a cash subsidy, since the guarantee holds out the possibility of avoiding any loss.

Broad and narrow frames—Framing affects decisions about risk in another way. The effect of bearing a given risk depends on the correlation of the risk with other risks (see chapter 7). Unless risks are perfectly correlated, a portfolio of small exposures to many risks tends to be less risky than a large exposure to a single risk. Making good decisions about exposure to a new risk therefore requires consideration not only of the new risk by itself, but also of its correlation with other risks. Often, however, we frame choices about new risks narrowly. We focus on the risk by itself, not on its effects on the risk of our portfolio. Such narrow framing encourages us to be more risk averse than we should be (Kahneman and Lovallo 1993). If governments consider guarantees in isolation, they may be too risk averse.

Problems Judging Probabilities

The decision-making problems just described occur even when the probabilities of the possible outcomes are known. But probabilities are seldom known. In practice, people must form their own judgments. Those judgments are sometimes remarkably good, sometimes systematically astray.[1]

Overconfidence—First, we seem to be too confident of the accuracy of our judgments: we seem to underestimate the uncertainty of the world.

---

[1]   On how good simple heuristic reasoning can be, see Gigerenzer, Todd, and the ABC Research Group (1999). For biases, see Gilovich, Griffin, and Kahneman (2002) and Kahneman, Slovic, and Tversky (1982).

Figure 3.3. Intuitive Forecasts

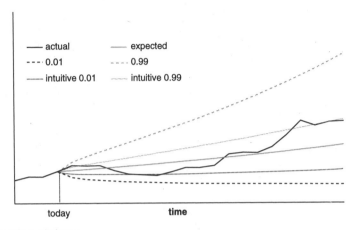

Source: Author's calculations.
Note: The actual and expected values and the true confidence interval assume that the risk factor follows a geo-metric Brownian motion with an expected growth rate of 3 percent and volatility of 10 percent (see "Measuring Exposure" in chapter 7). The figure assumes the intuitive 98 percent confidence interval is the same as a true 70 percent confidence interval.

Psychologists have assessed overconfidence by asking people to state their confidence intervals for the answers to each of a set of questions. For example, they might ask, "What is the length of the Nile? Specify an interval that you're 98 percent sure the true length lies within." A possible answer is 3,000 kilometers plus or minus 1,000. Asked 100 such questions, we ought to get about 98 right, however much or however little we know about the subject. But we typically get only 60 to 70 percent right.[2] When we're confident, it seems we're overconfident.

The evidence about overconfidence suggests that intuitive judgments about exposure to risk may underestimate the true exposure. Other things being equal, governments will tend to judge the likelihood of a guarantee's being triggered as lower than it is. Indeed, they may judge a call on the guarantee to be impossible and then discover that "events judged to be impossible happen 20 percent of the time" (Camerer 1995, 591).

Figure 3.3 illustrates. It depicts the path of a hypothetical risk factor—such as demand or the exchange rate—up to the present. It then shows an

---

2   Colin Camerer (1995, 593) reports a study giving 60 as the number. Philip Tetlock (2002, 752) reports a study of experts on politics and writes, "Across all predictions elicited across domains, experts who assigned confidence estimates of 80 percent or higher were correct only 45 percent of the time."

optimal forecast of the risk factor (labeled "expected"), the true 98 percent confidence interval for the risk factor (between the lines labeled "0.01" and "0.99"), and an intuitive confidence interval (between the dashed lines). Last, it shows one possible path taken by the risk factor. Because the intuitive confidence interval lies inside the true confidence interval, a government relying on intuitive judgments is likely to be surprised.

Hindsight bias—We also tend to overestimate the extent to which the present was predictable. We tend to think that what *did* happen *had* to happen. Put differently, when we look back, we see less risk than there really was. Yet to evaluate the predictability of an event, we must imagine not knowing what we know now. After the East Asian crisis of 1997 and 1998, when both governments and investors lost large sums in infrastructure projects, it may have seemed obvious that people made errors of judgment—that investors were too optimistic, that governments bore too many risks. Yet it's hard to judge the decisions retrospectively.

The deceptive wisdom of hindsight also encourages overconfidence; if the past seems more predictable than it was, the future will tend to seem more predictable than it is.

Availability—Estimates of the probability of an event depend on how readily events of its kind come to mind or, in other words, on the mental availability of such events. Other things being equal, the more readily an event comes to mind, the more probable it is judged to be. This is not unreasonable: the more likely an event is, the more often it will happen, and the more likely we are to think of it. But following this rule of thumb also leads us to overestimate the probability of uncommon but vivid, recently realized events and to underestimate the probability of common but unremarkable events. In the wake of the financial crises of the late 1990s and early 2000s, when memories of large devaluations were vivid, policy makers and investors alike may have been inclined to overestimate exchange-rate risk.[3]

The unpacking of events—Judgments of the probability of an event also depend on the detail in which the event is described or "unpacked" (Rottenstreich and Tversky 1997; Tversky and Koehler 1994). Suppose that a revenue guarantee might be triggered because demand falls during a recession or because a competing business enters the market or

---

3   Richard Zeckhauser and W. Kip Viscusi (1990, 560) state, "We are particularly likely to overestimate previously unrecognized risks in the aftermath of an unfavorable outcome."

because the government imposes price controls that are harsher than expected. An intuitive answer to the question, "What is the probability of the guarantee being triggered?" is likely to be lower than an intuitive answer to the question, "What is the probability of the guarantee being triggered because of a recession, a competing development, or harsher-than-expected price control?" A government that wishes to avoid under-estimating the risks of a guarantee might want to try to list all the events that could trigger the guarantee.

Representativeness—Judgments of probabilities are also guided by the extent to which events fit an existing mental representation. Sometimes the approach serves us well. Other times, our mental representations bias our judgment. For example, most of us have an inaccurate mental picture of the way chance events manifest themselves; we tend to think we recognize patterns where there is only randomness. Asked to pick a plausible sequence of heads (H) and tails (T) from six tosses of a fair coin, for example, we might choose one such as H T H H T H. A sequence such as H H H T T T, which is just as likely, seems less representatively random. (This tendency helps explain the gambler's fallacy of thinking a series of bad outcomes makes the next outcome more likely to be good.)

One consequence of the importance of representativeness to judgment is that estimates of probabilities are less sensitive to sample size than they should be. Statistical theory says that our confidence in the accuracy of an estimate should depend on the size of the sample considered. But a small sample can seem as representative of a population as a large one, and in making judgments, we tend not to adjust our views to the sample size. (Experts aren't exempt. Hoping to get econometricians to take small sample sizes as seriously as such polysyllabic problems as heteroskedasticity and multicollinearity, Arthur Goldberger [1991] chose to call the problem "micronumerosity.")

Problems for Governments as Well as for Individuals

This evidence about human judgments and decisions comes mainly from studies of individuals. Decisions by groups—and by governments in particular—might be better. Major governmental decisions are often made by a committee; even when they are made by an individual, such as a regulator, minister, or president, the individual has access to professional advice and may be obliged to consider it. Should we conclude that governments probably make good decisions in the presence of risk? One of the premises of this book is that structured decision making that draws on expert advice is better than intuitive decision making. But the evidence is troubling.

First, groups can make worse decisions than their members would make individually. One might think that groups would be more conservative than individuals are, but this seems not to be the case. Instead, group discussions seem to have a polarizing effect, and groups gravitate to views more extreme than the average view of their members (Ajzen 1996, 315).

Second, there's evidence that the agents of irrational principals make decisions that reflect the principals' irrationality. The managers of investment funds, for example, may choose to invest in fashionable stocks even if they think the stocks are overvalued, because they would otherwise lose the support of their irrational clients. The investment fund managers may be smart about investment, but their clients are not and can't easily judge managers' skills, because observed performance depends in the short term mainly on chance. Clients tend to judge managers most harshly if they do poorly while other managers do well, so the smart thing for many managers is to follow the crowd (Shiller 2002). As agents of their citizens, ministers are in a position similar to that of fund managers; even if they are rational, they may feel pressure to make irrational decisions.

A third piece of evidence comes from the regulation by government of risks presented by hazardous activities and chemicals. Researchers have evaluated the U.S. government's regulation of such activities and chemicals by estimating the economic cost imposed by a regulation for every life it saves. Regulating to remove lead from gasoline, for example, increases the cost of gasoline and therefore many other goods and services, but the resulting cleaner air saves lives. Similarly, requiring airlines to adopt new safety measures increases the cost of flying but may reduce deaths from accidents. Other things being equal, rational choices could be expected to require spending similar amounts to save lives in different domains: if it was worth spending $1 million to save a life by mitigating one danger, it would seem to be worth spending $1 million to save a life by mitigating a different danger. Yet cost-benefit analyses of risk regulations suggest large disparities in the cost per life saved. Some regulations impose a cost of only $100,000 per life saved; others impose a cost of $100 million or more (Breyer 1993, table 5; Sunstein 2001; Zeckhauser and Viscusi 1990). Part of the explanation seems to be that politicians share or respond to our fear of vivid, mentally available risks.

Overall, it is clear that making good decisions about guarantees is difficult. The net effect of the cognitive obstacles is, however, hard to discern. The bias created by political obstacles is much clearer.

Political Obstacles

According to Voltaire, the art of government consists in taking as much as possible from one group of citizens in order to give it to another.[4] We might be more optimistic, hoping that governments also devote time to solving problems that require collective public action, but it is clear that governments don't act solely with a view to promoting the public interest. Their decisions also depend on the interplay of interest groups and their need to win and maintain political support. This struggle for resources means that, even if government decision makers were perfectly rational, they wouldn't necessarily make decisions about guarantees that are in the public interest. Thus, to understand the obstacles to good decisions, we need to understand some of the pressures that politics brings to bear on government decision makers.

Strategies for Claiming Value

Some redistribution is usually considered legitimate. Though disputes about the details are fierce, most people agree that governments can reasonably redistribute some resources from the rich to the poor and from the healthy to the sick. Redistribution may also be grudgingly accepted when it is part of a policy that, to use a clichéd but helpful metaphor, simultaneously enlarges the pie. But in democracies, obvious attempts by a group no more deserving than others to grab a larger slice of an unenlarged or even diminished pie usually fail. Those who would lose recognize the threat and resist it. A firm that proposes a special tax for its own benefit can expect to be quickly rebuffed. Would-be acquirers of a larger slice of an unenlarged pie need a strategy for justifying or disguising their gains.

Clever proposals satisfy three criteria. First, they have a rationale that suggests they maximize value or at least redistribute it to deserving groups. A policy of minimum prices for agricultural products, for example, might be advocated on the grounds that it helps poor farmers manage otherwise unmanageable risk, greatly increasing their welfare at little cost to any one else.[5] A proposed tariff on imports might be advocated on the grounds that it creates jobs for the unemployed.

---

4   "En général, l'art du gouvernement consiste à prendre le plus d'argent qu'on peut à une grande partie des citoyens, pour le donner à une autre partie" (http://www.voltaire-integral.com/17/argent.htm).

5   According to Brian Wright (1993), helping farmers manage risks is one of the common rationales for mainly resource-transferring agricultural schemes in the United States.

Second, smart proposals ask for a little from many, rather than much from a few (see Mueller 2003, chapter 20; Olson 1965). Although many people have an incentive to oppose such proposals, none individually loses enough to warrant analyzing and opposing the proposals. A tariff on an imported good used by only a few big customers may be hard to establish, because the loss it imposes on those customers will probably be large enough to prompt them to organize and resist. And because they are few, they can organize easily. But a tariff on an imported product that everyone buys a little of may not elicit much opposition. People may not like the tariff, but they don't care about it much and couldn't easily organize to oppose it if they did.

Third, smart proposals conceal the transfers from the involuntary benefactors. The effect of import tariffs on the price of imported goods is clear, but their effect on the price of domestically manufactured items may be less obvious, making tariffs a reasonable way for domestic manufacturers to claim value. Quotas that restrict the volume of imports might be better, because their effect on the price of imports is more obscure. Safety-related restrictions on imports might be even better.

The Appeal of Guarantees

A proposal for a guarantee may satisfy these three criteria. First, a guarantee can easily be given a rationale—being necessary, say, to elicit much-needed investment or to make use of the government's superior risk-bearing potential. Second, the costs of the guarantee are distributed among many taxpayers and among many others who might have benefited from expenditure, each of whom bears only a small cost. Third, the costs are opaque, involving no immediate transfer of cash.

The opacity is increased by traditional government budgeting and accounting, which deal with the complexity of risk by ignoring it. Traditional government accounting and budgeting is cash based. Revenue is recognized when cash is received. An expense is recognized when cash is disbursed. Decisions to incur risk that involve no immediate spending therefore require no appropriation in the budget and make no difference to the reported budget deficit in the period in which the risk is assumed. They have an effect only when cash is received or disbursed. Guarantees thus allow governments to transfer value to firms without revealing to the benefactors the extent of their generosity. Guarantees are all the more attractive when governments are under pressure to cut their deficits.

Politics seem therefore to encourage governments to bear too much risk. Two qualifications to this conclusion are in order, however. First, even if politics tempt governments to bear too much risk, it doesn't follow that governments should never bear risk. As we will see in the next chapter, governments should be sympathetic to requests to bear project-specific policy risk, and when they want to ensure investment occurs, they should expect to bear demand risk.

Second, firms won't necessarily retain the benefits of guarantees. In particular, when a government chooses the firm in a competition, the firm's ability to capture the benefits of any subsidy, including a guarantee, is limited. The same will be true when a regulator sets prices to mimic the effect of competition. In each case, the transfer is at least partly from taxpayers to customers. As a result, arguments for guarantees may not come only—or most vociferously—from firms. The struggle for public resources may also take place between a ministry eager to secure invest-ment and a finance ministry anxious to limit spending.

Overcoming the Obstacles

Judicious decisions about guarantees are thus difficult. Some risks may be overestimated; others underestimated. Even when risks are accurately esti-mated, making good decisions is psychologically difficult. In addition, political pressures encourage governments to bear risk rather than spend cash.

What can governments do to overcome the cognitive and political obstacles to good decisions? Three options are explored in the rest of this book.

First, governments can improve their understanding of the appropriate allocation of risk. Import quotas and tariffs are, in some respects, perfect stealth transfers: their costs are opaque and widely distributed, and they come with seemingly plausible rationales. Yet understanding among policy advisers of the benefits of trade helps counteract the pressure for quotas and tariffs. Ideas as well as interests matter. Indeed, ideas may have been crucial in shaping the U.S. government's approach to bearing and regu-lating risk over the past two centuries (Moss 2002).

Second, governments can improve their ability to value exposure to risk. Several of the psychologists that have identified problems in human decision making have argued that the solution lies in quantifying choices— something few economists would disagree with.[6] The better governments

---

6 For arguments in favor of quantification as a way of mitigating decision-making prob-lems, see, for example, Dawes, Faust, and Meehl (1989); Kahneman and Tversky (1982); Posner (2001); and Sunstein (2001).

can estimate the cost of a guarantee and compare it with the cost of other policies, the better their decisions are likely to be.

Third, governments can change the rules that shape their decisions about guarantees. To name just three possible changes: accounting standards can be revised to better recognize the cost of guarantees; budgets can be changed to better capture those costs; and laws can be passed to require governments to disclose contracts with private infrastructure investors, so that people outside government can assess the government's exposure to risk.

We return to rules in chapter 6. The next two chapters consider the appropriate allocation of risk.

CHAPTER 4

Allocating Exposure to Risk

To determine which of a project's risks a government should bear, it helps to have a more general framework for deciding how risks should be allocated. In this chapter, we set out such a framework and then consider modifying it to deal with the special features of governments.

Definitions

To set out the framework, we need to clarify several terms. For example, what is risk and what does allocating it mean? Before we get to these terms, though, we need to be sure of the meaning of simpler ones.

A Riskless Project

A *project*, as the term is used here, is any kind of business. It needn't be new. Our focus is infrastructure, but the definitions and principle that follow are not specific to infrastructure.

Stakeholders in (or *parties* to) the project are those that have an economic interest in it. In a toll-road project, for example, the firm is one stakeholder, collecting tolls and paying for construction, maintenance, and operations. Customers are another, using the road and paying the tolls. The government is a third, perhaps collecting taxes and sharing in revenue, perhaps paying out on guarantees and subsidies. Many others also stand to win or lose from the project, including workers, insurers, subcontracted construction companies, the owners and users of other transport projects, and businesses in the neighborhood.

We focus on three parties: the firm, customers, and the government. We usually lump together all customers and make no distinction between taxpayers and other citizens who ultimately pay the costs or enjoy the benefits that accrue to the government (often referring to the group as "taxpayers" for the sake of brevity). We sometimes distinguish, however, between two stakeholders in the firm, namely its shareholders and its creditors, because their relationship can affect customers and the government (see "Insolvency Risk" in chapter 5).

The value of a party's interest in a project can be quantified: the costs the party incurs can be subtracted from the value of the benefits it receives. The sponsor of a project usually estimates the present value of the cash flows the project will generate for the firm undertaking it. The firm's value can then be decomposed into the value accruing to shareholders and the value accruing to creditors. It is also possible to consider the value of customers' interest in the project, namely the difference between the present value of the services customers receive and the present value of the bills they pay (the present value of the consumer surplus). Likewise, it is possible to consider the value of the government's interest in a project, or the difference in present values between any revenue the government receives and any payments it makes.

Total project value is the sum of the values accruing to each party. It is the economic value of a project and is closely related to the project's economic rate of return: it is positive if the project's economic rate of return exceeds the cost of capital. Projects with positive total project value should go ahead; projects with negative total project value should not. Put differently, projects with an economic rate of return greater than their cost of capital should go ahead; others shouldn't.

All stakeholders have an indirect interest in maximizing total project value. The greater that value is, the more they stand to gain from the project. Yet they have a direct interest in maximizing the value of their own interest in the project, regardless of total project value. Their attempts to increase the value of their own interest may increase the value of the project or may leave it unchanged, merely redistributing value from others. Those attempts may even reduce total project value. For example, a toll-road firm may lobby the government to increase tolls, thereby redistributing value from drivers to the firm. If the increase is big enough, the toll will discourage use of the service even when the benefits to drivers of using the road exceed the costs the toll road incurs in providing the service.

Risk

Project design is complicated by uncertainty or risk.[1] There are many possible future states of the world, many ways the world might be; which state will obtain is unknown, and value depends on which state does obtain. Total project value can hence be estimated in advance, but its ultimate value is unknown.

The word *risk* is commonly used to refer to the possibility of loss, of uncertain but possible bad outcomes. Thus, we might speak of the risk of a road being damaged by heavy rains or an earthquake or of demand for the road being lower than forecast. We wouldn't normally speak of the risk of the road not being damaged or of demand being greater than forecast. It's useful, however, to think of risk as encompassing the possibilities of good as well as bad outcomes—to talk of the risk of damage not occurring and the risk of traffic being greater than forecast. Though this use of the word deviates from tradition, it is now widespread in professional contexts, where people often talk of upside as well as downside risks.[2] We define *risk* to be unpredictable variation in value.

Total-project-value risk is unpredictable variation in total project value. It can be characterized by describing the probability distribution of total project value—that is, by describing the possible values of the project and their respective probabilities. Figure 4.1 illustrates by showing a histogram of the probabilities of possible values, in ranges, of a hypothetical project. In this example, the most likely outcome is total project value between 20 and 30, which has a probability of about 20 percent. But value is uncertain, and there are roughly equal probabilities of better or

---

1 Following Knight (1921), researchers sometimes distinguish *risk* from *uncertainty*. Risk in Knight's sense exists when the probabilities of different outcomes are known, uncertainty when they are not. In most real cases of interest, probabilities are unknown. Yet people can, in principle, always assign a subjective probability (see Jeffreys 2004, for example), so the distinction may not matter in practice. We use *risk* to refer to both Knightian risk and Knightian uncertainty.

2 Although the *Oxford English Dictionary* (CD-ROM version 3.1, 2004) does not include a definition of *risk* that allows for uncertain benefits, the fourth edition of the *American Heritage Dictionary* includes as one definition "the variability of returns from an investment." As an example from the field, Nevitt and Fabozzi (2000, 428) define risk as "instability; uncertainty about the future; more specifically, the degree of uncertainty involved with a loan or investment."

Figure 4.1. Characterizing Total-Project-Value Risk

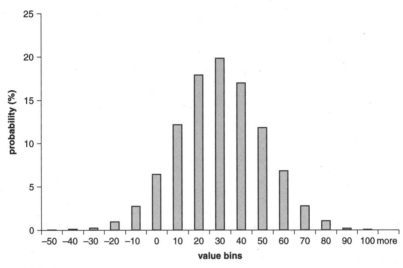

Source: Author's calculations.
Note: The first bin on the left, labeled "–50," shows the probability of values less than –50; the bin on the far right shows the probability of values greater than 100. The bins in between show the probabilities for ranges of 10: the second from left, labeled "–40," shows the probability of values between –50 and –40; the third, labeled "–30," the probability of values between –40 and –30; and so on. It is assumed that value is normally distributed, with a mean of 25 and a standard deviation of 20.

worse outcomes. There's a small chance that total project value might be negative, for instance, and a tiny chance that it might be 100 or more.

A *stakeholder's* or *party's risk* is unpredictable variation in the value of that party's interest in the project. It can be characterized by the probability distribution of the value of the party's interest in the project and depicted by a histogram. Because the values of the parties' interests in a project add up to total project value, the probability distributions of the values of the parties' interests add up to the probability distribution of total project value.

Figure 4.2 illustrates for two stakeholders—the firm and its customers. It is like figure 4.1, except that it shows frequency polygons (the outlines of the bars of histograms) so the distributions can be seen more easily. Total project value is divided between the firm and its customers. Thus, the distribution of total project value lies to the right of the distributions of the values of the firm's and customers' interests in the project. In this case, the firm and customers share the expected value of the project equally, but the firm bears more risk: the distribution of the value of the firm's interest is more spread out.

Figure 4.2. Stakeholders' Risks and Total-Project-Value Risk

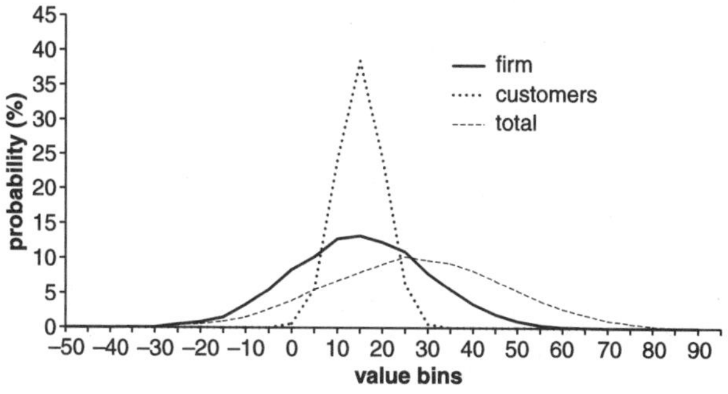

Source: Author's calculations.

Note: Like figure 4.1, this figure assumes a project with normally distributed total project value, with a mean of 25 and a standard deviation of 20. The value of the firm's interest in the project is three-quarters of total project value less one-quarter of expected total project value. The value of customers' interest is one-quarter of total project value plus one-quarter of expected total project value. The firm and customers therefore share expected total project value equally (12.5 each), but the firm bears three-quarters of the risk.

Particular Risks

Risk has many sources. For a toll road, it comes from uncertainty about demand, construction costs, whether various unlikely but possible events such as earthquakes occur, and so on. We can define *a (particular) risk* as unpredictable variation in value arising from unpredictable variation in a risk factor, where a *risk factor* is a variable whose outcome affects total project value and whose value is uncertain.[3] Thus, construction-cost risk is unpredictable variation in value arising from unpredictable variation in construction costs. Demand risk is unpredictable variation in value arising from unpredictable variation in demand. Earthquake risk is unpredictable variation in value arising from unpredictable variation in the occurrence of earthquakes. More generally, x risk is unpredictable variation in value caused by unpredictable variation in x, where x is a risk factor. (Risk in the first sense—unpredictable variation in value—might be called "risk in general" to distinguish it from particular risks.)

Some risks are *project specific*, some *economywide*. The value of an unbuilt tunnel may depend, for instance, on the rock that will be encountered during construction (a project-specific risk factor) and on the interest

---

3 In the language of probability, risk factors are, or can be expressed as, random variables or processes. *Random variables* are functions that map states of the world to real numbers. Whether there is an earthquake can be expressed as a random variable if we assign, say, the number 1 to the outcome of an earthquake's occurring and the number 0 to the outcome of an earthquake's not occurring.

rates that will prevail (an economywide risk factor). The distinction becomes important when we examine how risks should be allocated.

To illustrate the relationship between risk in general and particular risks, consider a toll road again and suppose that only two risk factors affect the project's value: demand and earthquakes. Suppose that, in the absence of an earthquake, total project value depends only on demand and has the distribution shown in figure 4.1. Suppose that earthquakes happen with a probability of 0.1 and create a cost of 50 in damage and lost business. To simplify, we assume that the effects of demand and earthquakes sum and that the two risk factors are independent.[4]

Demand risk and earthquake risk can then be described by their effects on total project value. To describe earthquake risk, we can show the probability distribution of total project value, holding demand constant at its average value. To describe demand risk, we can show the probability distribution of total project value, assuming that the earthquake makes its average contribution to value: a loss of 5 (10 percent of 50). Figure 4.3 shows that total-project-value risk is similar to demand risk, except that the possibility of an earthquake skews its distribution to the left.

Although risk factors must be partly random, they needn't be purely so: they can have a deterministic as well as a stochastic element. Thus, demand risk can result from a combination of purely random variation in traffic and variation that depends, say, on the quality of the service (for example, how well the road is maintained) and is therefore controlled by the firm.[5]

Allocating Total-Project-Value Risk

To *allocate* risk is to determine the extent to which each party bears unpredictable variation in value. To allocate total-project-value risk is to determine the extent to which each party bears variations in total project value. To allocate a particular risk is to determine the extent to which each party bears unpredictable variation in total project value arising from unpredictable variation in just that risk factor. Put differently, to

---

4 Specifically, we assume that total project value is the sum of two terms: (a) a random drawing from a normally distributed variable, representing demand risk, with a mean of 25 and a standard deviation of 20, and (b) a random drawing from a binomially distributed variable, representing earthquake risk, that takes a value of 0 with a probability of 0.9 and a value of –50 with a probability of 0.1.

5 Further, what is a risk for one party need not be for another: one party may be able to predict the value of the risk factor, while the other may not. Sellers, for example, know more about the quality of their wares than buyers do. This implies that the kind of risk that matters is subjective, not objective (see Jeffreys 2004).

Figure 4.3. Total-Project-Value Risk and Its Components—Demand and Earthquake Risk

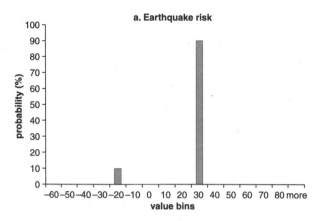

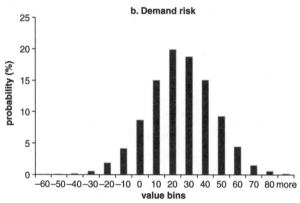

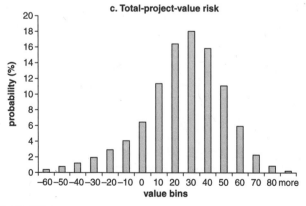

Source: Author's calculations.
Note: The labels on the horizontal axes have the meanings given in the note to figure 4.1.

allocate risk is to determine how value is shared among stakeholders in each possible state of the world.

In principle, risk could be allocated whole, without regard to its sources. All risks could be allocated to the firm, for example, and the firm could then pass them equally to its shareholders. In practice, different risks are allocated to different parties (figure 4.4). The maxim is "divide and manage."

To allocate a risk entirely to one party is to ensure that the other parties are unaffected by it. If customers bear all demand risk, for example, the firm's value is independent of demand. In practice, fully allocating a risk to one party may be difficult or impossible; risks are usually shared. Even if tolls are periodically adjusted in response to changes in demand in order to allocate demand risk to customers, the firm still bears demand risk between adjustments. Allocating demand risk only to the firm is similarly difficult. Even if tolls are fixed for many years, they may eventually be adjusted in a way that transfers risk to customers.

Risk is allocated by many instruments. Rules for adjusting tolls have just been mentioned, and government guarantees are, of course, another instrument that allocates risk. There are others. The structure, as well as the adjustment, of prices allocates risk. If a tariff contains a large fixed charge and a small volumetric charge, more demand risk is borne by customers and less by the firm. By contrast, if all revenue comes from a volumetric charge, the firm bears more of the risk. Insurance contracts allocate risk between the firm and its insurers. Contracts between the firm and its subcontractors allocate construction- and operating-cost risks between the firm and its subcontractors. Last, taxation means that the government shares in the profits of projects, as a sort of silent partner.

Distributional Risk

As well as being exposed to total-project-value risk, a stakeholder may be exposed to risk arising from unpredictable variation in the way an unchanging total project value is distributed. *Distributional risk* (in general) can be defined as unpredictable variation in the distribution of value among stakeholders, holding total project value constant. *A (particular) distributional risk* can be defined as unpredictable variation in the distribution of value arising from unpredictable variation in that distributional risk factor.

Distributional risk arises from unpredictable variation in the price and quality of a service and in the taxes and subsidies that the government levies or grants. Variation in all these things can affect total project value,

Figure 4.4. Risks and Stakeholders

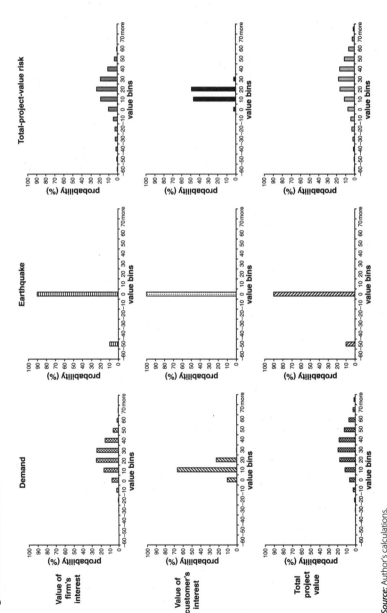

Source: Author's calculations.
Note: Demand and earthquake risk are as in figure 4.3. Demand risk is shared, as in figure 4.2. The firm bears all earthquake risk. The firm makes a payment of 3.75 to customers to equalize their expected values, the amount necessary taking account of the firm's expected benefits from bearing the most demand risk and its expected losses from bearing the earthquake risk. Demand and earthquake risks are shown holding the contribution of the other factor constant at zero.

as well its distribution. A price increase, for example, may reduce the use of the service and thereby reduce total project value. But variation in prices and quality standards and in taxes and subsidies also tends to redistribute value among stakeholders, an effect that may be much greater than any change in total project value.

In infrastructure businesses, price risk and other distributional risks are usually governed and thereby mitigated by rules set out in laws, regulations, or contracts. But distributional risk still arises from uncertainty about how the rules will be applied and whether they will be changed. If the rules say that the price of the service will increase with average consumer prices and the government unexpectedly refuses to allow such an increase, it changes the distribution of value that was expected, given average consumer prices. Such risks are reduced by courts and other institutions designed to ensure that all parties fulfill their contractual obligations or else compensate the others, but these institutions cannot eliminate the distributional risk created by nonperformance. It costs time and money to get a judge to enforce performance or compensation, so everyone can get away with some nonperformance.

A Principle

Having defined these terms, we can state the following principle of risk allocation: Each risk should be allocated, along with rights to make related decisions, so as to maximize total project value, taking account of each party's ability to

1. Influence the corresponding risk factor.
2. Influence the sensitivity of total project value to the corresponding risk factor—for example, by anticipating or responding to the risk factor.
3. Absorb the risk.

This principle is in the spirit of advice to allocate a risk to those who can manage it best.[6] The formulation is intended, however, to clarify what managing a risk entails and to specify a criterion—total project value—for assessing how well a risk is managed.

---

6 See, for example, Government of Victoria, Australia (2001); IMF (2005); and Quiggin (2004).

The principle calls for maximizing the sum of the values accruing to all stakeholders, measured in dollars or another unit of currency, without regard to the distribution of value. It might be criticized, therefore, for treating a dollar in the hands of a customer (any customer) as no more valuable than a dollar in the hands of the firm or the government. Yet allocating risk isn't the same as allocating value. Allocating a risk to a party doesn't mean reducing the value of the party's interest in the project. It means reducing the value of the party's interest in worlds in which the corresponding risk factor turns out badly and increasing the value of the party's interest in worlds in which the corresponding risk factor turns out well. Allocating earthquake risk to an insurance company, for example, doesn't reduce the value of the insurance company unless the premium is too low. Of course, if an earthquake occurs, the insurer will do poorly, and if no earthquake occurs, the insurer will do well—but this is a different matter. Governments can reasonably allocate risk to maximize total project value and then use other policies—toward prices and subsidies, in particular—to achieve the desired distribution of value.[7]

The principle identifies three ways of managing a risk: influencing the risk factor, anticipating or responding to the risk factor, and absorbing the risk. These three parts of the principle may push in different directions. The party best placed to influence a risk factor may not be the party best placed to anticipate or respond to it. Neither of those parties may be best placed to absorb the risk. Thus, tradeoffs may have to be made, using total project value as the criterion.

Allocate a Risk to the Party Best Able to Influence the Risk Factor

The first part of the principle says that, other things being equal, a risk should be allocated to the party that has the most influence over the corresponding risk factor.[8] The idea is simple: if one party can influence the risk factor and bears the corresponding risk, it gets the benefit of improving the risk factor's outcome and pays the cost of doing so. It has an incentive to spend resources to improve the outcome, until the extra

---

7 This is an application of the idea that most policies should be judged on their efficiency, not their distributional effects, on which see, for example, Posner (2001).

8 This part of the principle is related to the idea of moral hazard. It says, "Other things being equal, allocate risk to minimize moral hazard." The idea of moral hazard comes from insurance, where the risks of interest are on the downside, but can be generalized to apply also to the upside. People can take care to secure positive outcomes as well as to avoid negative outcomes. For early economic discussions of moral hazard, see Arrow (1971) and Stiglitz (1974).

cost of improvement is as great as the extra benefit. If it gets all the benefits and pays all the costs, it has an incentive to maximize total project value with respect to the risk factor.

It is on this ground, for example, that construction-cost risk is usually allocated to the firm, which, in turn, allocates it to the construction company. The idea is that the construction company can influence construction costs through its choice of materials and construction techniques and the diligence with which it manages the construction. As long as the quality of construction can be monitored, the total value of the project will tend to be higher if the construction company bears the construction-cost risk—that is, if it profits when construction costs less than expected and loses when it costs more. Construction-cost risk can be allocated to the company by avoiding construction-cost guarantees and by setting a price that does not vary with actual (as opposed to expected) construction costs.

Although the construction company may have the most influence over construction costs, the government may influence others. For example, the government may have the power to expropriate land for the road and may not be able to delegate this power. It then has more influence than any other party over the cost of acquiring land. The risk associated with the cost of acquiring land can be allocated to the government by requiring the government to pay the actual costs of acquisition after receiving from the firm a payment equal to the expected cost. Assuming the government also bears the risk related to the cost of delays in the acquisition of land, such an allocation gives the government an incentive to minimize the total costs of acquiring land.

Other risks can also be allocated by reference to the first part of the principle. The firm strongly influences at least some of the operating costs of the project, and allocating the associated risks to the firm is likely to maximize total project value. As before, effecting the allocation requires not doing something—in this case, not giving a rate-of-return guarantee or adjusting prices for actual operating costs. For this reason, pricing rules often adjust prices in response to changes in economywide or industry-wide price indexes that are beyond the control of the firm, but not in response to changes in actual costs, which after controlling for prices are often influenced by the firm.

Allocate a Risk to the Party Best Able to Anticipate or Respond to the Risk Factor

Sometimes no one can influence a risk factor. The first part of the principle is then of no use in deciding how to allocate a risk. Even when no one can influence the risk factor, however, one party may be able to anticipate or respond to it. By doing so, that party may be able to influence the sensitivity of total project value to the risk factor, taking steps to reduce sensitivity if outcomes are—or are expected to be—bad and taking steps to increase sensitivity if outcomes are—or are expected to be—good. In other words, the party may be able to mitigate downside risk and exploit upside risk. The second part of the principle, therefore, is to allocate the risk to the party that can most influence the sensitivity of total project value to the risk factor.[9]

No one, for example, can influence whether an earthquake occurs. But that doesn't imply that nothing can be done to mitigate the risk of an earthquake. If one party knew more about earthquakes and had responsibility for locating the project, it could choose a location less vulnerable to earthquakes. Or if everyone has the same knowledge, one party may be better at mitigating the risk by choice of building methods and materials. In either case, that party is best at anticipating the risk.

Likewise, no one may have much influence over demand, but one party may be better than others at forecasting it and adjusting the design of the project accordingly. Whether a toll road has positive total project value may depend, for instance, on demand. If we suppose that no one can influence demand, allocating demand risk to the party that can best forecast demand may maximize total project value by encouraging better decisions about whether to build the road.

Alternatively, one party may be better placed to respond to variation in the risk factor once it occurs. Consider a power-generation project, whose ideal size depends on demand. Suppose the investment need not be undertaken all at once but can be carried out in stages. Then the optimal investment program may be to start small and consider adding capacity if demand turns out to be high. If the firm is better at responding quickly to changes, allocating demand risk to the firm may maximize total project value by encouraging value-adding responses to changes in demand.

---

9 This part of the principle is related to the idea of adverse selection. Like the idea of moral hazard, the idea of adverse selection comes from insurance, where the risks of interest are on the downside. The problem of adverse selection in insurance is that people exposed to risk seek insurance, while the safe shun it. The idea of adverse selection can, however, be generalized to the case of positive as well as negative risk. Akerlof (1970) notes that one consequence of adverse selection when sellers know more than buyers about quality is that risk is naturally borne by the seller. For other early applications of the idea of adverse selection, see Rothschild and Stiglitz (1976) and Stiglitz and Weiss (1981).

This last idea is related to the idea that projects include valuable real options, such as the options to defer, expand, contract, or abandon the project and to switch between different inputs (see, for example, Copeland and Antikarov 2001; Dixit and Pindyck 1994). Allocating risk to the party that can best respond to the corresponding risk factor means allocating risk to the party best placed to exercise the associated real options.

Allocate a Risk to the Party Best Able to Absorb the Risk

The two parts of the principle just discussed are probably the most important for allocating risks in private infrastructure projects. One party is likely to be best placed to influence the risk factor or, failing that, to influence the sensitivity of the project's total value to the risk factor, and usually that party should bear the risk. If people were all risk neutral—if they cared only about the expected value of outcomes and not their variability—only the first two parts of the principle would matter. Further, only the first two parts would matter if financial markets were perfect. Everyone would then buy and sell exposure to risk until nobody differed in ability to absorb further risk.[10] Undiversifiable risk would still matter, but it would matter equally to everyone. People aren't risk neutral, however, nor are financial markets perfect. So the third part of the principle comes into play: people's ability to absorb risk must be considered.

A party's ability to absorb a risk depends on four things. First, it depends on the extent to which the risk factor is correlated with the value of the party's other assets and liabilities. If the new risk is small and uncorrelated with the risk of the party's existing portfolio, the party's cost of bearing the risk is small. If the new risk is large or highly correlated with the risk of the existing portfolio, the cost may be high. For example, demand for a toll road may be correlated with the strength of the local economy and therefore with the value of the government's portfolio of assets and liabilities (its tax revenue tending to rise and its spending on social welfare tending to fall when the economy is strong). For the same reasons, demand risk may be strongly correlated with customers' portfolios. It may be less correlated, however, with the portfolio of an international firm.[11]

---

10 This idea is related to the Modigliani and Miller's (1958) theorem that, in perfect financial markets, firms cannot change their value by changing their capital structure.

11 According to plausible financial theories, what matters is not the correlation with the firm's portfolio, but with the portfolios of its shareholders and, ultimately, with the portfolios of all shareholders. See chapter 7.

Second, a party's ability to bear a risk also varies with its ability to pass the risk on to others. The firm and government may be able to buy derivatives that protect them from changes in interest and exchange rates and the prices of commodities such as oil. Residential customers, by contrast, usually have no such ability. Other things being equal, then, the firm and the government may have a lower cost of absorbing these risks than residential customers do.

Third, the parties may differ in their ability to spread risk among other ultimate risk bearers. Governments and firms, for example, don't ultimately bear risk (though politicians and managers may). Risk allocated to the government is ultimately borne by the government's taxpayers and the potential beneficiaries of its spending: if the government does well, taxes can fall or spending rise; if it does poorly, taxes must rise or spending fall. Risk allocated to a firm is ultimately borne by its creditors, insurers, subcontractors, and shareholders.

Finally, the ultimate stakeholders may differ in their degree of risk aversion. Poor customers, for example, might be more risk averse than the average taxpayer or shareholder.

Matching Risks and Rights

Which party is best at managing a risk is not fixed but depends on how rights to make decisions are allocated among the parties. Risks and rights must therefore be allocated together.

Consider once more demand risk for a toll road. The most important choice dependent on demand is whether to build the road. To keep things simple, suppose that it is the only choice that depends on demand, that there are no differences among the parties in ability to absorb risk, and that the firm has no role in deciding whether the road is built: the government is prepared to offer whatever subsidy is necessary to get the firm to build the road. Then nothing is gained by allocating demand risk to the firm, even if the firm is better than the government at forecasting demand. Either the risk should lie with the government, to encourage it to forecast as well as it can, or the firm should be given some responsibility for determining whether the road is built. This doesn't mean that the firm need decide itself whether the road is built. The government can fix a subsidy, allocate demand risk to the firm, and see whether any firm wants to take the project on. If no firm thinks demand will be high enough to make the road profitable at the given subsidy, there will be no takers and no road. If firms are the best forecasters of demand and the subsidy was well chosen, this outcome is the right one: no road should be built.

Or consider demand risk for power projects. There may be reasons for thinking that firms are best at forecasting demand and thus reasons for allocating demand risk to them. But if the government is to benefit from firms' forecasting ability, it must give firms the right to make decisions that can anticipate or respond to demand. It must allow the firm to choose when to invest, what technology to use, and so on. A government that wants to make these decisions itself while contracting out new generation to independent power producers may have no choice but to bear the demand risk. It may, that is, have to enter into long-term purchase commitments in which it agrees through its state-owned utility to pay for the availability of power regardless of whether the power is used.

Applying the Principle to Four Kinds of Risks

Risks can be divided into four categories, according to whether they are project specific or economywide and whether they affect total project value or only its distribution among stakeholders (table 4.1). All parts of the principle of risk allocation are relevant to allocating project-specific total-project-value risks. However, only some parts of the principle are usually relevant to allocating other risks (table 4.2).

Project-specific distributional risks are often controlled by one party. The price of a service, for example, may be controlled either by the government, if the price is regulated, or the by firm, if it is not. In the

Table 4.1. Four Kinds of Risk and Examples Thereof

		Nature	
		Total project value	Distributional
Scope	Project-specific	Unpredictable variation in value arising from unpredictable variation in construction costs specific to the project	Unpredictable variation in the distribution of value among stakeholders arising from unpredictable variation in the regulated price of the service
	Economywide	Unpredictable variation in value arising from unpredictable variation in the wages of construction workers	Unpredictable variation in the distribution of value among stakeholders arising from unpredictable variation in the exchange rate and foreign currency debt

Source: Author's representation.

Table 4.2. The Principle for Four Kinds of Risk

		Nature	
		Total project value	*Distributional*
Scope	Project-specific	Influence the risk factor Influence the sensitivity of total project value to the risk factor Absorb the risk	Influence the risk factor
	Economywide	Influence the sensitivity of total project value to the risk factor Absorb the risk	Influence the sensitivity of the distribution of total project value to the factor Absorb the risk

Source: Author's representation.
Note: Risks and related rights should be allocated among parties so as to maximize project value, taking account of each party's ability to do the things noted in the relevant cell of the table.

case of such risks, attention should be devoted to controlling the risk, rather than anticipating it, responding to it, or absorbing it. This can be done by allocating the risk to the party that controls it. Thus, the second and third parts of principle are relatively unimportant for project-specific distributional risks.

Economywide risks differ from project-specific risks in that most stakeholders cannot influence the risk factor. Or, in the case of the government, which may be able to influence the risk factor, deciding what to do by reference to the project alone is usually inappropriate. Thus, when one is considering the allocation of risk in the context of a particular project, the first part of the principle of risk allocation, which refers to influencing the risk factor, has little application to economy-wide risks. Instead, attention must be devoted to anticipating and responding to the risk factor or absorbing the risk. That is, economywide risks should usually be allocated according to the second two parts of the principle of risk allocation.

Transaction Costs

Transaction costs limit the benefits of certain allocations of risks.[12] In principle, risks can be subdivided almost infinitely: construction-cost risks can be divided into risks related to different stages of construction and to the prices of different kinds of labor and materials, demand risk

---

12 Arrow (1971) is an early reference that makes this point.

can be divided into risks related to each type of customer, operating-cost risks can be divided into risks related to each component of operating costs, and so on.

Other things being equal, fine allocations may maximize value, since they allow each risk to be allocated to the party best able to manage it. But it costs money to analyze risks and the ways they interact, to negotiate the allocation of risks, to draft contracts that effect the negotiated allocation, and then to monitor whether all the parties are complying with their contractual obligations. For a large, expensive project, a very fine allocation may make sense. But at some point the transaction costs of finer and finer subdivisions and allocations of risk must outweigh the benefits of better management.[13]

Even when an allocation is not too expensive to design, it may be too expensive to apply. It would be straightforward, for example, to draft a law stating that all policy risks should be borne by the government, thereby requiring the government to compensate those who lose from a policy change. But such a rule would be extremely costly to apply. Consider a regulation banning lead in gasoline. It may be costly for drivers, but good for pedestrians. It may be good for children, but bad for oil companies and car manufacturers. The ultimate incidence of the costs and benefits is obscure: whether firms and their workers and shareholders suffer depends on how prices change in response to the change in regulation, which in turn depends on the competition the firms face.

More generally, if the government bore all policy risk, every change in policy that redistributed value—that is, every change in policy— would require the government to compensate all the losers and tax all the winners. There would be costs associated with designing the tax-benefit system to effect the compensating taxes and subsidies. There would be costs associated with estimating how much each person and firm had gained or lost from the change. And there would be costs associated with litigation over the amounts. Many losers would find any proposed compensation inadequate. Many winners would doubt they had gained enough to justify their taxes. In short, the transaction costs would be impossibly high.

This does not mean that the transaction costs of a government's bearing a risk are always too high. Certain policy changes affect some

---

13 Klein, So, and Shin (1996) discuss transaction costs in privately financed projects.

people or firms disproportionately. When the government takes land to build a road (a policy change as we define it), for example, the transaction costs of compensating the owner are not prohibitive. Moreover, if the government didn't compensate the owner, it would have less incentive to take account of the cost of land. Valuing land is often done for other reasons, so it is not too costly to do for the purposes of compensation.[14]

But the principle of risk allocation should really be restated as follows: allocate risks and related rights so as to maximize total project value, taking account of each party's ability to influence, anticipate, and absorb risk—and transaction costs.

Governments' Special Features

Governments have special features that change the analysis in certain respects.

Ability to Absorb Risk

Governments are sometimes better able to absorb risk than firms are, because they can spread risk among millions of taxpayers and beneficiaries of government spending (see Arrow and Lind 1970; Whitman 1965, 54). The United States, for example, has some 100 million individual taxpayers, and nearly all its 300 million residents benefit from federal spending and therefore bear risk allocated in the first instance to the U.S. government.[15] When governments are better at absorbing risk, the third part of the principle favors allocating risk to governments.

This may not greatly affect the appropriate allocation of infrastructure risks. On the one hand, the cost of absorbing risk is probably not the decisive factor in the allocation of risks in infrastructure projects. If one party can influence, anticipate, or respond to the risk, allocating the risk to that party probably has a greater effect on total project value than allocating the risk to the party that can best absorb it. On the other hand, large private firms can also spread risk among millions of shareholders, taking account of the ultimate beneficial owners of shares owned by mutual funds, pension funds, and insurance companies. The

---

14 For an analysis of compensation for the taking of land, see Shavell (2004, chapter 6).

15 A U.S. Treasury press release notes that in 1999 approximately 98 million individual income tax returns were filed (http://www.treas.gov/press/releases/docs/count.pdf).

extent of private risk spreading may indeed be greater than that achieved by the governments of small countries.[16]

Ability to Spread Risk Coercively

Even when governments cannot spread risk among more people than firms can, they do have an advantage over firms: they can spread risk coercively. They can compel their citizens to bear risk. The ability to compel has a disadvantage: governments can fund harebrained ventures, giving their citizens no choice but to bear the risks. But it also allows governments to solve problems that markets cannot.

Because people hoping to sell a risk often know more about the risk than the would-be buyers do, markets don't insure all risks.[17] Insurers may not be able to distinguish between good risks and bad, and at any given insurance premium, people with high risks will be more likely to buy insurance, leaving the insurer with risks that are poorer than average. Trying to solve the problem by increasing the premium won't necessarily work, because it may scare off more good risks, leaving the insurer with an even riskier portfolio. Thus, insurance for some risks may be scarce or unavailable. In principle, governments can solve this problem of adverse selection by providing the insurance themselves and

---

16 A closely related question is whether the government's cost of capital is lower than firms' cost of capital. Most governments can borrow at an interest rate lower than that available to most private firms, which leads some to think that public finance is cheaper than private finance. This argument is unsound, however, because the cost of investing in a project is not the interest rate paid by the investing entity (see for example, Brealey, Cooper, and Habib 1997; Flemming and Mayer 1997; Jenkinson 2003; Klein 1997). A government's low borrowing rate reflects in part the government's ability to tax; it is as though taxpayers give their governments a free guarantee of the government's borrowing. The full cost of the borrowing would have to account for this guarantee. A similar point applies to firms. A large, diversified, profitable firm can borrow for less than other firms can, but its cost of capital for a new project is not therefore lower; the firm's other projects effectively guarantee the loan for the new project. The argument considered in the text is more sophisticated: it is that the public cost of capital is lower because governments can spread risk among more ultimate risk bearers. See Klein (1997) for more. There are other arguments, including the possibility that the private cost of capital reflects an irrational degree of risk aversion for reasons including those discussed in "Cognitive Obstacles" in chapter 3 (see Quiggin 2004; Siegel and Thaler 1997). Here we take the view that the cost of capital for both public and private investment is its opportunity cost, which depends on the riskless rate of interest and the risk of the project (Brealey, Cooper, and Habib 1997).

17 For an influential early discussion of this fact, see Rothschild and Stiglitz (1976), and for a recent summary discussing the implications for the government's role as a risk manager, see Moss (2002).

compelling the payment of the premium through taxation—or by making private insurance compulsory.[18]

The ability to compel may also allow the reduction of an asymmetry of information. Governments can use their coercive powers to get information that firms and private insurers cannot. By tackling the underlying information problems, governments may reduce adverse selection and also moral hazard—that is, people's taking less care to improve a risk factor, and therefore to avoid a loss or capture a gain, if they don't bear the associated risks (Moss 2002, 50).

For these reasons, it is often said that governments should provide or mandate health insurance. It's not clear whether the arguments justify more risk bearing by governments in infrastructure projects, but it's worth looking out for similar possibilities in such projects.

Ability to Subsidize Lending

Coercive power also enables governments to tax and, therefore, to subsidize—in particular, to subsidize borrowing, either by contributing to interest payments or by guaranteeing loans and thereby encouraging commercial lenders to lend at a lower interest rate. It is sometimes argued that governments should use this power to solve another problem caused by moral hazard and adverse selection.

The problem is that lenders, like insurers, know less than their clients do about the risks involved in the transactions they enter into. They know less about the risks of the borrowers' projects and about the actions the borrowers will take that may reduce or increase those risks. Lenders can charge a higher interest rate to offset this problem, but as in the case of insurance, this may not solve the problem. Raising the interest rate may increase the average risk of the loans, as some potential borrowers with low-risk, low-return projects drop out and some remaining borrowers increase the risk in their projects.[19] In such a situation, credit is rationed: interest rates do not clear the market, and some firms wanting to borrow at prevailing rates cannot.

Credit rationing may create a rationale for government debt guarantees.[20] In particular, some theoretical models show that government interventions that favor lending increase national welfare and that,

---

18 Governments can even spread risks among generations. By borrowing, a shock to the current generation can be passed on to future generations (Stiglitz 1993).

19 See Stiglitz and Weiss (1981) for a discussion, and, for a textbook treatment, see Tirole (2006).

20 See Eichengreen (1996) for an example.

in some circumstances, guarantees are better than interest subsidies.[21] The theoretical literature focuses on debt guarantees, but other guarantees that reduce the firm's exposure to risk and facilitate financing might serve the same purpose. If these models are realistic, governments should be more sympathetic to requests for guarantees that help infrastructure firms raise finance.

Yet credit-rationing arguments for guarantees may not be very strong. Different models in the same tradition lead to different conclusions; some suggest governments should tax or otherwise discourage borrowing (de Meza and Webb 2000), and an attempt to use a credit-rating model to quantify the effects of the U.S. government's subsidies and guarantees of borrowing found they did more harm than good (Gale 1991). Joseph Stiglitz, a pioneer of the theory of credit rationing who has often argued for interventions to remedy other problems of imperfect information, has also expressed skepticism about government intervention in the lending market (Stiglitz 1989, 202). Last, if there are useful government interventions that respond to credit rationing, they seem more likely, given the pervasive nature of the information problems, to be economywide than infrastructure specific.

Role in Redistributing Resources

Their power to compel allows governments to perform another function that distinguishes them from other stakeholders. They can coercively redistribute resources between citizens (see "Policy Obstacles" in chapter 3). Not everyone thinks the function is legitimate, but probably most people do. Moreover, most people probably believe that governments may from time to time change the extent and nature of redistribution. If redistributive policies are to change, however, the government cannot bear all policy risks; it cannot agree to compensate for all changes in policy.

Limited Sensitivity to Financial Incentives

Stakeholders may differ in the way they respond to the incentives created by risk bearing. Firms, for example, are run by managers who don't necessarily have any direct incentive to respond to the risks their firms bear. Corporate governance aims, however, to ensure that managers do better when their firms are profitable. Although corporate governance is far from perfect, it usually does encourage managers to seek to lower

---

21 Innes (1991) and Janda (2005) provide examples.

costs and increase revenue. Thus, allocating a risk to a firm can be expected to change the firm's behavior.

Government decisions are also made by people who have no direct financial interest in furthering the government's interests. Politicians' pay and other rewards do not necessarily vary with the government's financial performance. On the whole, political governance does not seem to be as effective as corporate governance in making decision makers sensitive to financial incentives. This, at any rate, is at the heart of many arguments for involving private firms in providing infrastructure.

If governments are less sensitive to the financial consequences of bearing a risk, the benefits of allocating risk to them are reduced. Even when the government *could* influence, anticipate, or respond to the risk factor, it may not. If the firm or customers have some ability to influence, anticipate, or respond to the risk factor and are more sensitive than the government to financial incentives, allocating the risk to either of them may do more to maximize total project value.

CHAPTER 5

The Allocation of Three Risks

In the last chapter, we set out a framework for allocating risks and discussed in passing its implications for the allocation of demand and construction-cost risks. In this chapter, we focus on three difficult cases: exchange-rate risk, insolvency risk, and policy risk.

Exchange-Rate Risk

Exchange rates are often volatile, especially in the developing world (figure 5.1). This volatility creates two types of risk for infrastructure projects.

First, most infrastructure firms use tradable inputs, the costs of which depend on the exchange rate. The cost of the fuel used by many power generators, for example, depends on the world price of the fuel, irrespective of whether the fuel is imported or locally produced. Its price in local currency therefore depends on the exchange rate. A few infrastructure projects produce a tradable service whose value also rises and falls with the local currency. Some power plants, for example, are linked by transmission lines to markets in neighboring countries. But most projects sell untradable services. For them, a lower exchange rate doesn't directly cause customers to value their service more highly in local currency. Thus, the value of the project tends to vary inversely with the value of the local currency.

Figure 5.1. Currencies of Five Developing Countries against the U.S. Dollar, 1985–2002

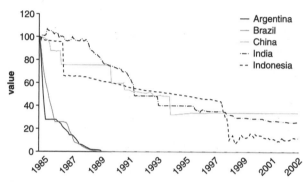

Source: Gray and Irwin 2003a.

Second, even if a firm uses no tradable inputs, its financing may introduce exchange-rate risk. In developing countries, the firm may have difficulty borrowing in local currency, especially for long terms at fixed rates. Local banks may lend at fixed rates only for short terms, and local-currency bond markets may not exist at all. Moreover, there may be no derivative markets that allow floating-rate or foreign-currency payments to be swapped with fixed-rate or local-currency ones. So the firm often borrows in foreign currency and remains exposed to exchange-rate risk. If the local currency then depreciates sharply, shareholders may suffer large losses—unless prices are tied to the exchange rate, in which case customers may suffer large losses, or the government has given an exchange-rate guarantee, in which case the government may suffer large losses.[1]

Argentina's recent history illustrates the issue. The prices charged by privatized Argentine utilities in the 1990s were set in U.S. dollars (Estache 2002). As a result, customers bore exchange-rate risk. For many years, the value of the peso was fixed at one U.S. dollar. But then, during a macroeconomic crisis, the government ended the policy of convertibility, and the peso fell in value to about a third of a dollar. The pricing rule called for roughly a tripling of peso prices. Not surprisingly, the government refused to allow such an increase. Thus,

---

1 Many governments have also borne exchange-rate risk, often through subsidiaries, by making long-term commitments to buy power and water at prices denominated in foreign currency.

customers bore less exchange-rate risk in practice than they did on paper, while the utilities bore more. Having to pay world prices for some inputs and having to service foreign-currency borrowing, some utilities made big losses and defaulted on their debts. Many have sought compensation from the government, and depending on the decisions of arbitrators, the government may turn out to have borne some of the exchange-rate risk.

Many governments have explicitly borne exchange-rate risk. Guarantees on Spanish toll roads in the 1960s and early 1970s were mentioned in chapter 2. Chile and the Republic of Korea have also given exchange-rate guarantees to private toll roads.[2] They have so far been luckier than Spain, because their currencies have mainly appreciated since they issued their guarantees. A standard Korean exchange-rate guarantee says the government will compensate the concessionaire for half the loss caused by depreciation greater than 20 percent, while requiring the company to give the government half the gain associated with appreciation of more than 20 percent (Hahm 2003). Chile's guarantees have the same form, but the government bears all the risk outside the thresholds.

Governments have more influence over the exchange rate than anyone else does, which leads some to think the exchange-rate risk should be allocated to governments. Others say it should be allocated to customers, perhaps because risks allocated to the government are ultimately allocated to taxpayers, who in practice may be the same people as customers. Either way, it is argued, allocating the risk to the firm makes no sense because the firm has no control over the risk factor. Yet firms can change the project's sensitivity to the risk factor, leading others to think the firm should bear the risk.[3]

Categorizing Currency Risks

Exchange-rate risk is economywide: the risk factor affects not only the project at hand but also almost all businesses. Risk related to the cost of project inputs is a total-project-value risk: rising input prices lower the value of the project. Risk related to borrowing in foreign currency

---

2 Other countries to have given exchange-rate guarantees include Colombia (Christopher, Lewis, and Mody 1997), the Dominican Republic (Guasch 2004), and Malaysia (Fishbein and Babbar 1996).

3 For different views, see Gray and Irwin (2003b), Mas (1997), and Matsukawa, Sheppard, and Wright (2003).

is partly distributional: when the firm borrows in foreign currency, the exchange rate affects the distribution of the value of the firm between shareholders and creditors—or, with an indexed price or government guarantee, between the firm, customers, and government.

Currency risk also depends on whether the exchange rate is fixed or floating. When the rate is fixed, exchange-rate risk arises from the possibility of devaluation or revaluation—and from the possibility that the government will abandon its policy and allow the currency to float, an occurrence likely to be associated with a devaluation or revaluation.

In countries with fixed exchange rates, the government may restrict the conversion of local currency into foreign currency and the transfer of foreign currency out of the country. These possibilities create convertibility and transferability risks. The government controls the convertibility and transferability of its currency, and if it fixes the exchange rate, it controls the exchange rate as well. In such a case, currency risk is a policy risk, and the discussion later in this chapter is relevant. In countries with floating exchange rates, the main currency risk is the exchange-rate risk, which is the focus of the rest of this section.

The Price of Tradable Inputs

We start with the allocation of exchange-rate risk related to the price of tradable project inputs: that is, unpredictable variation in the value of the project arising from unpredictable variation in the price of inputs caused by unpredictable variation in the exchange rate. Chapter 4 argued that economywide total-project-value risks should usually be allocated according to the parties' ability to influence the sensitivity of project value to the risk factor and to absorb the risk. Suppose we take the allocation of rights as given. Then if one party strongly influences the sensitivity, that party should bear the risk. If distinguishing between the parties on this ground is difficult, the party best able to absorb the risk should bear it.[4]

---

4 We assume here that economywide risks shouldn't be allocated according to the parties' ability to influence the risk factor. It might be argued that this assumption is unwarranted here and that the government's ability to use fiscal and monetary policies to influence the exchange rate needs to be considered. If this argument is right, the case for allocating some exchange-rate risk for input prices to the government is stronger. To make the case, one would have to argue that the government's fiscal and monetary policy would be influenced by the allocation of risk in a particular project and that it ought to be. That would be more likely the larger the project was relative to the rest of the economy.

Sometimes no one has much influence over the sensitivity of total project value to the exchange rate. Depending on the allocation of rights, however, firms or customers may have some influence over it. Firms can sometimes choose among technologies that use different inputs and thus influence the sensitivity of total project value to the exchange rate. For example, a power-generating company might be able to choose between building hydroelectric and gas-fired plants. In other cases, it might be able to switch between inputs as their relative price fluctuated with the exchange rate. A company that owns both hydroelectric and gas-fired plants can switch between them as the price of fuel and the scarcity value of water change. The firm might also be able to enter into long-term purchase contracts that fix the price of inputs such as gas in local currency.

Customers' behavior may also influence the sensitivity of project value to the exchange rate. When the exchange rate and the costs of tradable inputs change, the marginal cost of the service changes. If the price of fuel rises, for instance, the marginal cost of power rises. When that happens, the level of consumption that maximizes total project value falls. Thus, there is an advantage in setting the marginal unit price faced by customers—especially industrial customers—equal to marginal cost, allowing the firm to impose fixed charges if revenue would otherwise fall short of costs. If the marginal unit price varies with marginal cost, customers bear exchange-rate risk.

The firm and its customers may also differ in their ability to absorb exchange-rate risks. In particular, customers' wealth and the firm's wealth (and, more specifically, that of the firm's shareholders) may be unequally correlated with the exchange rate. Dramatic depreciations often occur during macroeconomic crises, when local customers' wealth declines. By contrast, the firm's shareholders may be foreigners or wealthy locals who can hold some of their wealth outside the country and who can therefore absorb exchange-rate risk more easily than customers can.

Overall, the principle of risk allocation suggests that the exchange-rate risk for input prices should be shared between the firm and customers, according to their ability to anticipate or respond to changes in the exchange rate. And when neither party has that ability, the risk should be shared according to the parties' likely ability to absorb the risk, which probably implies allocating it to the firm.

Foreign-Currency Borrowing

But who should bear the economywide, partly distributional risk that comes from borrowing in foreign currency? Chapter 4 suggested that, given the allocation of rights, economywide risks should be allocated to the party most able to influence the sensitivity of total project value and its distribution to the risk factor and, failing that, to the party best able to absorb the risk.

The extent of foreign-currency borrowing determines the sensitivity of value and its distribution to the exchange rate. And the firm and its creditors normally decide how much foreign currency is borrowed. Thus, the principle of risk allocation suggests allocating the risk to the firm and its creditors, not allowing them to transfer the risk to customers or tax-payers. That, in turn, means not indexing the price to the exchange rate and not providing an exchange-rate guarantee.

If governments do give a guarantee or index the price to the exchange rate, the firm has an incentive to borrow as much as it can in the currency with the lowest interest rate.[5] Although this strategy may seem to lower costs, the low foreign interest rates probably imply expected depreciation of the local currency against the foreign currency. For example, if the local interest rate is 12 percent and the foreign equivalent is 2 percent, a good guess is that the local currency will depreciate—and the difference in rates, 10 percent, is not a bad estimate of the rate of depreciation.[6] So if the price is indexed, it can be expected to go up, and if the government gives a guarantee, it may well be called.

An alternative to allocating the risk to the firm and its creditors is to change the allocation of rights. When the firm and creditors choose foreign-currency borrowing, they should bear the associated risk. Conversely, if the government or customers bear the risk, the government should control foreign-currency borrowing. When the risk is shared—as, for example, in Korea when exchange-rate guarantees only partially protect the firm against exchange-rate risk—the firm and the government should jointly decide. One option is for the government to limit the firm's foreign-currency borrowing.

---

5 Gómez-Ibáñez and Meyer (1993, 130) describe the Spanish government's exchange-rate guarantee as "pernicious, since it encouraged the companies to search for foreign loans with the lowest nominal interest rates, regardless of the exchange risks."

6 The proposition known as *uncovered interest-rate parity* says that the expected depreciation is equal to the difference in interest rates. The proposition would be true if investors were rational and required no risk premium for holding one of the currencies instead of the other. The imperfect rationality of investors (see chapter 3) and the possibility of risk premiums imply that uncovered interest-rate parity need not hold—something confirmed by empirical evidence (see M. Taylor 1995). It still seems reasonable to assume that large differences in interest rates will be associated with a depreciation of the high-interest-rate currency against the low-interest-rate currency.

Figure 5.2. Annual Average Inflation and Currency Depreciation against the U.S. Dollar in a Sample of 89 Countries, 1976–2001

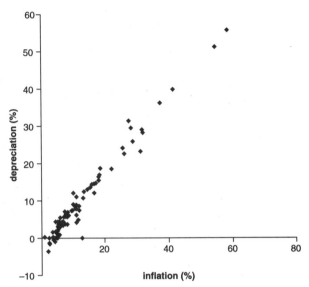

Source: Gray and Irwin 2003a.

Implications

Two implications of exposing the firm to financing-related exchange-rate risk should be mentioned. First, exposing the firm to the risk shouldn't be viewed as a strategy for reducing the firm's expected profits. As always, the allocation of risk needs to be distinguished from the distribution of value. A firm exposed to exchange-rate risk may need to charge a higher expected price than one protected by customers or the government from the risk. (Moreover, nothing in the preceding argument suggests changing a previously agreed allocation of exchange-rate risk.)

Second, if prices are not indexed to the exchange rate, they must be indexed to something else, such as average consumer prices or another weighted average of the local prices of goods and services. In the long run, changes in exchange rates and local prices are related (figure 5.2).[7] Thus, at the end of a long contract governing private investment, the price may not vary that much according to whether it was indexed to the exchange rate or to consumer prices. Yet in the short run, changes in the consumer

---

7 See also Rogoff (1996) and A. Taylor and M. Taylor (2004) for a discussion of the relation between exchange rates and local prices.

price index can diverge sharply from changes in the exchange rate, so the choice matters. Indexation to the price level won't permit as much foreign-currency borrowing. But nor will it require customers to endure a large nominal price increase before local inflation has had a chance to catch up with the exchange rate.

Insolvency Risk

Next we consider the allocation of insolvency risk, or unpredictable variation in value, and its distribution, arising from unpredictability in whether the firm will be able to pay its debts. The stakeholders to whom this risk is most important are, of course, creditors. But in private infrastructure projects, insolvency risk also matters to customers and the government, because the firm's financial distress may lead to an unscheduled increase in regulated prices or a taxpayer-funded bailout.

Insolvency risk increases with uncertainty about the value of the firm and with increases in the firm's leverage (its debt as a fraction of its value). For any given degree of uncertainty about the firm's value, an increase in leverage increases the probability of insolvency. To simplify, think of insolvency as occurring if and only if the value of the firm's assets falls below the value of its outstanding debt. If the value of its assets exceeds the value of its outstanding debt, creditors get everything they are owed. Otherwise, they get only the value of the assets (figure 5.3).

The nonlinear payoffs shown in figure 5.3 are like option payoffs. Conceptually speaking, shareholders have a call on the assets of the firm, with a strike price equal to the nominal value of the debt, while creditors have sold a put on the assets of the firm, with a strike price also equal to the nominal value of the debt.[8] One consequence is that we can use option-pricing techniques to value shareholders' and creditors' interests in a project (see "Insolvency Risk" in chapter 8). Here, however, we consider how the division of value between shareholders and creditors varies with insolvency risk.

Other things being equal, insolvency risk reduces the value of the creditors' interest in the project. Creditors take account of this when pricing loans, of course: borrowers with poorer credit pay more interest.

---

8 See Hull (2003, chapter 1). The value of the firm is equal to the value of the call plus the value of the debt, assuming the debt is riskless, less the value of the put. This relationship is known in option-pricing theory as *put-call parity* (see Hull 2003, chapter 8).

Figure 5.3. Creditors' and Shareholders' Interest in the Firm as a Function of the Value of the Firm at the Maturity of Its Debt

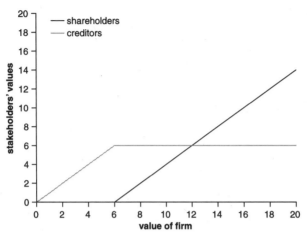

Source: Author's calculations.

Note: The figure assumes that the firm must make a debt payment of 6. The nature of the debt contract means the value at maturity of the creditors' interest in the project is at most 6. Limited liability (plus an assumption that the creditors' only security for the debt is the firm's assets) means that the value of the shareholders' interest is at least 0.

But insolvency risk can increase after the creditor has decided to lend. It can increase because the value of the firm's assets falls, hence reducing the buffer between the value of the assets and the value of the debt. Yet it can also increase, without any change in the value of the firm, simply because the firm's business becomes riskier (figure 5.4).

Explicit and Implicit Allocation of Insolvency Risk

In most industries, insolvency risk affects only creditors and shareholders. Creditors gauge the likelihood of insolvency and ensure that they are compensated for it. To prevent the shifting of value shown in figure 5.4, they may limit the firm's leverage and require the firm to keep business risks within certain bounds. If the firm defaults, creditors try to maximize the amount they recover, usually having the right to take over the running of the firm. But they normally have no recourse to taxpayers or customers.

In infrastructure, governments and customers can bear some insolvency risk normally borne by creditors. If the firm cannot pay its debts, the government and customers may share the losses normally borne by creditors. Creditors may even lose nothing, payments from the government or customers keeping them whole. Governments and

Figure 5.4. Creditors' and Shareholders' Shares of the Value of the Firm and the Volatility of the Firm's Value, Holding Debt, and the Value of the Firm Constant

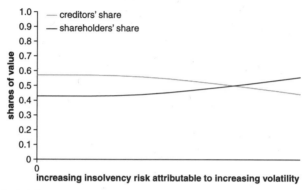

Source: Author's calculations.

customers bear insolvency risk in two ways: explicitly (de jure) and implicitly (de facto).

As we saw in chapter 2, governments sometimes guarantee the debts of infrastructure firms and therefore bear insolvency risk explicitly. They can also bear insolvency risk by guaranteeing the obligations of public enterprises in long-term purchase contracts.

A common long-term purchase contract in developing countries is the power-purchase agreement.[9] As an example, consider one in the Philippines, where in the 1980s and 1990s the state-owned power company Napocor signed dozens of power-purchase agreements with private companies. In one agreement, Keilco, a company mostly owned by the Korean power company Kepco, agreed to build a 1,200-megawatt gas-fired plant, at a cost of about $710 million, in return for Napocor agreeing to pay a monthly fee for 20 years for capital, operations, and maintenance of about $8 per kilowatt, as well as amounts in Philippine pesos for energy produced.[10] The agreement ensures that Napocor pays nothing unless the plant is available to generate power.

9 A typical power-purchase contract is described in Kerf and others (1998, annex 2). Overviews and comments on such contracts can be found in Albouy and Bousba (1998), Babbar and Schuster (1998), Gray and Schuster (1998), and Lovei (2000). Similar long-term contracts for purchasing bulk water and treating wastewater are also common (see Haarmeyer and Mody 1998).

10 See the World Bank's Private Participation in Infrastructure project database and Kepco's form 20-F for 2003, available at http://ppi.worldbank.org/ and http://www.kepco.co.kr/, respectively.

It also creates an economic liability similar to debt. The amount of the liability can be estimated by making an assumption about the plant's availability and then discounting back to the present the cost of paying for that availability. If we suppose that Keilco will make available a constant 80 percent of the plant's nominal capacity of 1,200 megawatts, Napocor will have to pay $7.7 million a month (1,200,000 kilowatts × 0.8 × $8 per kilowatt). If we discount the payments at 12 percent, we get a present value of $725 million—just slightly more than the reported cost of the plant. The government gets the power, but only by agreeing in advance to pay an amount roughly equal to the capital cost of the plant (conditional on its availability).

Projects like this one quickly brought new generation capacity to the Philippines and ended blackouts and brownouts that were extremely costly to the Philippine economy. But the economic crisis that hit the Philippines in the late 1990s meant that demand was lower than forecast, while costs, denominated in pesos, were higher. Furthermore, the Philippine power regulator allowed only some of the extra costs to be passed on to power consumers. As a result, Napocor ran out of money, and the government had to take over its debts.

When long-term contracts are signed by state-owned enterprises, rather than the government, the government often guarantees the obligations of the state-owned purchaser. Many of Napocor's power-purchase agreements were so backed, for example. Insofar as the contracts resemble debt, the guarantees resemble debt guarantees. Sometimes, as, for example, in Indonesia, governments may also write letters of support or comfort, giving a less formal, perhaps ambiguous degree of backing to the state-owned enterprise's obligations (World Bank 2004a, 65, 126, 136).

And when governments don't fully guarantee the repayment of debt, they may still treat debt more favorably than equity by agreeing to compensate lenders but not shareholders in the event of the project's early termination for certain reasons.

Governments sometimes bail out firms in financial distress even when they have no obligation to do so, which implies that they were bearing insolvency risk implicitly. Although they may have given no commitment to protect the lenders from insolvency—and may have expressly refused to do so—they may still find the prospect of the firm's bankruptcy politically unpalatable. Bankruptcy is contentious and disruptive. It may nullify the firm's supply contracts, calling into question the firm's ability to get critical inputs, and it may lead to the replacement of the firm's management. Whether services will continue to be provided may be uncertain. When the services in question are as vital as water and power, even the possibility of disruption can cause the government to intervene.

Bankruptcy may also seem to signal failure on the part of the government. In particular, if the government recently sold the firm, the firm's insolvency may seem to indicate that the sale was a mistake. The inference may be wrongheaded: part of the reason for selling may have been to shelter the government from the risks of owning or lending to the firm. The bankruptcy might even be taken as evidence of the prescience of the policy. But it seldom is. The failure of the firm looks like the failure of policy.

A government may therefore prefer to avoid the risk of bankruptcy by giving the firm a grant, a concessional loan, or a guarantee allowing the firm to borrow cheaply from others. The government may get something in return, such as future loan repayments or shares in the company, but the motivation for the bailout is unlikely to be purely commercial—otherwise it would probably have been unnecessary. The motivation is usually to reduce the likelihood of service disruption and political embarrassment.

Customers may take the place of taxpayers in bearing insolvency risk. First, they may offer a sort of explicit debt guarantee: that is, the rules governing prices may treat debt-service payments as a pass-through—requiring the price to increase enough to ensure that the firm can pay its debts. Second, they may offer a sort of implicit guarantee: regulators may increase prices to prevent insolvency despite the absence of any rule requiring such an increase.

Consider Great Britain's air-traffic-control organization, NATS (National Air Traffic Services), which was privatized in 2001.[11] The firm earned its revenue by charging planes that used British airports, the charge being fixed by regulation. As was standard in Britain, prices were fixed for five years by a "retail price index − x" formula that meant real prices would gradually fall over the period. The price-setting formula meant that the firm would bear most business risks, except for the risk associated with retail-price inflation for the five years. The purchaser of NATS borrowed to finance the purchase, and the combination of business risk (from the price-setting formula) and financial risk (from leverage) meant the firm was vulnerable to shocks.

---

11 For more about the privatization, see Ehrhardt and Irwin (2004) and the references therein.

After the terrorist attacks of September 11, 2001, air traffic declined. Given the pricing formula, however, the price NATS could charge didn't change, so the firm's revenue fell. Most of the firm's operating costs were fixed, as were its debt-service obligations. The decline in traffic therefore created severe problems for the firm. The firm and its bankers took their concerns to the regulator, the U.K. Civil Aviation Authority, seeking an increase in the regulated price to compensate the firm for the unexpected decline in demand.

The regulator was in a difficult position. Rejecting the request might jeopardize NATS's financial viability. That wouldn't necessarily cause any problems for air traffic control in Great Britain, because there were rules providing for smooth transition in case of bankruptcy. But the rules were untested, and it wasn't possible to be sure what would happen. Those responsible wouldn't have relished the prospect of being held responsible for disruptions in flights or worse, after having rejected an increase in prices and precipitated bankruptcy. But acceding to the request would seem like a change in the rules halfway through the game. Hadn't the firm willingly taken the risks in the price formula? Hadn't it willingly increased them by borrowing? Wouldn't it have argued forcefully against cutting prices if demand had risen unexpectedly?

In the end, the regulator agreed to an increase, and bankruptcy was avoided. Thus, customers bore the insolvency risk in practice, though not on paper, and some of the shift in value illustrated in figure 5.4 was actually from customers, not creditors.

Who Should Bear Insolvency Risk?

Unplanned, implicit risk bearing by governments or customers is generally undesirable. It means that the government's real policies differ from those written in laws, contracts, and regulations and that the true allocation of risk is vague. But should governments or customer bear insolvency risk explicitly?

Insolvency risk is the result of leverage and unpredictable variation in the value of the firm. Although unpredictable variation in the value of the firm has many causes, project specific and economywide, the crucial choice of leverage is project specific. Thus, insolvency risk is mainly project specific. Though insolvency can reduce project value—for example, by creating transaction costs associated with bankruptcy proceedings—insolvency risk is predominantly distributional. What is mostly at stake when a firm verges on insolvency is the distribution of the now-reduced value among customers, governments, creditors, and shareholders. Thus, insolvency risk is mainly a project-specific distributional risk. According to table 4.2, it should therefore be allocated to the party with the most influence over the risk factor.

Because insolvency risk depends in part on the risk in the firm's value, anyone who can influence this risk can influence insolvency risk. Risk in the firm's value has many sources, including demand risk and the extent of the firm's fixed costs. It also depends on the regulation of prices, especially the rules for changing prices: the more prices change to compensate the firm for changes in costs and demand, the more stable is the value of the firm.

Pricing rules almost always leave the firm bearing some risk. This is reasonable, because the firm is best at influencing, anticipating, and responding to some risk factors. Yet as long as pricing rules leave the firm bearing some risk, the firm and its creditors can choose the probability of insolvency by choosing leverage. If the pricing rules are changed to expose the firm to less risk, the firm and creditors can increase leverage until insolvency is as likely as it was before the change. And if the pricing rules are changed to expose the firm to more risk, the firm can reduce the probability of insolvency by reducing leverage. In the end, the firm and its creditors have the strongest influence over insolvency risk.

The principle suggests, therefore, that, if the firm and its creditors choose leverage, the firm and its creditors should bear the insolvency risk. It suggests that the government should not guarantee the debt and that rules for adjusting pricing should not allocate the risk to customers.[12] Alternatively, if the government or customers bear insolvency risk, the matching of risks and rights suggests that the government

---

12 Two further arguments for debt guarantees can be advanced. First, it can be asserted that debt is cheaper than equity because interest rates are lower than required returns on equity. Debt guarantees may then be advocated because they allow greater leverage. As well as ignoring the cost of debt guarantees, arguments from a lower cost of debt often appear to assume a simplistic relationship between leverage and the returns required by shareholders. Modigliani and Miller (1958) showed that the weighted average of the cost of debt and equity can be left unchanged as debt increases, because the lower cost of debt can be exactly offset by higher returns required by shareholders (for a textbook exposition, see Brealey and Myers 2000, chapter 17). A second argument is that governments should provide debt guarantees as a way of allowing the project to benefit from the government's putatively lower cost of capital. This view also seems simplistic; see chapter 4, note 16.

should control the firm's leverage, a topic further addressed in the section after next.

How Can Governments Avoid Implicitly Bearing the Risk?

If this approach is to work, however, governments need to avoid giving implicit guarantees. It is not much good declining to grant explicit guarantees if implicit guarantees remain. Indeed, if the implicit guarantee is sufficiently sure, the explicit guarantee may be better because clearer. So how can a government avoid implicit guarantees?

As a start, the government can announce that it won't bail the firm out. It might also state that the firm's bankruptcy, if it were to occur, would not be a sign of the failure of the government's policy. Even though an announcement is not binding, it may help. Having publicly committed itself to allowing the firm to go bankrupt, the government may be less inclined to give in to pressures to bail the firm out.[13] Having stated that it would not view bankruptcy as a sign of policy failure, it is in a better position to rebut arguments to the contrary.

Yet announcements are not commitments, and it may be difficult for governments to find ways of committing themselves not to intervene. Sometimes, however, they can make use of an international agreement. The French and British governments, for example, agreed in the Treaty of Canterbury that they would not bail out the company undertaking the channel tunnel.[14]

Allowing firms to go bankrupt was difficult, we argued, mainly because of the fear of service disruption during bankruptcy. So a second step is to make bankruptcy smoother. Governments need ways to make it easier for the ownership of the firm to move from its shareholders to its creditors and for the new creditors to appoint new managers, if they choose—all without the threat of service disruption.

Special rules for the bankruptcy of infrastructure firms may help. Such rules can impose obligations on the firm (and perhaps also on its creditors and critical suppliers) to ensure that service continues during bankruptcy. The rules might also allow the government to step in and

---

13 Cialdini (1998) describes evidence that the desire people have to be consistent means that public announcements do influence their subsequent behavior.

14 See, for example, the *Wall Street Journal* April 8–12, 2004 (European edition), p. M4, and Eurotunnel's 2002 prospectus for "the redemption of equity notes," available at http://www.eurotunnel.com.

manage the firm after bankruptcy. Yet special rules such as these haven't always prevented bailouts.[15]

Limiting Unavoidable Government Exposure to Insolvency Risk: Matching Risks and Rights

When governments doubt they can make bankruptcy smooth enough to be politically acceptable, they need to think about limiting the insolvency risk to which the public is exposed. One option is to limit the firm's exposure to business risks. This, however, has the disadvantage of moving away from the allocation of risk that looked best when considered on its own and, in any case, may not work, because firms and their creditors can reestablish the probability of bankruptcy they want by increasing leverage.

The only sure way to reduce the public's exposure to insolvency risk, if it cannot be avoided altogether, is to limit the firm's leverage. The government can do this in several ways. Most directly, it can require the firm to have a minimum amount of equity, for example, by specifying that the firm's equity must be more than a certain percentage of the accounting value of its assets. In Mexico, where the government previously suffered losses from bailing out private toll roads, the government now requires concessionaires to have a minimum of 20 percent equity.[16] Depending on the extent of risk to which the firm is exposed, higher requirements might be better.

Sometimes the government might be able to achieve a similar effect by requiring the project to be undertaken on the balance sheet of the project sponsors instead of on the nonrecourse or limited-recourse basis of project finance. If the sponsor of the project—the company or consortium that develops and takes a big stake in the equity of the project—is large relative to the project, the probability of bankruptcy is thereby

---

15 See Ehrhardt and Irwin (2004) for examples. Perhaps part of what is needed is for governments and customers to become familiar with bankruptcy in infrastructure, to see that it can occur without service disruptions. The United States seems to have found a way of allowing infrastructure firms, such as Enron and WorldCom among many others, to go bankrupt (Ruster 1995). So has Great Britain for its private finance initiative, under which private contractors have experienced financial distress without the government having to intervene (Timmins 2004).

16 On Mexico's problems, see Ehrhardt and Irwin (2004), which draws on Gómez-Ibáñez (1997) and Ruster (1997). On the new Mexican policy, see Government of Mexico, Secretaría de Comunicaciones y Transportes and Banco Nacional de Obras y Servicios Públicos (2003, 18). The requirement occurs in a context in which the government offers a guarantee whose cost increases with leverage.

reduced. Alternatively, the government might require the project company's parent companies to guarantee the debt.

In taking any of these steps, the government intervenes in a decision normally made by firms and their creditors. This intervention is likely to have a cost: it may prevent the firm from choosing a capital structure that would be optimal even in the absence of implicit government guarantees. But the situation is abnormal because the public bears some of the losses in insolvency. Unusual interventions may therefore be justified.[17]

Policy Risk

Finally, consider *policy risk*, which we define as unpredictable variation in value arising from unpredictable variation in government action. Perhaps the most important policy risk relates to the price the government allows the firm to charge for its services. Such risk arises from the possibility of the government's unexpectedly changing the rules governing controlled prices, as well as from the possibility of its applying the rules in an unexpected way. When prices are not controlled, policy risk arises from the possibility of the government's unexpectedly introducing price control. Policy risk also arises from the possibility of the government's unexpectedly changing quality standards, creating or abolishing a monopoly, expropriating without compensation, and raising taxes or cutting subsidies—or cutting taxes and raising subsidies.

The Importance of Policy Risk in Infrastructure

Policy risk matters for all businesses. All businesses care about taxes, for example, and prefer them to be not just low but stable. According to one survey of ordinary businesses in developing countries, policy risk is, in fact, the single biggest constraint on investment (World Bank 2004b, 5). Policy risk is exceptionally important, however, for infrastructure businesses.[18]

First, infrastructure investments are often sunk (that is, irreversible). A firm that builds a toll road does not end up with an asset that it can use for some purpose other than that originally intended. It can't use the

---

17 The approach is like a government's setting a minimum capital-adequacy ratio for banks, a policy that has a similar rationale: implicitly or explicitly, governments bear some of the risks of the banks' becoming insolvent.

18 See, for example, Gómez-Ibáñez (2003), Levy and Spiller (1994), Newbery (1999), Smith (1997a), and World Bank (2004b).

road to offer road-transport services in another location, and it can't do much with the road where it is other than offer it for use as a road. A water utility that creates dams, reservoirs, and a network of pipes can't do much with the investments except sell water in that particular location. To varying extents, investors in gas, power, and telecommunications face the same problems: much of the value of their investment is specific to its current use.

The problem can be analyzed in terms of real options. If a project becomes unprofitable, its owners can abandon it. In the language of real-options analysis, they have an abandonment option. Specifically, they have the right to put the project's assets in return for the assets' value in their next-best use. Firms whose investment is entirely sunk, however, have an abandonment option with a strike price of zero: they can give up the project, but they get nothing for it. Their abandonment option is therefore worthless.

However analyzed, sunk costs make the firm vulnerable to changes that happen after it invests. The firm is vulnerable to a reduction in demand, to an increase in operating costs, and to changes in government policy. If the government cuts the regulated price of the service the firm sells, the firm can lose almost everything. Yet as long as the government keeps the price high enough to cover the firm's operating costs, the firm won't abandon its investment. The firm has lost its initial investment, but it earns more by continuing than by closing.

Second, infrastructure firms are intensively regulated and politically contentious. As well as being subject to taxes, competition policy, financial reporting requirements, and so on, they are subject to industry- or firm-specific rules about the price and quality of the services they sell. They may also be subject to rules about the quantity of the services, being obliged to connect all new customers or to add customers at a certain rate. Sometimes, they are even subject to requirements to make particular investments, not just provide particular services.

These rules arise partly because the firms have monopolies or important market power, which creates a rationale for regulation. They also arise because infrastructure services tend to be politically important. Power, water, and road transport are important to nearly all customers and voters, and these customer-voters urge politicians to use their regulatory powers to keep prices low.

All this puts an infrastructure firm in a difficult position. It faces the risk that the price of its service will be cut or that other rules will be made less favorable, and because its investment is sunk, it is especially vulnerable to the risk.

Infrastructure-Investment Games

The problem can be represented as a game played by the firm and the government (figure 5.5). The firm chooses whether to invest, knowing that the government has promised not expropriate, but not knowing whether the government will keep its promise. (Expropriation here means taking the firm's assets without compensation or regulating to prevent its profitability.) If the firm invests, the government then decides whether to keep its promise. Total project value—that is, value accruing to the firm and the government—is maximized when the firm invests; but if the firm invests, the government maximizes the value of its interest in the project by expropriating. So the government expropriates. As Machiavelli (1992, 46) said, "a prudent prince neither can nor ought to keep his word when to keep it is hurtful to him and the causes which led him to pledge it are removed . . . and no prince was ever at a loss for plausible reasons to cloak a breach of faith." Recognizing that the government gains by expropriating, the rational firm decides not

Figure 5.5. An Infrastructure Investment Game

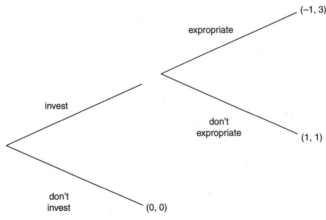

Source: Author's representation.
Note: The firm's decision is represented by the first branching of the tree. In the first, deterministic version of the game discussed in the text, the second branching represents the government's decision. In the second, probabilistic version, the government is modeled not as making decisions but as expropriating with a probability of p and not expropriating with a probability of $1 - p$. In both, the firm's value is given by the first of the numbers in parentheses, the government's by the second. The figure assumes total project value of investment is 2, whether the government expropriates the firm or keeps its promise.

to invest. Instead of sharing the benefit of investment—the payoff (1, 1) in the middle of the tree in figure 5.5—the firm and government get nothing.

One response to this fundamental problem of infrastructure investment[19] is for the government itself to invest. Because the government need not act commercially, it can invest even if it thinks it will later expropriate itself, as it were, by cutting prices. Thus, the benefits of infrastructure investment can be gained in the presence of policy risk (see, for example, Flemming and Mayer 1997; Jenkinson 2003). But the government must then forgo the possible advantages of private investment, such as stronger incentives to operate efficiently and stronger discipline on the government to maintain cost-covering prices.

Infrastructure investment choices are not as cut and dried as the game just described and depicted in figure 5.5. Sometimes the firm may make not just one investment decision but a series of them, and the government wants to preserve its reputation with the firm. At other times, the government cares about its reputation for keeping its promises because it wants to attract other investors. In either case, the real game is repeated.

Yet enough of the features of the game are reflected in the world to make attracting private investment difficult. The bigger the investment is, and the less closely linked it is to future investments, the greater is the government's temptation to sacrifice reputation for immediate gain. The temptation will be harder still to resist if the politicians in office give little weight to the government's long-term reputation.

Another simple representation of the infrastructure investment game makes the government's choice a risk factor. The game just described doesn't contain any real risk. Although the firm must decide whether to invest before the government decides whether to keep its promise, the firm can deduce that the government will renege. In reality, the firm doesn't know what the government will do. Its decision whether to invest therefore depends on its estimate of the probability of the investment being expropriated and the values of the investment when the government keeps the promise and when the government expropriates.

---

19 The fundamental problem in infrastructure investment is like the "fundamental transformation" in investments in specific assets (Williamson 1989), the obsolescing bargain in foreign investment by multinationals (Vernon 1971), and the time-inconsistency problem in policy (for example, Merton and Bodie 1992).

Figure 5.6. Expropriation Risk and the Price Required for Investment

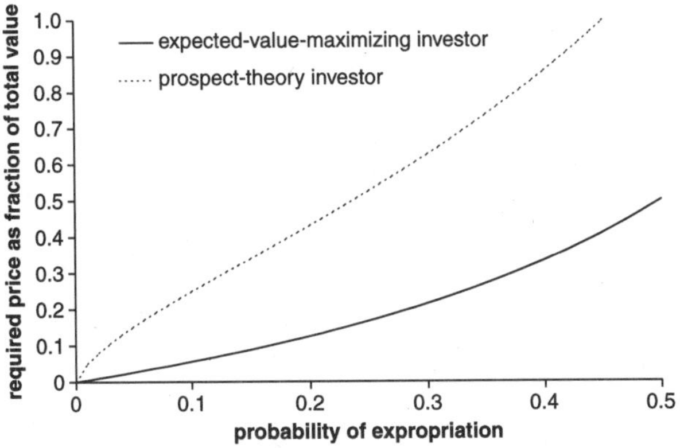

Source: Author's calculations.
Note: The figure shows the price, as a fraction of total project value, that the government must promise the firm, as a function of the probability that the government will expropriate the firm (ignoring any feedback from the price to the probability), according to two theories of the firm's behavior.

If government wants private investment in a probabilistic infrastructure investment game, it must promise a price high enough to compensate the firm for the possibility of expropriation.[20] The greater the probability of expropriation, the higher the price must be—in other words, the greater the fraction of total project value that must be promised to the firm. Exactly how much more must be offered to the firm depends on the firm's attitude toward risk. Figure 5.6 illustrates this point for a firm that maximizes expected value and for a firm that conforms to prospect theory (see chapter 3).

In this simple game, a high price reduces the value of the government's interest in the project. In practice, it might reduce the value of customers' interest in the project. Either way, private investment may still make sense if its benefits are great enough, but the government will do better if it can reduce the probability of expropriation. More generally, since expropriation risk is just a stark example of policy risk, the government will do better if it can reduce policy risk.

---

20 The effect of policy risk on required prices is sometimes said to be mediated by the firm's cost of capital: when policy risk is high, it is said, the firm's cost of capital is high, so prices must be high. But this characterization of the effect confounds changes in expected cash flows with changes in the risk of those cash flows. The problem arises even if the firm's cost of capital is unaffected by policy risk (perhaps because the cost of capital is given by the capital-asset pricing model and policy risk is uncorrelated with the return on the market; see "Valuing Exposure" in chapter 7).

Who Should Bear Policy Risk?

Who should bear policy risk in infrastructure projects—the firm, its customers, or the government? The infrastructure investment games suggest the firm shouldn't, because if it does, it will either refuse to invest (the deterministic game) or invest only if it is promised a higher price than would otherwise be necessary (the probabilistic game). This analysis conforms to the overarching principle of risk allocation set out in chapter 4, which is to allocate risks to maximize total project value. Does further consideration of the principle—and ability to influence, anticipate, respond to, and absorb the risk—suggest a different answer?

Policy risk is sometimes project-specific, as, for example, when the policy is project-specific price control. It can also be economywide, as, for example, when the policy is part of competition law, corporate taxation, or financial reporting requirements.

Whether project specific or economywide, policy risk can affect total project value. For example, if project value is maximized for some particular price, and the price unexpectedly diverges from this optimum, the value of the project falls. But the most direct result of many unexpected changes in policy is to redistribute value. If the government unexpectedly reduces prices, for example, and makes no other changes, it transfers value from the firm to customers. If it nationalizes the firm without fair compensation, it transfers value from the firm to itself. If it unexpectedly lowers the firm's taxes, it transfers value in the opposite direction.

The principle laid out in chapter 4 suggests that the allocation of project-specific distributional risks should be guided by the parties' ability to influence or control the risk. By definition, governments control policy risk. When the government controls price, for example, it controls price risk.[21] Thus, the principle of risk allocation implies that governments should generally bear project-specific policy risk. If the government lowers a controlled price—in a way not foreseen by the pricing rule, that is—it should pay the firm a compensating amount.

The principle laid out in chapter 4 suggests that economywide risks should not normally be allocated according to the parties' ability to

---

21 The analysis changes if prices are set by a regulator that is independent of the government and in particular of the authorities that have the power to tax and spend—and therefore to compensate financially. If a regulator is independent, the government does not control its decisions; thus, risks arising from uncertainty about an independent regulator's decisions are not policy risks as we have defined them.

influence the corresponding risk factor. Though it may influence or even control the risk factor, the government shouldn't determine its policy toward an economywide risk factor by reference to any particular project. The transaction costs of the government bearing economywide policy risks may give further weight to this view—as, for some policies, may the government's role in legitimate redistribution (see chapter 4).

But is there a case for taking a different approach to economywide policy risk that affects infrastructure projects? When investments are sunk, the firm is as vulnerable to economywide policy risk as to project-specific policy risk, and the benefits of protecting the firm from the risk may be large. Moreover, the transaction costs of compensating the firm, positively and negatively, for at least some changes in economywide policy may not be exorbitant. The effects of policy changes that have a direct influence on the firm can be estimated using the sort of the financial model already developed by the firm's regulator.

Consider economywide taxes. The government could agree to freeze them at their current levels for certain infrastructure firms. Or it could expose the firms to the risk of changes in taxes but allow the changes in costs to be passed on quickly to customers. Or it could agree to bear only the risk of discriminatory changes in taxes, requiring firms to bear the costs of general tax increases and enjoy the benefits of general tax cuts. Which option is best depends on analysis of the details of the case, such as the extent of the risk and the extent to which the firm is vulnerable to it.

How Is Policy Risk Usually Allocated?

Governments are often ambivalent about policy risk. They agree to bear some policy risks themselves, and they allocate others to customers by allowing prices to compensate the firm for costs imposed by policy. But by no means do governments protect all firms from all policy risks. When reviewing government decisions, the courts have also been ambivalent, protecting firms in some cases, but not others.

Contracts—In many countries, infrastructure firms enter into contracts with the government before investing. These contracts set out the rights of the firm, as well as its obligations, and generally protect the firm from most adverse changes in project-specific policy and some adverse changes in economywide policy. Insofar as the government respects them, the contracts protect the firm from policy risk.

The contract governs the price the firm can charge, so that any change in pricing rule has to be agreed to by the firm. For example, the contract may set a starting price and a formula for periodically adjusting the price. Alternatively, it may contain a vaguer rule, such as "The price will be set to give the firm enough revenue to cover its reasonable costs and no more."

Neither kind of rule eliminates price risk for the firm. Even precise rules may have uncertain application. A rule that adjusts prices for inflation, for example, can specify a measure of inflation, such as a certain consumer-price inflation series published by the national statistical agency. But what if the agency discontinues the publication of that series? General rules, such as that the price will be set to cover the firm's reasonable costs, allow many interpretations. What is cost? What is reasonable? Even if there were no uncertainty about the application, the firm faces the risk that the government won't permit the rule to be applied. Yet if the rules are reasonable, and do not prescribe prices too different from those demanded by economics and politics, they reduce price risk faced by the firm.

Such rules require the government to maintain policies that are stable in some sense. In the case of prices, they require the government to maintain a predictable price or, more commonly, a price predictable given the outcomes of certain risk factors. For example, the price may be predictable once inflation is known. Because the world and the government's preferences change unpredictably, perfectly stable policies are not necessarily best. If the rate of change of the firm's costs diverges markedly from the rate of consumer-price inflation, the price after adjusting for consumer-price inflation may drift far from the optimal price. Even if nothing changes, the government may come to prefer a lower or higher price. It may want to cut the price paid by the poor, for example, or increase the price to reflect the environmental costs of the service.

Does this mean that contracts are undesirably rigid? Not necessarily. The government can change the rules in any way it wants, provided it persuades the firm to accept the change. Unless the firm can be persuaded that the change is in its interest, this condition will require the government to ensure the firm is compensated in some way.

Sometimes, the government may provide the compensation itself. In 1993, the Telecommunications Agency of Singapore granted SingTel an exclusive right to sell certain services. At the time, the benefits of competition in telecommunications were perhaps smaller or less widely understood than they are today, and temporary monopoly franchises were common. By 1997, however, the government of Singapore wanted to end the monopoly. To do so, it paid about $1 billion. Something similar happened in Malaysia. There, the government had entered into a concession contract for a toll road; the contract established that tolls would increase according to a formula. The government later decided not to permit the full increase and had to compensate the firm (Mody 2002, 378).

When the policy in question is not about price, compensation can come from customers in the form of a higher price. If quality standards are increased, the price may be increased to compensate the firm for the attendant increase in cost. Or if the policy is about price, compensation can come from customers in the form of lower quality or lesser quantity. The firm's obligation to connect new customers might be relaxed, for example.

Some policy changes benefit the firm, and the firm won't object if these changes are made without compensation—that is, without the firm's giving the government or customers something. Changes of policy that benefit the firm may be rarer than those that hurt it, if the government tries to start with policies that encourage investment. But when the government wants to change policy in a way that increases profits, it may want to seek compensation from the firm.

Policy risk without contracts—Contracts are the norm for private infrastructure projects in many countries, including France and countries with similar legal systems (former French colonies and other continental European countries such as Spain and Portugal and their colonies). They are also the norm in most developing countries, where policy risks are big enough that firms usually insist on contractual protection.

But not all private infrastructure projects are governed by contracts. In the United States, many early private infrastructure companies signed franchise contracts with municipal governments (Gómez-Ibáñez 2003). But the arrangements evolved, and municipal franchise contracts were replaced by arrangements in which firms operated without contracts with any government. In Great Britain, private gas, power, water, and telecommunications companies operate under licenses, not contracts.

Even when policy is not set out in contracts, however, legal rules have developed to protect firms from policy risk, at least where private investment in infrastructure has been sustained. In the United States, for example, utility prices are set by regulatory agencies. As regulation by state regulatory agencies developed in the 19th and early 20th centuries, the courts often had to adjudicate on the powers of the states to change prices and other policies governing the utilities. The degree of a firm's appropriate exposure to policy risk was a matter of legal controversy, and in the 19th century, firms did not have any clear protection from adverse regulatory decisions.[22] But policy gradually changed. In 1898, the Supreme Court ruled that regulatory agencies could not change policy in ways that prevented utilities from making a fair return on the value of their assets. And by now, utilities in the United States appear, despite the absence of contracts, reasonably well protected from policy risk. Usually, it is customers who compensate, not governments. For example, when greater competition was permitted in power in the 1990s, firms that had invested in high-cost plants under monopoly protection and some regulatory direction were protected from lower prices by taxes on power paid by customers.

A large part of the protection of U.S. utilities, according to commentators such as José Gómez-Ibáñez (2003, 117), is the U.S. constitution, whose fifth amendment, passed in 1789, states that

> No person shall . . . be deprived of life, liberty, or property, without the due process of the law; nor shall private property be taken for public use, without just compensation.

The 14th amendment clarifies that this rule applies to states as well as the federal government:

> No State shall . . . deprive any person of life, liberty, or property, without due process of law; nor deny any person within its jurisdiction the equal protection of its law.

In Canada, by contrast, the constitution included no such protections for firms, which explains in part why private Canadian utilities were mostly nationalized, while their U.S. counterparts remained private (Gómez-Ibáñez 2003).

In Great Britain, many utilities, having been nationalized earlier in the century, were privatized in the 1980s and 1990s. Important parts of the rules governing the utilities are set out in licenses issued by the government. These licenses, which include pricing rules, are not contracts. Yet the law has features designed to reduce policy risk. The regulator cannot change prices without the firm's consent, except with the approval of

---

22 See, for example, the description of *Munn v. Illinois* in Gómez-Ibáñez (2003, 188).

another government agency, the Competition Commission. Both agencies are part of the British government, but they are independent of each other and of politicians. The laws governing utility regulation moreover require the regulator to ensure that utilities can finance their activities, which, with a history of the rule of law, further reduces policy risk.

Policy risk for utilities in Great Britain is probably greater than it would be if pricing and other important rules were set out in contracts—as they are for firms providing services under Great Britain's private finance initiative. One can argue that the policy risk is too great. In 1997, the incoming Labour government in Great Britain imposed a windfall tax on private utilities on the grounds that they were sold too cheaply and their shareholders had earned excessive profits. To many commentators, the tax looked like partial expropriation in the infrastructure investment game—an arbitrary change in the rules after investment.[23] The government might get more investment and, hence, better services at a given price if it reduced policy risk.

Quasi-contracts in the civil-law tradition—Sometimes policy rules are set out in contracts subject to the same law as contracts between firms. When there are contracts in countries with common-law traditions, such as Great Britain and its former colonies, the contracts are like that. In countries with a civil-law tradition, by contrast, a distinction has developed between private and administrative contracts. Contracts between firms or individuals are private and cannot be changed unilaterally. Contracts between the government and a firm may also be private, but some such contracts—notably those between a government and a firm about the provision of services to the public—are considered administrative and are governed by special administrative law, not the ordinary law of private contracts.[24]

In contrast to private contracts, certain aspects of French administrative contracts can be changed by the government unilaterally. The government can, for example, impose quality standards that are more demanding and prevent a contractually determined price increase from being applied. However, it must compensate the firm—by paying in cash, by allowing the price to rise, or by reducing the firm's obligations.

Moreover, the principle that requires compensation extends beyond changes in contractual provisions. A doctrine known as *fait du prince*

---

23 For comments on the tax, see Gómez-Ibáñez (2003) and Helm (2004).
24 For the case of France, see, for example, du Marais (2004) and Lachaume (2002).

requires the government to compensate the concessionaire for substantial changes to policy outside the contract that adversely and disproportionately affect the concessionaire. Thus, in France, infrastructure firms are protected from much policy risk, even though the rules are not set out in conventional contracts changeable only by common consent of the contracting parties.

Protection from too much risk?—In countries with long histories of sustained private provision in infrastructure, such as France and the United States, firms are thus protected from much policy risk. The government does not always have to get the firm's agreement to changes in policies, but it must generally keep the firm whole. The durability of these arrangements and the apparent convergence of countries as different as France and the United States caution against radical changes. Yet one aspect of the approach looks wrong, according to the principle of risk allocation set out in chapter 4: the rules that protect investors from policy risk also protect them from other risks.

In France, a doctrine called the theory of *imprévision*, similar to *fait du prince*, provides that the firm should be compensated for certain major, unpredictable changes in the business environment. A sudden collapse in demand might count. Furthermore, the law appears to create a general presumption that the firm should be profitable: the financial equilibrium (*équilibre financier*) of the contract must be maintained. The interpretation of the law is unclear, but it limits the firm's exposure to business as well as policy risks. In the United States, cost-of-service (rate-of-return) regulation protects regulated firms from policy risk but is often criticized for protecting the firm from risk generally and thus for dulling its incentives to lower costs.

Governments Really Bearing Policy Risk

Even when a government agrees to bear policy risk, it may struggle to persuade firms that it will actually do so. The government may promise stable policy and compensation for adverse changes, but will it keep its promise? Putting the promises in a contract helps, but will the government respect the contract? If it doesn't, can the firm enforce its rights? Governments need to think carefully about how they can effectively bear the policy risks they choose to bear.

Putting policies into contracts is probably beneficial for all governments except those with other well-accepted mechanisms for protecting firms from excessive policy risk. But to be effective, the contracting parties must be able to enforce their rights by appealing to a competent, independent body that has the power to impose its decisions on both parties. In many developing countries, courts don't have these attributes. Firms fear that national courts will be unable or unwilling to impose penalties on the government. Thus, contracts often provide for disputes to be settled by bodies other than local courts, such as independent experts and arbitrators. Foreign firms often prefer international experts and international arbitration—conducted by people unaffiliated with the host country of the investment. Governments can make international arbitration work more effectively if they enter into bilateral investment treaties and various multilateral agreements, such as the New York Convention and the Washington Convention on the Settlement of Investment Disputes (see, for example, Smith 1997a).

Such contracts also need to be interpreted and applied on a regular basis, even before disputes arise. The classic contractual solution is for the parties to decide jointly, negotiating until they reach agreement. This approach can work, but it is vulnerable to holdup: one party may withhold consent to delay the change as part of a bargaining strategy. Another solution is often sought, at least as a backup to be used if the parties can't agree.

One such solution is for the decision to be made by an independent expert or panel of independent experts, chosen jointly by the government and the firm, with possible recourse to the courts or arbitration.[25] Another is for such tasks to be performed by independent regulatory agencies (Gómez-Ibáñez 2003; Shugart 1988; Smith 1997b, 1997c, 1997d). Machiavelli might have approved of both approaches; he wrote, "Princes should devolve on others those matters that entail responsibility, and reserve to themselves those that relate to grace and favor" (1992, 50).

Neither approach, as usually practiced, is entirely satisfactory. Developing countries, especially, have struggled to create systems that ensure competent, impartial decisions and preserve the advantages of contractual protection for firms against policy risks. The regulator may have too little expertise, too much discretion, or too little independence from the political pressures that encourage governments to expropriate the firm in the infrastructure investment game.

Decisions by independent experts and arbitrators ensure independence and, if accepted, can limit policy risks. But they are not always accepted by customers. Independent experts and arbitrators have traditionally been

---

25 This is a change in the allocation of decision rights. For more on such approaches, see Bertolini (2004).

used to resolve disputes in commercial contracts. In such a context, confidentiality is the norm, and third parties have no right to be heard. Contracts that set out pricing rules and other matters of public policy are quite different. Customers, for example, have a legitimate interest in decisions about prices. While the government may represent them in two-party negotiations, customers and customer representatives expect to be able to follow the discussions and have their say. If they can't, they may have little faith in the outcome. Decisions by independent experts and arbitrators can therefore be perceived as unfair and may lack legitimacy.

Lack of legitimacy, in turn, can undermine the apparent reduction in policy risk faced by the firm. If customer-voters think decisions about prices—or other policies—are made illegitimately, they may complain, demonstrate, withhold payment, and finally force the government to renege on its promises to abide by the decisions of the experts and arbitrators. The approach may backfire.

The relationship between the strength of an investor's protection against expropriation and the price the investor must be promised thus depends on the perceived fairness, or legitimacy, of the protections (figure 5.7).

Figure 5.7. Legitimacy, Legal Protection, and Promised Prices

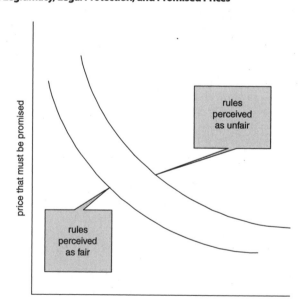

Source: World Bank 2004b.

Each of the two approaches—independent regulation and decisions by independent experts and arbitrators—might benefit from drawing on the strengths of the other. In countries without established norms protecting firms from policy risk, decision making by independent regulatory agencies might work better if more constrained by contracts. That is, the approach might work better if the rules followed by the agency were set out in a contract between the firm and the government and if the agency's power derived from the contract, not from a law over which the firm had no control.

Decisions by independent experts and arbitrators, by contrast, may work better if the decision makers adopt some of the procedures used by many regulatory agencies, as well as those used by courts. Customers and other third parties could have the opportunity to be consulted, arguments could be heard in public, written submissions could be published, the reasoning behind decisions could be disclosed, and so on.

CHAPTER 6

Rules

Governments can try to make better decisions about guarantees in particular cases, using a framework such as that set out and applied in the last two chapters. But that can be difficult. To make the task easier, governments can also step back and try to improve the rules that influence their decisions about particular cases—that is, the laws, regulations, standards, and guidelines that govern those decisions.

The quality of a decision depends in part on the characteristics of the decision makers—and thus on the person or body that is assigned by law to make the decision. It also depends on the context in which the decision is made. For example, what information do standards for accounting and cost-benefit analysis generate for the decision makers? What criteria must the decision makers apply? What incentives do they face? With whom must they consult? To whom must they explain their decision? And who monitors the outcome of the decision? For decisions about guarantees, what information do the decision makers have about the costs and benefits of the guarantee and alternative policies, and what incentives do they have to increase the benefits of the decision and reduce its costs?

Figure 6.1. Decision Makers, Incentives, and Information

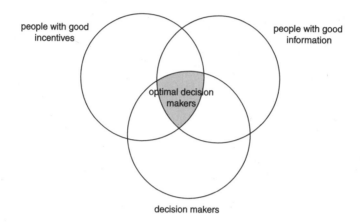

decision makers

Source: Irwin 2003.

With this framework in mind, one can think of two approaches to improving decisions: first, reassigning the right to make the decision to someone better placed to make it, and second, improving the information and incentives of the current decision maker (figure 6.1). The goal can be thought of as ensuring that the set of decision makers is in the intersection of the set of the people with good information and the set of people with good incentives.[1]

In practice, improving incentives and improving information may be intertwined. Policies that create information and make it public may also improve decision makers' incentives. Decision makers may be less likely to use a guarantee as a disguised subsidy, for example, if they know that the cost of the guarantee will be made public.[2]

This chapter discusses several ways to improve the incentives or information of government decision makers:

1. Involve officials and ministers with an interest in future costs in advice and decisions.

---

1 Although information and incentives are crucial, the capability of decision makers also matters. That is, some decision makers may be better than others at using information to reach their goals. The allocation of decision makers' attention, a scarce resource, also matters (March and Shapira 1987).

2 See, for example, Scott (2001).

2. Charge guarantee fees.
3. Set criteria that guarantees must meet and require analysis.
4. Use markets to value guarantees.
5. Report according to modern accounting standards.
6. Disclose additional information.
7. Budget for guarantees.

Some of these options are relevant to many government decisions, not only those about guarantees for infrastructure projects. Thus, choices about which options to use need to take account of more than just their effects on decisions about guarantees for infrastructure projects.[3]

Involving People with an Interest in Future Costs

Good decisions are more likely if the decision makers and their advisers have a strong interest in and, to the extent possible, internalize both the costs and the benefits of decisions. A decision maker who has good incentives, for example, will be as concerned about reducing the costs of the decision as increasing its benefits, even when the costs may not be realized for many years, if ever.

Ministers responsible for infrastructure may be more concerned about realizing the benefits of a project than about reducing its future costs. They are likely to be well aware of the benefits of infrastructure and may gain prestige or be paid bribes if the project goes ahead. The costs borne by future taxpayers may, however, seem abstract. In these circumstances, the government may suffer from the tragedy of the commons: the costs of a project are a common resource, but some of its benefits are private.

By contrast, ministers of finance, prime ministers, presidents, and other officials with broad responsibilities may be concerned about minimizing costs. Thus, ensuring that the minister of finance, or someone else with similar interests, can veto guarantees can help ensure that costs are properly considered. A closely related approach is to ensure that decisions are made collectively by a body such as the cabinet, the council of ministers, or in

---

3 This chapter draws on work on the government's management of its overall exposure to risk, including Brixi and Mody (2002), Petrie (2002), Schick (2002a, 2002b), and other papers in Brixi and Schick (2002); IMF (2001a); Merton and Bodie (1992); Sniderman (1993); and Towe (1993). It also draws on similar work that does focus on private infrastructure, including Hemming and Staff Team of the IMF (2006); Irwin (2003); Irwin and others (1997); and Mody and Patro (1996).

some cases the legislature. The legislature, for example, might set a limit on the total value of guarantees to be issued. Decisions to grant a guarantee of more than a certain value might then need the approval of the minister of finance or, above a higher threshold, the cabinet.

One way to ensure that the costs of guarantees are considered alongside their benefits is to agree to them in the budget. If the government sets a limit on total spending and the budget rules count the cost of guarantees, a decision to grant a guarantee can require dropping another spending proposal. The cost of a guarantee therefore becomes the loss of the benefits of the project it displaces. If the costs of guarantees are truly captured in the budget, the need to involve the minister of finance or the cabinet in decisions about particular guarantees is much reduced (see "Budgeting for Guarantees" below).

Good decisions also require good advice. A government can get advice from consultants, academics, investment banks, think tanks, and other outside experts (some ways of drawing on such expertise are considered below), but it also needs some in-house capability. The best approach is probably to get advice from at least two agencies. The ministry of finance may be best placed to advise decision makers on the costs and risks of guarantees. Only the ministry of finance is likely to care much about a guarantee's effect on the government's total exposure to risk, considering all assets and liabilities. Within the ministry, the debt management office may be most likely to have the expertise to value guarantees or to review and use valuations made by outside experts.[4] The relevant infrastructure ministry may know most about the benefits of guarantees, and the government should also get advice from this perspective. The government might also benefit from getting advice from an agency that has expertise in infrastructure policy but doesn't carry out projects, since such an agency may have more industry-specific expertise than the ministry of finance, yet be more critical than a project-implementing ministry.

Letting all these groups give advice and criticize each other's advice helps ensure that the government sees the whole picture. Coordination among advisers has its advantages, but disagreement and contestation are useful, in ensuring that governments overcome the problems of individual and group reasoning discussed in chapter 3.

---

4 Debt management offices play an important role in managing liabilities associated with power-purchase agreements in Turkey and with debt guarantees, mostly for public enterprises, in Sweden (see E. Currie n.d.).

Charging Fees

A second way to improve incentives by ensuring that costs as well as benefits are considered is to charge the beneficiary of the guarantee. The charge could be set equal to the estimated value of the guarantee, plus, perhaps, a premium to cover the government's administrative costs. The beneficiary of the guarantee might be considered to be the firm, its lenders or investors, or the ministry promoting the project. If the beneficiary is charged, it must compare the price with the benefits of the guarantee and decide whether the guarantee is worth taking. Charging can thus reduce the chance of the government's issuing guarantees less valuable to the beneficiary than they are costly to the government.

Charging can also help draw the government's attention to two possible purposes of a guarantee: to subsidize and to reallocate risk. Charging for a subsidy is, of course, self-defeating. But if the purpose is to subsidize, giving a guarantee may not make sense. Yet if the government's purpose is to protect the firm from risk rather than to subsidize it, charging may be justified (Schick 2002a, 96).[5]

Charging won't necessarily affect the firm's profits. If the government offers a guarantee at a fixed price when it solicits bids for a project, the bidders can be expected to reflect the costs and benefits of the guarantee in the price they offer to charge. Thus, the winning firm's expected profits won't depend on the guarantee fee, even if the firm takes the guarantee and pays the fee. The guarantee can be expected to change the distribution of value between customers and taxpayers, but not the distribution of value between these two groups, on the one hand, and the firm, on the other. The main value of charging for the guarantee in this case is to prevent the government from giving the guarantee when the firm values it at less than the price.

One way to charge for guarantees is to demand exposure to upside risk in return for bearing downside risk. If the government offers a revenue guarantee, it can insist on sharing revenue above some threshold. If it gives an exchange-rate guarantee protecting the firm from depreciation, it can insist on getting a comparable guarantee from the firm that means

---

5 See also Merton and Bodie (1992), who discuss several techniques for managing debt guarantees: monitoring the value of the collateral assets and seizing and liquidating them if their value declines to the point where a call on the guarantee is likely, requiring the firm to increase its equity or quasi-equity, restricting the firm's investments to better match its assets and liabilities, and charging risk-based premiums.

the government, not the firm, benefits from appreciation. Doing so also limits the firm's profits when things go well, which may be advantageous if the firm's profits are public knowledge. It is more complex than charging in cash, however: getting the in-kind fee right requires estimating the cost of the revenue-sharing agreement as well as the guarantee.

Charging for the guarantee in cash can make one matter worse. It means that guarantees not only have an opaque cost, which is difficult to incorporate in decisions, but also have a transparent cash benefit. If the government's budget counts only immediate cash revenue and spending, issuing a guarantee for a fee may look profitable even when it is nothing of the sort. So a policy of charging for guarantees makes it all the more important to get the accounting and budgeting right.

Setting Criteria and Requiring Analysis

It is also helpful to set the criteria to be satisfied before the government gives a guarantee, along with setting a requirement that any proposal to grant a guarantee be accompanied by an analysis of whether the proposal satisfies the criteria.

Governments could require a full cost-benefit analysis—in which both costs and benefits were quantified—of every proposed guarantee. The cost of a guarantee could be estimated using the techniques set out in chapters 7 and 8. The benefits could be quantified using other techniques. The analysis would then conclude whether the policy has net benefits or net costs. The decision makers would still decide: they could issue a guarantee even if its estimated cost exceeded its estimated benefit, and they could reject a proposed guarantee even if its estimated benefit exceeded its estimated cost. But the decision would be informed by analysis.

Quantifying the benefits of a guarantee may be extremely hard, however, and an alternative to requiring full cost-benefit analysis is to require an analysis in which only the cost is quantified. The decision makers must form an impressionistic view of the benefits and then judge whether the benefits justify incurring the estimated cost.

Requiring quantification is, of course, no panacea. The analysis will depend on many judgments about which reasonable, competent advisers can disagree. Analysts can reasonably differ about the correct model of an underlying risk factor and the correct estimates of crucial parameters, such as the volatility of the risk factor (see chapters 7 and 8). Analyses can therefore be designed to give a desired answer. If the cost of the guarantee seems too high, the analyst can change the model, choose a lower estimate of volatility, and so on.

For example, Australia and Great Britain carry out value-for-money tests when deciding whether to use private finance to procure a public service. Such tests take the project as given and then compare the cost of private finance with that of a public-sector comparator. They incorporate the expected cost of the government's exposure to risk[6] and therefore require judgments about the probabilities of various outcomes. It is a subject of controversy, however, whether the analysis determines the choice or whether the choice determines the analysis (see, for example, Quiggin 2004).

Despite the problems, setting criteria and requiring analysis have the advantage of focusing the attention of advisers and decision makers on the rationale for the guarantee and on its cost.[7] There are limits to the ability of analysts to generate convenient estimates, and if advice is contestable, others can dispute the analysis and present their own.

Several governments have come up with interesting qualitative criteria or guidelines for decisions. Great Britain, South Africa, and the state of Victoria in Australia, for example, have published extensive guidelines on the allocation of risks in privately financed infrastructure projects.[8] Canada offers the following criterion specifically for issuing a debt guarantee: "The sponsoring department must analyze the project and demonstrate that it cannot be financed without government assistance, and that cash flow will be adequate to cover repayment of the debt as well as interest and operating costs and yield a satisfactory rate of return" (Schick 2002a, 93).

---

6 See Government of United Kingdom, Her Majesty's Treasury (2003), and Government of Victoria, Australia (2001). The government of Victoria explains how it recommends that the cost of bearing risk be calculated; the approach doesn't incorporate what we describe in chapter 7 as the risk premium; it simply discounts an estimate of the expected cash flow at a fixed discount rate.

7 Setting aside the practical considerations, there are also theoretical problems about the appropriate way to do cost-benefit analysis. See, for example, the discussion in Adler and Posner (2001). As Posner (2001) and Sunstein (2001) argue, however, cost-benefit analysis can be useful even among people who disagree about some of the underlying theory and even when the analyses are not especially accurate. As Sunstein (2001) argues, its main value may not be to give a precise estimate of the net value of a policy but to counteract flawed intuitive decision making (see "Cognitive Obstacles" in chapter 3).

8 For examples of such guidelines, see Government of United Kingdom, Her Majesty's Treasury (2004); Government of South Africa, National Treasury (2004); and Government of Victoria, Australia (2001).

Colombia has made a concerted effort to improve its guarantee decisions by writing guidelines and requiring risks to be quantified before decisions are made. In the 1990s, it guaranteed revenue on toll roads and an airport and payments by utilities that entered into long-term power-purchase agreements with independent power producers. (The state-owned telecommunication company also guaranteed the returns of its joint-venture partners.) Although the guarantees encouraged valuable investments, lower-than-expected demand and other problems required the government to make payments of $2 billion by 2005.[9] Concerned by the payments, the government undertook to improve future decisions about guarantees and to improve its monitoring and management of outstanding liabilities.

The government commissioned a study that estimated the liabilities associated with the power, toll-road, and telecommunication guarantees (Christopher Lewis and Mody 1997). Then it created new rules. Guidelines set out appropriate public risk bearing in each infrastructure industry. For transport, for example, the guidelines state that the firm should generally bear risks related to the costs of construction, operation, and maintenance and risks related to demand, exchange rates, customer payment, and availability and terms of financing. The government should generally bear risks related to the cost and timing of land acquisition. It may also bear some construction-cost risk when, as in projects involving tunnels, information on likely costs is poor, and it may sometimes bear demand and exchange-rate risk. In particular, it may offer "liquidity support," to help a concessionaire service debt when faced with a demand or exchange-rate shock. Although the firm is expected to bear general regulatory risks, the government may agree to compensate it for changes in rules about prices and subsidies. The conformity of proposed allocations of risk with the government's guidelines is checked by a planning agency.[10]

The government also requires that public entities intending to offer guarantees estimate the government's resulting exposure to risk, before the public entity can bid out or directly award a contract. It must use techniques approved by the ministry of finance (Government of Colombia, Ministerio de Hacienda y Crédito Público, Dirección General de Crédito Público, División de Pasivos Contingentes n.d.).

---

9 See Echeverry and others (2002); IMF (2005, 28); and Christopher Lewis and Mody (1997) on the early guarantees and associated problems.
10 See Government of Colombia, Department of National Planning (2001a and 2001b), which implement Decree 423 of 2001, which, in turn, implements Law 448 of 1998.

Another possible approach is to adopt a rule such as the following. The government will grant a guarantee to a privately financed project only if the guarantee satisfies these criteria:

- The guarantee complies with the law.
- The project benefiting from the guarantee has been chosen in the normal planning process, and the firm undertaking the project has been chosen in a fair competition.
- The government has acted to limit the cost and risk of the guarantee and, if appropriate, will charge a fee for it.
- The guarantee does not breach any budget limits.
- The guarantee has greater net benefits for the country than alternative uses of the government's money, including other kinds of subsidy.
- The guarantee is as transparent as is consistent with good targeting, and the guarantee contract will be made public, along with a description of its possible fiscal implications.

In 2006, the Indonesian government adopted a similar, though simpler, version of these criteria—focusing on legality, project quality, fiscal costs and fiscal risks, and transparency (Government of Indonesia 2006).

Using Markets to Value Guarantees

Governments might sometimes use markets to value their guarantees. One option is to try to sell guarantees to a bank, insurer, reinsurer, or other financial company (Schick 2002a). In principle, the price that the government gets is the market's assessment of the value of the guarantee. This approach should work when the risks are similar to those already traded or understood. When they are not, buyers of the risk may demand much more than the government's estimate of the guarantee's value. Among other problems, credible public information about the risk factor may be scarce, and the government's desire to sell may be taken as evidence that exposure to the risk is costly.[11] More generally, the attempt to sell the guarantees may run into the very market failures that led the government to assume the risk in the first place: if private firms had been willing to bear the risk, the government could have avoided it.

---

11 The market would thus be subject to the lemons problem (Akerlof 1970), and the prices offered by potential buyers of risk wouldn't reflect the prices they would offer with more information.

These problems need not stop the government from exploring the sale of risks. By fully disclosing its information about the risks over several years, the government may persuade possible buyers that it is not hiding information. Moreover, the government may have given the guarantee, not as a reasoned response to a market failure, but as a way of disguising a subsidy, in which case financial markets may allow the government to convert its exposure to risk into a straightforward subsidy. Financial markets may also be willing to take on more risks than they were when the guarantees were granted. And, to serve the function of providing information, the government need sell only a fraction of its exposure. Conceivably, financial markets may be prepared to bear some of the risk, even if they are unwilling to bear all of it.

Daniel Cohen (2002) proposes another way of selling some or all of the government's exposure to risk and obtaining a market value for any remaining exposure. Suppose the government plans to assume certain risks and creates a limited-liability fund to make payments resulting from the guarantees. Limited liability means the guarantees have the credit-worthiness of the fund, not the government. The government could sell some or all of its shares in the fund, the shareholders receiving any surplus in the fund at a certain date, after all obligations had been met. The government could then infer an estimate of the value of the guarantees from the price at which shares traded. Alternatively, if the government had already issued the guarantees under its own name and therefore couldn't limit its liability to the size of the fund, the government could sell securities in a fund that would be the first to be used to pay calls on guarantees. The proposal invites the questions raised in response to other ways of selling risk. Is it feasible? Could the government get a reasonable deal? But like the earlier proposals, it may be worth exploring.

Last, a government might also get insiders or outsiders to value its exposure to risk by creating a parallel market in which individuals can speculate on guarantee payments. For example, officials in government agencies might be asked to bet on guarantee outcomes, perhaps confidentially. Consider a guarantee of a policy risk arising from an agreement to increase prices. Suppose the government wants an estimate of whether it will decline to permit the contractual price in one year's time and be required to pay. Now imagine a contract that pays $1 for every $10,000 that the government pays in that year for that reason. Such a market would be controversial, but the price of the contract would give an estimate of the cost of the commitment.[12]

---

12 Surowiecki (2004) describes the uses of such markets.

Reporting According to Modern Accounting Standards

Traditional accounting standards contribute to the problems of government risk bearing, because they ignore the cost of risk. Improvements in accounting standards can therefore help solve the problems. Governments are routinely under pressure—whether imposed autonomously or with the help of foreign lenders—to reduce their debt and deficits. More precisely, they are under pressure to reduce their *reported* debt and deficits. And it is the standards for financial reporting adopted by the government and its foreign lenders that determine what is reported.

Crucially, the standards determine whether the cost of granting a guarantee shows up in the government's reported debt and deficits. Under the primitive cash accounting used by most but not all governments, guarantees do not affect the reported deficit or the volume of reported liabilities in the year they are issued. They show up only when the guarantees are called.

Financial reporting standards also determine whether governments report as a financial liability the obligations they incur in long-term purchase contracts (see "Insolvency Risk" in chapter 5). The standards followed by state-owned utilities, for example, determine whether a power-purchase agreement is treated as creating a liability similar to debt. State-owned utilities tend to follow the financial reporting standards followed by commercial firms, which are more advanced that those followed by most governments. Some standards, such as those applied by Napocor of the Philippines, require the obligations in power-purchase agreements to be reported as a liability—and the rights as leased assets.[13] Likewise, the auditor-general of New South Wales determined that the assets and liabilities associated with privately financed bulk-water treatment plants properly belonged on the public purchaser's balance sheet (Harris 1998). Other standards don't require such reporting, thereby possibly disguising the utility's true liabilities. Last, the standards the government follows for the consolidation of subsidiaries, including state-owned utilities, determine whether the assets and liabilities of a state-owned utility created by a long-term purchase agreement are counted as debts and assets of the government.

Indirectly, the standards also affect the pressure on the government to bear risk in private projects by determining how public investment

---

13 See Napocor's annual report for the year ended 31 December 2002 at http://www.napocor.gov.ph/.

affects the government's reported deficit. Traditional cash accounting reports the cash disbursed to buy or create an asset, but not the value of the asset. So if the government spends $100 million one year on a new power plant, the deficit increases by $100 million, even though the government's net worth—the value of its assets less the value of its liabilities—may not change.[14] By contrast, guaranteeing a power-purchase contract signed by an unconsolidated state-owned utility that excludes long-term power-purchase obligations from its reported debts may seem to cost nothing.

Financial reporting standards also matter for information disclosure because they create legal obligations. If the information that must be reported is of the right type, the standards make it hard for governments to keep an estimate of a cost confidential without good reason. Critically, the publication of the information in periodic financial reporting does not depend on the government deciding ad hoc to disclose information or on vigilant members of the public asking for it under a freedom-of-information act. It is regular and routine.

Moreover, accounting standards come with an apparatus of verification. Financial reports must be audited by an independent body: in governments, a public or supreme audit office. Auditing is no guarantee of accuracy, as accounting scandals repeatedly reveal. And some governments publish accounts that an auditor qualifies as unsatisfactory without being embarrassed enough to improve their financial reporting. But despite its limitations, auditing is surely better than no auditing.

The Move to Better Accounting Standards

The governments of many industrial countries, including Australia, Canada, Great Britain, New Zealand, and the United States, have adopted new standards. And the governments of developing countries as diverse as Chile, Indonesia, the Philippines, and South Africa are following this trend. The new standards are similar to those that apply to firms. They require the publication of cash flows—in a cash-flow statement—just as in traditional government accounting, but they also require the reporting of many noncash costs and revenues in an income statement. The standards also require the reporting of assets and liabilities in a balance sheet: that is, they require the reporting of stocks as well as flows. Thus, they encompass the traditional government cash accounts but go beyond them. As we will see, they are far from perfect, but they are better than standards that require only cash accounting.

---

14 For a discussion of this problem, see Easterly and Servén (2003).

Adopting an existing set of standards is easier than designing new standards from scratch, and governments overhauling their accounting practices have often based their new standards on existing local or international standards. Those standards often go by the name of GAAP, an acronym standing for generally accepted accounting principles in the United States and generally accepted accounting practices in Great Britain.

Most local GAAP seem destined to be largely replaced by international standards. The International Accounting Standards Board has developed a set of international accounting standards—now called International Financial Reporting Standards (IFRS)—for adoption by anyone who chooses. The setters of accounting standards in many countries have already decided that these international standards will largely replace their local standards. Notably, the European Union has decided that listed firms in its jurisdiction must now follow the international standards. The United States is perhaps the only major country not likely to adopt the international standards, and setters of accounting standards there are working with the International Accounting Standards Board to bring the two standards closer to each other. Since the accounting practices of reforming governments are strongly influenced by local GAAP, they will be strongly influenced by IFRS.

Similar standards have been developed specifically for governments. The International Public Sector Accounting Standards Board has created International Public Sector Accounting Standards, based on IFRS, but adapted to fit the special features of governments. The International Monetary Fund has created accrual accounting standards for government finance statistics (IMF 2001b).[15]

International Public Sector Accounting Standards, IFRS, and the like are living standards, changing and for the most part improving. So even when those standards are flawed, agreeing to follow them may lead to progressive improvement. By contrast, a government that relies on its own standards, developed during a time of passing enthusiasm for better financial reporting, may report according to increasingly out-of-date standards if the enthusiasm passes. By adopting a standard outside its control, a government also ties its hands and increases the credibility of its financial reporting. If the government designs its own standard, it may be tempted to alter a standard that produces a deficit it doesn't like. That is harder to do if the standard is set by an international or independent

---

15 Strictly speaking, the International Monetary Fund's standards are for statistical, not financial reporting. Statistical reports are not audited, but they include similar information.

local body. Although the government can discard a previously adopted independent set of standards, such a rejection calls attention to itself and frustrates an attempt to conceal a fiscal problem.

When Are Guarantees and Long-Term Purchase Contracts Recognized?

Yet no set of financial reporting standards deals adequately with all the ways a government can expose itself to risk. Modern standards require the recording of assets and of liabilities other than debt and don't, as a rule, ignore costs requiring no immediate cash expenditure. But they don't always require recognition of guarantees and other commitments.

To be concrete, we need to consider a specific set of standards. U.S. GAAP are perhaps the most fully developed, comprehensive set of standards available, and they may do the best job of capturing the costs and risks of guarantees and other commitments. But IFRS are mostly similar and are of wider interest. They also form the basis of International Public Sector Accounting Standards. The public-sector standards, however, do not so far treat guarantee-like obligations in the same detail as IFRS do, and when the public-sector standards are silent, IFRS offers guidance. So we focus on IFRS. The application of IFRS to the guarantees we have been describing is complex. Several particular standards are relevant.[16]

International Accounting Standard (IAS) 37 treats "Provisions, Contingent Liabilities, and Contingent Assets." Some guarantees may be considered contingent liabilities for the purposes of this standard. The standard's complex definition of a contingent liability is as follows (International Accounting Standards Board 2004, 1531–32):

(a) a possible obligation that arises from past events and whose existence will be confirmed only by the occurrence or nonoccurrence of one or more uncertain future events not wholly within the control of the entity; or

(b) a present obligation that arises from past events but is not recognized because:

    (i) it is not probable that an outflow of resources embodying economic benefits will be required to settle the obligation; or

    (ii) the amount of the obligation cannot be measured with sufficient reliability.

---

16 See also International Accounting Standard (IAS) 21 on government grants, which says, rather pessimistically, "Examples of assistance that cannot reasonably have a value placed upon them [include] government guarantees" (International Accounting Standards Board 2004, 1019, paragraph 35).

Contingent liabilities, as defined, are not recognized. That is, incurring a contingent liability doesn't increase the government's liabilities or its accrual deficit. A guarantee might create a contingent liability. If so, it would not be recognized.

Although a government's exposure to risk from guarantees is often referred to under the rubric of contingent liabilities, guarantees need not create contingent liabilities as defined by IFRS, for there are two other categories into which guarantees might fall: derivatives and insurance contracts. (Indeed, the International Accounting Standards Board has proposed doing away with the term *contingent liability*.)

IAS 39, "Financial Instruments: Recognition and Measurement," defines a derivative as follows (International Accounting Standards Board 2004, 1651):

> a financial instrument or other contract within the scope of this Standard . . . with all three of the following characteristics:
> (a) its value changes in response to the change in a specified interest rate, financial instrument price, commodity price, foreign exchange rate, index of prices or rates, credit rating or credit index, or other variable, provided in the case of a non-financial variable that the variable is not specific to a party to the contract (sometimes called the "underlying");
> (b) it requires no initial net investment or an initial net investment that is smaller than would be required for other types of contracts that would be expected to have a similar response to changes in market factors; and
> (c) it is settled at a later date.

Exchange-rate and interest-rate guarantees might be derivatives according to IAS 39, and a government following IFRS and issuing such guarantees would generally be required to recognize their cost in its deficit and balance sheet.

By contrast, guarantees written on risk factors specific to the firm might count as insurance contracts, which are excluded from the scope of IAS 39 but included in the scope of IFRS 4 on insurance contracts. An insurance contract is defined as follows (International Accounting Standards Board 2004, 387):

> A contract under which one party (the insurer) accepts significant insurance risk from another party (the policyholder) by agreeing to compensate the policyholder if a specified uncertain future event . . . adversely affects the policyholder.

Insurer and *policyholder* are defined broadly to include not just insurance companies and their clients. The government could be an insurer, and a private infrastructure firm a policyholder. Exposure to insurance risks is exposure to risks that are "nonfinancial"—that is, those whose value doesn't vary in response to the factors mentioned in paragraph (a) of the definition of a derivative. A government guarantee that compensates the firm for an increase in a construction-cost price index might count as a derivative, subject to IAS 39; a construction-cost guarantee that depends on the firm's actual construction costs might count as insurance. So too might traffic and revenue guarantees, as well as debt guarantees (financial guarantees in the language of IFRS).

IFRS 4 is intended as a stopgap, applying until a more comprehensive standard on the subject is promulgated. Its requirements are permissive, often allowing firms to maintain elements of their existing treatment of insurance contracts. Yet it allows insurance contracts to be recognized at fair value, and the new insurance standard promised by the International Accounting Standards Board may require recognition at fair value (see International Accounting Standards Board 2004, 377).

The treatment of guarantees in IFRS is complex and less than fully satisfactory. Some guarantees would have to be recorded at fair value; others wouldn't. The trend appears to be in the right direction, though: the International Accounting Standards Board appears to want to move toward standards that, wherever practicable, require contractual liabilities such as guarantees to be recognized at fair value.

Likewise, it is unclear exactly how well IFRS deal with the accounting problems created by long-term purchase contracts, such as power-purchase agreements and typical public-private partnerships. The standards would generally require consolidation of the state-owned utility that entered into such contracts. And, depending on the details, the standards might treat the contracts as financial leases—contracts tantamount to the purchase of an asset with money borrowed from the nominal lessor (which, from an economic point of view, is a seller also providing finance). If so, the contracts would create an asset and a liability on the utility's—and therefore the government's—balance sheet. But the contracts might be considered executory, under which both parties have yet to fully perform their obligations. If so, no assets and liabilities would be recognized.[17]

---

17 On consolidation, see IAS 27; on leases, see IAS 17. The Accounting Standards Board of Great Britain has issued perhaps the most detailed guidance on the treatment of what we have described as long-term purchase contracts. The guidance is found in a note on "Private Finance Initiative and Similar Contracts," which is appended to its Financial Reporting Standard 5, "Reporting the Substance of Transactions," included in Institute of Chartered Accountants of England and Wales (2003).

IFRS have only recently been adopted by many firms around the world, and the required treatment of long-term purchase contracts under the standards may soon become clear. In any case, there is evidence—as in the case of guarantees—that mainstream accounting standards are gradually moving toward greater recognition, at fair value, of contractual rights and obligations.

Disclosing Additional Information

A government that adopted, say, International Public Sector Accounting Standards would be signing up to standards that, though imperfect, are better than most of the realistic alternatives and are likely to improve. Such a government's financial reporting would be among the best in the world. To address all the accounting problems that might tempt it to make poor decisions about exposure to risk, however, it would have to go beyond the requirements of the standards. Moreover, few governments report according to modern accrual accounting standards. In the short term, the best that these governments can do is to disclose additional information to supplement their cash accounting.

The Chilean government, for example, discloses information that is not required by the financial reporting standards it currently follows. In a report on public finances that accompanies the budget, the government discloses information on the costs of the revenue and exchange-rate guarantees it has granted to toll roads. It presents estimates of the amounts it expects to pay or receive over the next 20 years under the revenue and exchange-rate guarantees (lumping together all the different concessions). It also presents estimates of the value of each of the revenue and exchange-rate guarantees by concession. Table 6.1 extracts an example of the information it discloses (Government of Chile 2003).[18]

Disclosed information need not be purely quantitative. For example, a government can describe the guarantees it has issued and the risks to which it is therefore exposed. It can also publish the contracts that include the guarantees, allowing others to identify and assess the risks.

When disclosed, such information may spur others to improve the government's information. Academics, consultants, and others may offer opinions on whether giving the guarantees is good policy and on how much they are worth. Outside review can also discipline the government's advisers and decision makers. If they know their advice and their decisions may be scrutinized, they have another reason to get the advice right.

---

18 The estimates are derived using the approach set out in chapters 7 and 8.

Table 6.1. Chile's Disclosure of Guarantee Costs
Expected cash flows (Ch$ billion)

Year	Guaranteed minimum income	Income sharing	Exchange-rate guarantees	Total
2003	−1.257	0.000	−0.853	−2.110
2004	−1.584	0.000	−0.044	−1.629
2005	−2.587	0.010	−0.354	−2.931
...	...	...	...	...
2020	−18.428	0.985	0.000	−17.444

Values (Ch$ billion)

Project	Net minimum income	Exchange rate	Total
El Melon Tunnel	0.000	0.000	0.000
Santiago–Colina–Los Andes	3.054	0.000	3.054
Camino de la Madera	−1.257	0.000	−1.247
Route 5, Los Vilos–La Serena	2.335	3.413	5.748
...	...	...	...
Total	128.556	10.605	139.161

Note: *Net minimum income* is the net value of the guaranteed-minimum-income agreements and income-sharing agreements.
Source: Government of Chile 2003.

For this very reason, officials and politicians often resist the disclosure of information when they address the question in a particular case. Yet governments sometimes do decide, when considering the issue from a broader perspective, to adopt laws and regulations that generate transparency. Some adopt financial reporting standards that require extensive disclosure. Some adopt freedom-of-information laws. Some publish infrastructure concession contracts.[19]

Transparency isn't an unmitigated good for the public. The release of reams of official documents can hide critical information. Freedom-of-information laws can encourage advisers to speak their mind only behind closed doors. Decision makers who must explain their decisions can later become unreasonably committed to them, committing the sunk-cost fallacy of throwing good money after bad (Mellers, Schwartz, and Cooke 1998, 461). The design of freedom-of-information laws can reduce some of these problems—protecting certain types of advice in certain circumstances—but tradeoffs are inevitable.

---

19 Some contracts are available at http://rru.worldbank.org.

Budgeting for Guarantees

Incorporating the cost of bearing risk into budgets is central. If budget rules require governments to take account of the cost of a guarantee when it is issued, the temptation to use guarantees as disguised subsidies instead of instruments for improving the allocation of risk is much reduced. We consider several options here.[20]

Caps on Exposure and on the Value of Guarantees
Perhaps the simplest option is for the government or legislature to set a cap on the increase in the government's maximum possible loss (or, to use a different term, exposure; see "Measuring Exposure" in chapter 7).[21] If the legislature sets the cap, it might approve each guarantee separately, but more likely it would set one limit on total exposure or a set of limits for each of several categories—one for power projects, say, another for transport projects, and so on.

Such a parallel budget for guarantees allows the government to control the issuance of new guarantees and therefore the increase in maximum possible loss new guarantees could cause. It also forces tradeoffs between guarantees: once the limit on new exposure is reached, issuing a guarantee means forgoing another. Poland limits new guarantees in this way. When it guaranteed a large borrowing by the A2 motorway company (see chapter 2), complaints were heard that this guarantee used up much of the guarantee budget, displacing other possible guarantees (Esty 2004, 318).

This approach is simple and useful. But because guarantees with the same maximum possible loss can have different values, the approach doesn't adequately control the incurrence of costs. Further, it doesn't allow comparisons between guarantees and direct expenditure.

To get around this problem, governments could establish a cap on the policy-related increase in the value of outstanding guarantees. The reason for adding the qualification that the increase be policy related is that the value of a guarantee, as opposed (usually) to the maximum possible loss, can change for reasons unrelated to policy. The cost of a revenue guarantee,

---

20 A simpler but still important task is to ensure that the coming year's expected guarantee cash flows are included in the cash budget, so that cash forecasts are reliable and cash needs can be managed. A law in Hungary addresses this problem by requiring the government to appropriate the expected cost of guarantees in the coming year (Brixi, Schick, and Zlaoui 2002, 219).

21 The U.S. government used this approach in the years after World War II (Whitman 1965, 69–70). See also Brixi, Schick, and Zlaoui (2002) and Schick (2002a, 87–88).

for example, could fall because demand fell, even if the government did nothing to make the guarantee more generous. Estimating the value of a guarantee is also much harder than simply determining the maximum possible loss (see chapter 7). Otherwise, this cap would operate in the same way as the cap on exposure.

Although a cap on the policy-related increase in the value of outstanding guarantees can be considered as an alternative to a cap on exposure, a government might want to establish both. The cap on value is relevant because the value of the guarantee is the best estimate of its cost to the government and is most relevant in comparing guarantees with other policies. The cap on exposure is also relevant, however, because a prudent government will care not only about the value of its commitments, but also about the risks of much higher payments. A cap on exposure is also less vulnerable to manipulation. (The difference between value, risks, and maximum losses is clarified in chapter 7.)

Budgeting According to an Accrual Accounting Standard

An alternative is to tackle the fundamental problem with traditional budgets: their reliance on traditional government accounting, with its focus on cash expenditure in the coming year, to the exclusion of deferred, contingent expenditure. A government can address the problems of traditional budgeting by moving from appropriations of cash flows to appropriations of costs according to an accrual accounting standard. It can shift its budgetary focus, that is, from the cash-flow statement to the operating statement—or from the cash-flow statement alone to both statements. (Nothing in modern accounting suggests that governments should ignore current cash flows.)

If the standards adopted require the economic liability created by a guarantee to be recognized, they solve the budgeting problem. For budgeting purposes, the cost of issuing a guarantee is the same as the cost of disbursing cash of an equal value. The required approvals are the same, and the requirements to confront tradeoffs are the same: issuing the guarantee requires the government to cut a dollar somewhere else, raise taxes by a dollar, or increase the accrual deficit by a dollar. The risk created by the guarantee must still be managed, but the central issue of ensuring that decisions reflect estimates of costs and benefits is addressed.

Yet, as we saw, even the best existing accrual accounting standards don't require recognition of all guarantees. For the foreseeable future, financial reporting standards won't solve the problem. One way around them is to create a custom-made standard to deal with the biggest problems.

This is in effect what the United States did with the Federal Credit Reform Act of 1990.[22] The United States generally budgets on a cash basis, and before the act, its budget reflected only the immediate cash flows associated with guarantees. Guarantee fees showed up as revenue; guarantee calls as expenditure. The act changed this by requiring that Congress appropriate the long-term cost of debt guarantees in the year they are issued. It requires the cost of debt guarantees to be estimated as the value, discounting at the risk-free rate, of the cash flows the guarantee is expected to generate, including fees, payments on defaults, and any subsequent recoveries. Actual cash flows go through a separate financing account.

Suppose, for example, that the government guarantees a $10 million loan for an upfront fee of $1 million and that the present value of expected payments resulting from default, less any recoveries, is $3 million. The net cost of issuing the guarantee is therefore $2 million. And suppose that the borrower defaults later in the year, requiring the government to pay $10 million, and that no recoveries are possible. Given these assumptions, the legislature must appropriate $2 million in year 1. That appropriation and the $1 million fee received in year 1 go into the financing account. Later in the year, the government pays $10 million from the financing account, the remaining $7 million coming from the Treasury. No new appropriation is needed, however.

The Federal Credit Reform Act also deals with changes in the value of a guarantee that happen after the guarantee is issued. If the government changes policies in a way that increases the estimated cost of an outstanding guarantee, it must appropriate the increase in cost. If the estimated cost of outstanding guarantees increases for reasons other than a change in the government's guarantee policy (such as a change in the prevailing riskless interest rate), the increase is also appropriated, but under a provision providing for automatic appropriations. The two types of change are shown separately.

The Federal Credit Reform Act does not solve all the budgeting and accounting problems created by government risk bearing. It covers only certain debt guarantees, excluding such important programs as pension guarantees and insurance of bank deposits. The estimates also ignore any risk premium (see "Valuing Exposure" in chapter 7). Expected cash flows are neither adjusted for risk nor discounted at a risk-adjusted rate. Thus,

---

22 The Federal Credit Reform Act of 1990 is available at http://www.fms.treas.gov/ussgl/ creditreform/fcra.html. See also Phaup (1993) and Mody and Patro (1996).

the cost of guarantees is generally underestimated.[23] Yet the act is a major improvement on prior practice.

An alternative to developing a new accrual standard for budgeting is to work around the problem created by inadequate standards, by creating a fund. The idea is to manage guarantees in a way that provokes recognition of their costs in a cash budget or an accrual budget based on imperfect standards.

Using a Fund

A fund can be used to manage liabilities arising from guarantees and other sources of uncertain cash expenditure. It can also be used, as in Colombia, to reassure investors that the government will meet its obligations (Echeverry and others 2002). Might it also obviate the problems created by poor accounting?

Suppose the government puts money into a fund when it gives a guarantee and takes money from the fund when the guarantee is called. Specifically, suppose a spending ministry giving a guarantee must contribute cash to the fund equal to the estimated value of the guarantee. In this case, the ministry must get an appropriation to spend that cash. The use of the fund therefore works to reveal a cost in the budget of the ministry issuing the guarantee, possibly imposing more discipline on it to make tradeoffs.

To impose the same discipline on the government as a whole, however, the fund must be off budget; it can't be consolidated for the purposes of estimating the budget deficit. Otherwise, the payment to the fund counts as both revenue and an expense for the government, and the net effect on its measured debt and deficit is zero. For governments with primitive accounting, it may be easy to keep the fund out of the government's accounts. For others, it may not be. For them, the fund may not solve the accounting problem for the government as a whole—though it may still improve the incentives of the ministry issuing the guarantee.

The fund can also be used to make payments when they fall due, possibly avoiding the need to get a new appropriation to meet an unexpected call on the guarantee. Yet the fund has limitations in this area as well. If it is to circumvent the problems of poor accounting, the contribution to the fund should equal an estimate of the value of the guarantee. If the guarantee has an estimated value of $1 million, the spending ministry should put $1 million in the fund. Withdrawals and further contributions

---

23 The government is aware of the problem, and there are proposals to address it; see Government of United States, Congressional Budget Office (2004).

will in general be needed in future years as the estimated value of the guarantee changes. If circumstances cause the value of the guarantee to rise by $1 million over the course of the year, the spending ministry must contribute another $1 million. If circumstances improve, it must make a withdrawal.[24]

But setting contributions and withdrawals according to the value of the guarantee may frustrate the achievement of the government's cash-management goals. Specifically, the government may hope the fund will prevent it from having to make cash payments out of its ordinary budget when guarantees fall due (Echeverry and others 2002; Christopher Lewis and Mody 1997). Contributions equal to the value of the guarantee will help in this respect but won't be ideal. Unless the contributions to the fund equal the present value of the maximum possible loss, the fund cannot cover all losses with certainty. There is always a chance the government will have to dip into another of its pockets to meet calls. For the purposes of cash management, for example, the government may want a fund that can meet calls at least 90 percent of the time. The contributions that create such a fund, however, won't generally equal the value of the guarantees. For a fund with only a few guarantees, they will almost certainly be higher. The more guarantees the fund covers and the less correlated they are with each other, the more likely is a fund equal in value to the guarantees to have the cash needed to meet calls. Yet the approach that addresses the accounting problem cannot optimally address the cash-management problem.

Although a fund can help with cash management, it also has a cash-management disadvantage. It segregates the government's cash and other financial assets and liabilities into different pools. If the government has net debt, keeping cash in the fund prevents the government from reducing its debt. If the government pays a higher rate of interest on its debt than it receives on cash invested in the fund, maintaining the fund costs more than the alternative of reducing debt. It also makes cash management harder by denying the government the full benefit of diversification. And use of a fund encourages those managing the fund to view the government's exposure to risk too narrowly (see "Cognitive Obstacles" in chapter 3).

---

24 An alternative allocation of risk within the government is possible. The initial contribution by the spending ministry could be treated as the purchase of insurance from, say, the ministry of finance. In that case, the ministry of finance would make the additional contributions and withdrawals.

CHAPTER 7

Valuing Exposure to Risk

Governments can better choose whether to bear a risk if they have measured and valued their prospective exposure—that is, if they have described it quantitatively and estimated its cost. If the risk is especially complex or ambiguous, measurement and valuation may prove too rough or too difficult to be useful. If the risk is very small, measurement and valuation may be unnecessary. But approximate measurement and valuation are often possible, and if the risk is large, approximations are better than nothing.

The measurement of risk is part of risk management, the practice of monitoring and controlling the risks to which an organization is exposed. Risk management is designed to help organizations avoid financial distress and its attendant costs. In some countries, risk management might require careful analysis of government guarantees, because guarantees are most likely to be triggered during a financial crisis and may significantly contribute to financial distress.

In some cases, the avoidance of fiscal distress may be the main goal of measuring a government's exposure to risk in private projects. The risk of a portfolio of exposures, however, is generally less than the sum of the risks of the component exposures. So risk management is most valuably done for the entire portfolio of exposures of a government—all its assets and liabilities, all its revenues and expenditures—not for a single infrastructure project or even for its portfolio of infrastructure projects.

Our focus is therefore not risk management in this sense. It is the valuation of guarantees that we take to be the ultimate goal of analysis, because an estimate of the value is what a government chiefly needs if it is to decide what to do—if it is to compare the cost of bearing a risk with other options and to choose the most cost-effective. Before turning to valuation, however, we consider the measurement of risk, which is a step on the way to both valuation and risk management. Measurement is also useful because it helps ministries plan. Knowing the probability of having to spend more than a certain amount next year isn't the same as knowing the cost of a guarantee—and may not be crucial for a government for which the guarantee is but one small part of a large portfolio of assets and liabilities subject to risk. But it may be crucial for the financial management of the ministry responsible for guarantees.

Identifying Exposure

The first step in measuring and valuing exposure to risk is to identify the major risk factors. What might cause outcomes to differ from forecasts? What might make them worse? What might make them better?

In its role as policy maker, a government may need to think about all the main risk factors that enter into the total-project-value function (see "Definitions" in chapter 4). If a government regulates the price of a service, it needs to think about how its regulatory policy allocates risks between the firm and customers. In its fiscal role, a government needs to think about the sources of its own exposure. In principle, this is a matter of specifying the function that determines the value of the government's interest in the project. Identifying all the risk factors—thinking about implicit as well as explicit obligations—is impossible, but many of the major risks can be found by looking in laws, licenses, regulations, concessions, guarantee contracts, and other instruments that allocate risk. Many of the major risks will already have been identified by project sponsors, ministries, and outside advisers.

For example, a concession contract for a toll road might include the following rules, implying payments to or from the government in certain states of the world:

- The concessionaire may increase tolls with inflation. If the government wishes, it can avert the increase as long as it compensates the concessionaire.

- The government guarantees that the concessionaire's revenue will not fall below a specified threshold. If revenue would otherwise fall below the threshold, the government will top it up.
- The concessionaire will pay the government a proportion of any revenue it gets above a specified threshold.
- The government can cancel the concession at any time if it compensates the concessionaire for past investment and forgone profits.
- The road reverts to the government after 30 years, at which time the government will pay the concessionaire the accounting value of the road.

All such rules expose the government to risk. It should be possible to express each one in an equation that specifies how much the government gets or pays. For example, the government's guarantee of the concessionaire's revenue might be expressed as

$$p_t = \max\left\{0, k_t - x_t\right\} \tag{7.1}$$

where p is the government's payment, k is guaranteed revenue, x is toll revenue, and the subscript t refers to the year. Note that the right-hand side of the equation refers to revenue, which is a risk factor and whose value is therefore unknown. So the formula does not unconditionally predict the amount of the payment; it predicts the payment given an outcome of the risk factor.

Sometimes, the true formulas may be extremely complex; many conditions may have to be met before the government makes or gets a payment, and the amount of any payment may depend on many things. Payments under a revenue guarantee, for example, might depend on the road's being properly maintained and the number of accidents not exceeding a threshold. In quantifying exposure to risk, we must work out how much simplification is appropriate: too much and the analysis becomes unrealistic; too little and it becomes unwieldy. We need to know which risk factors are so important they must be modeled and which can be ignored without introducing undue error.

Measuring Exposure

Having identified the main risk factors and the rules that link these risk factors to payments to or from the government, we can measure risk. Before describing techniques for measuring exposure to risk, we need to clarify what we mean by measuring exposure to risk.

The Probability Distribution of Gains and Losses

Fully measuring exposure to risk means specifying the probability distribution of payments over the period of the exposure. For an exposure that relates to just one moment in time, such as the obligation to make a termination payment to a concessionaire at the end of its concession, a single probability distribution is involved, and a single graph is sufficient to represent it. Figure 7.1 shows a histogram, derived from made-up data, depicting a possible frequency distribution for such a payment.

For exposures that relate to an extended period, a single probability distribution is insufficient. For example, if payments may be made each month over five years, we need, in principle, 60 probability distributions. We might simplify, however, by considering annual payments instead of monthly payments, which would reduce the required number of probability distributions to five. Sometimes the appropriate period for analysis is determined by the risk. For example, if a revenue guarantee specifies that revenue will be calculated at the end of each year and any payment made then, the year is the natural unit of analysis. At other times, we must choose somewhat arbitrarily.

Figure 7.1. Termination-Payment Risk

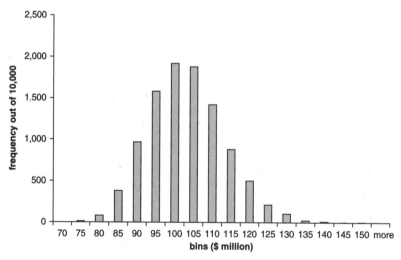

Source: Author's calculations.
Note: The figure shows payments of up to $70 million, those between $70 million and $75 million, those between $75 million and $80 million, and so on. The labels indicate the upper limit of each bin, except for the last ("more"), which includes all payments higher than the last numerical label. Payments between $95 million and $100 million are the most common, occurring about 2,000 times in 10,000, or about 20 percent of the time. The frequency distribution assumes the payment is lognormally distributed.

Figure 7.2. Revenue Guarantee: Relative Frequency of Payments in Various Ranges

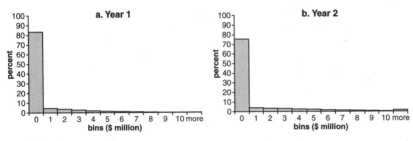

Source: Author's calculations.
Note: The labeling of the bins follows the pattern of figure 7.1. The estimates are based on a sample of 100,000.

Figure 7.2 shows histograms of government payments under a revenue guarantee for each of two years. It assumes that revenue starts at $100 million in year 0 and is expected to grow by 5 percent a year and that the government has guaranteed the firm revenue of at least $100 million in year 1 and $105 million in year 2. Note that the dispersion of payments is greater in year 2 than in year 1.

Estimates of the whole probability distribution, such as those shown in the histograms above, are extremely useful. Indeed, for fully measuring risk they are essential. Their disadvantage is their lack of concision. For some purposes, we'd prefer to summarize the government's exposure to risk in just one or two numbers.

Maximum and Minimum Payments

Two simple but useful measures are the government's maximum possible gain and its maximum possible loss. The government's maximum possible loss, in particular, is sometimes described as the government's exposure. The maximum possible loss on the revenue guarantee just discussed is $100 million in the first year and $105 million in the second year. The maximum possible loss under a debt guarantee may be the amount of the loan.

Other instruments may give the government exposure to upside risk but cap the possible gain. The government might share in the revenue of a project up to some limit. Or, as part of an exchange-rate guarantee linked to foreign-currency debt, the government might agree to protect the concessionaire from depreciation on condition that the government benefit from appreciation. The government's gain, expressed in foreign currency, is limited by the value of the debt.

At other times, the government's loss or gain is unlimited. Measured in local currency, for example, the possible loss created by exposure to exchange-rate risk is infinite: there is no limit to the amount of local currency the government might have to spend to meet its obligation. Gains too may be unlimited. A typical revenue-sharing agreement places no cap on the government's gains—nor does an agreement to share in the equity of a project.

Expected Payments

Another useful measure is the expected payment or receipt. The expected payment, in this sense of expected, is probability weighted. Consider a simple example: if the government were to offer to toss a fair coin and to give a firm $1 if the coin landed heads up and nothing otherwise, the government would have a 50 percent chance of paying $1 and a 50 percent chance of paying nothing. Its probability-weighted, or expected, payment would be 50 cents.

Expected payments can be estimated from the data underlying histograms such as those shown in figures 7.1 and 7.2. These graphs are based on large samples of possible outcomes. (Later we explain how we generated them.) In figure 7.1, the 10,000 possible outcomes are possible termination payments. The average of those payments is an estimate of the government's expected payment. The average payment in the dataset turns out to be about $100 million, so $100 million is an estimate of the expected payment. In figure 7.2, the 100,000 possible outcomes are revenue-guarantee payments. The averages of these turn out to be $0.43 million in year 1 and $1.04 million in year 2.

Cash Flow at Risk, Excess-Payment Probability, and More

Other measures of risk focus on bad outcomes, defined in various ways. One such measure is the probability of having to pay more than a certain amount. For the revenue guarantee illustrated in figure 7.2, the government might want to know the probability of having to pay more than $5 million in year 1. In the example, it happens to be 2 percent. This measure might be called the *excess-payment probability*.

Another closely related measure is cash flow at risk. Its definition is rather long-winded: it is the smallest payment that the government can expect, with a particular degree of confidence, not to pay more than. There is thus a cash flow at risk for each degree of confidence. For the revenue guarantee, cash flow at risk at the 98 percent confidence level is $5 million. At the 99 percent level, it is $7 million. Cash flow at risk is a close relation of value at risk, which focuses on loss of value rather than on cash disbursed.[1] Be careful not to be misled by the expression *at risk*: in the ordinary sense, cash flow at risk would be the most the government can lose, not the most it can lose with a particular degree of confidence.

Another measure of risk is the standard deviation of the payment or its square, the variance. If the payments follow a known distribution of a certain type, such as the normal distribution, knowing the expected payment and the standard deviation is sufficient for describing the entire probability distribution (for drawing the histogram). It is therefore sufficient for specifying other measures described here, such as cash flow at risk and the excess-payment probability. If the payments are normally distributed, for example, the government can be about 95 percent sure its payment will lie within two standard deviations of the expected payment. If the expected payment is $10 million and the standard deviation is $1 million, the government can, therefore, be about 95 percent sure its payment will be between $8 million and $12 million.

When the distribution is unknown or unusual, as in figure 7.2, knowing the standard deviation is less useful. The payments under the revenue guarantee in year 1 have a standard deviation of $1.3 million, and the expected payment is, as just noted, $0.43 million. But it isn't obvious what this tells us about the probability of payments above, say, $2 million. To work that out, we must look at the underlying data.

Other measures are possible and may sometimes be useful. When risks relate to events that may or may not occur, it may be useful to estimate the probability of the event occurring. Another possibility is to estimate the expected payment, given that losses exceed a certain cash flow at risk. For the revenue guarantee, the expected loss, given a loss of at least the 99 percent cash flow at risk, is $8 million.[2]

Portfolios and Correlations

So far, we've considered risks one at a time. Expected payments simply add: the expected total payment from two or more guarantees is the

---

1 Value at risk is an application of the quantile function in probability theory (see, for example, DeGroot and Schervish 2002, 114). For discussions, see Baumol (1963), Dowd (1998), and Jorion (1997).

2 Dowd (1998) and Duffie and Singleton (2003) discuss various measures of risk and criteria for comparing them. G. Boyle and Irwin (2005) illustrate the application of cash flow at risk and the excess-payment probability to government payments in infrastructure projects.

sum of the expected payments for each guarantee. Thus, it is possible to estimate the expected total payment for a portfolio of guarantees by adding results from independent analyses of each guarantee. Values add in the same way. But the standard deviation of the value of a portfolio is not, in general, the sum of the standard deviations of the values of the parts of the portfolio. The same is true for cash flow at risk and the excess-payment probability. Thus, estimates of these measures of risk for a portfolio cannot be derived simply by adding results from several independent analyses.

To illustrate the point, suppose the government must make two payments of uncertain amounts. If the standard deviations of the payments are σ_a and σ_b, respectively, the standard deviation of the sum of the payments σ_p is given by

$$\sigma_p = \sqrt{\sigma_a^2 + \sigma_b^2 + 2\rho\sigma_a\,\sigma_b},$$

where ρ is the coefficient of correlation between the two payments, which measures the extent to which their values move together. It is defined as

$$\rho = \frac{\text{cov}(a,b)}{\sigma_a\,\sigma_b},$$

where $\text{cov}(a,b)$ is the covariance between the two payments. The coefficient ranges from -1 to $+1$. If $\rho = 1$, the values of the two payments are perfectly correlated, and the standard deviation of the portfolio is at its highest. In this case, the standard deviation of the portfolio is the sum of the standard deviations of the constituents. At the other extreme, where $\rho = -1$, the standard deviation of the portfolio is at its lowest. If $\rho = -1$ and the two payments have the same standard deviation, the standard deviation of the portfolio is zero: risk has been eliminated. In between, where $\rho = 0$, again assuming equal standard deviations, the standard deviation of the portfolio is about 1.4 times the standard deviation of the individual payments.[3]

---

3 If $\rho = 1$, then $\sigma_p = \sqrt{\sigma_a^2 + \sigma_b^2 + 2\sigma_a\sigma_b} = \sqrt{(\sigma_a + \sigma_b)^2} = \sigma_a + \sigma_b$. If $\rho = -1$, then $\sigma_p = \sqrt{\sigma_a^2 + \sigma_b^2 - 2\sigma_a\sigma_b} = \sqrt{(\sigma_a - \sigma_b)^2} = \sigma_a - \sigma_b$. If $\sigma_a = \sigma_b$, the standard deviation of the portfolio of liabilities is zero. If $\rho = 0$, then $\sigma_p = \sqrt{\sigma_a^2 + \sigma_b^2}$. If it is also the case that $\sigma_a = \sigma_b = \sigma$, then $\sigma_p = \sqrt{2\sigma^2} = \sqrt{2}\sigma$. Statistics and finance textbooks generalize these results for more than two assets. See, for example, DeGroot and Schervish (2002).

Having identified the risk factors—or rather, having identified some of them (the main ones, it is to be hoped)—and having decided what measures of risk to focus on, we must next choose a set of models that characterize the probability distributions of the risk factors.

Modeling the Risk Factor at a Point in Time

Choosing a model may sometimes be a matter of picking a single probability distribution that describes the risk factor at a specific time. For example, suppose the government has agreed to bear some construction-cost risk in a project—perhaps it will pay half of any construction costs above a certain threshold. One way to estimate the risk of this exposure is to assume, for analytical purposes, that construction costs are incurred at a single point in time and to make an assumption about the probability distribution that describes the risk of the costs at that time. In choosing the distribution, the government may be able to use its own data on the construction costs of similar projects or to draw on the research of others (see Flyvbjerg, Holm, and Buhl 2002; Skamris and Flyvbjerg 1997; Trujillo, Quinet, and Estache 2002).

Suppose that a combination of research and guesswork suggests that construction costs are lognormally distributed. This implies that the log of construction costs is normally distributed and means that construction costs cannot be negative. (An assumption that construction costs themselves were normally distributed would imply that construction costs might be negative.) The choice also means that the distribution of costs is skewed to the right. Suppose also that the project's proponents have estimated the cost of construction at $100 million, but that our experience leads us to think that this figure is on the low side. With our combination of research and guesswork, we conclude that the true expected cost is $120 million and that the standard deviation of the cost is about $25 million. Suppose, finally, that the government has agreed to bear half of any construction costs over $150 million. Figure 7.3 shows histograms of estimated construction costs and government payments.

Modeling an Evolving Risk Factor

Often we are interested in risk factors that change over time. If the government has guaranteed the concessionaire's revenue, for example, we are interested in how revenue changes. Now we need to choose a stochastic (random) process, not just a single probability distribution. A random walk is an example of a simple stochastic process in which the value of the risk factor equals its value in the last period plus a random number.

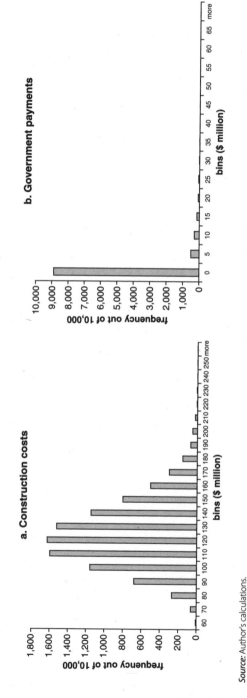

Figure 7.3. Construction-Cost Risk and Government Payments

a. Construction costs

b. Government payments

Source: Author's calculations.

Note: The data are derived by assuming that construction costs are lognormally distributed, with a mean of $120 million and a standard deviation of $25 million and that the government's payment in millions of dollars is 0.5 max(0, cost − 150).

One frequently useful choice is to assume that the risk factor of interest follows a geometric Brownian motion.[4] This allows the risk factor to have a trend rate of growth or decline as well as a random element, and it makes the trend rate of growth and the size of the random elements proportional to the current value of the risk factor. It also means that negative values are impossible, which is often right for the risk factors of interest, such as costs, prices, revenues, and asset values. Mathematically, a risk factor x that follows a geometric Brownian motion changes as

$$dx = \mu x dt + \sigma x \sqrt{dt} z, \tag{7.2}$$

where μ is the expected rate of growth of x, dt is an increment of time, σ is the volatility of the growth of x, and z is a random drawing from a standard normal distribution—that is, a normally distributed variable with a mean of 0 and a variance of 1. In words, the proportional growth of the risk factor over an increment of time is equal to a constant rate of growth multiplied by the increment of time and a random element proportional to its volatility multiplied by the square root of the increment of time.

Equation 7.2 gives the change in the value of the risk factor from one instant to the next. It implies the following equations for the current value of the risk factor as a function of previous values (see "Equations for Geometric Brownian Motion" in appendix A):

$$x_t = x_{t-1} \exp\left(\left(\mu - \frac{\sigma^2}{2}\right) + \sigma z\right) \tag{7.3}$$

and

$$x_t = x_0 \exp\left(\left(\mu - \frac{\sigma^2}{2}\right) t + \sigma \sqrt{t} z\right). \tag{7.4}$$

Noting that the Microsoft Excel function NORMSINV(RAND()) generates random numbers with a standard normal distribution, we can use these equations to implement geometric Brownian motion in a spreadsheet.

Superficial or Structural Modeling?
Often we must choose how deep the analysis of a risk factor should go. Suppose, for example, we're interested in revenue. One option is to

---

4 For more on geometric Brownian motion, see, for example, Dixit and Pindyck (1994, chapter 3) and Hull (2003, chapter 11).

assume that revenue follows a given process such as a geometric Brownian motion. Another is to take advantage of the dependence of revenue on more fundamental risk factors, such as price, demand, and billing and collection. If we do this, we could choose to model the underlying risk factors and build our estimate of revenue from them. We might, for example, assume that demand followed a geometric Brownian motion, that the rate of billing and collection followed some other process, and that the price was constant. In the one case, we treat revenue as a primitive in the analysis; in the other, we treat revenue as the result of other risk factors that are themselves the primitives.

Which approach is better may depend on the circumstances. In the example, treating revenue as the primitive has the advantage of being simpler; it doesn't add new risk factors to the analysis. Treating it as a function of other primitives may be useful if we start with a good sense of the how the underlying factors change and know the relationship between the underlying factors and revenue. It may also make the analysis seem more realistic to people used to forecasting the risk factor of interest in terms of other variables.

Formulas and Monte Carlo Simulation

Sometimes we can use formulas to measure risk. But the complexity of the instruments that create exposure to risk often means that formulas for measuring the relevant risk are either unknown or nonexistent. When formulas don't exist or are unknown, we can use other techniques that give approximate solutions.

Perhaps the most useful is Monte Carlo simulation.[5] In Monte Carlo simulation, we use a random-number generator to take a sample of outcomes of the risk factor or risk factors, and for each outcome, we record the payment to or by the government. For a revenue guarantee, for example, we would sample revenue and record the resulting guarantee payments by the government. As we increase the size of the sample, we build up an increasingly reliable estimate of the probability distribution of the possible outcomes.

Return to the example of the revenue guarantee illustrated in figure 7.2, and suppose that we want a probabilistic forecast of revenue for the next two years. Suppose that we think traffic revenue follows a geometric Brownian motion as in equation 7.3 and that, as before, this year's

---

5 Others include numerical methods such as binomial trees. For more on Monte Carlo simulation, see, for example, P. Boyle (1977) and Hull (2003, chapter 18).

revenue is $100 million and that revenue is forecast to grow at 5 percent a year. Suppose also that data on past revenue on the road suggest an estimate of the volatility of growth of 5 percent a year. We can then use a random-number generator in Excel to get values of z to plug into equation 7.3 to get possible outcomes for revenue. Figure 7.4 shows the forecast and three possible paths, labeled a, b, and c. In path a, revenue remains quite close to the forecast. In path b, it grows less strongly. In path c, it grows more strongly.

If our model and our choice of parameters are good, and if we take a big enough sample of possible paths—perhaps 100,000—we will get a reasonable estimate of the probability distribution of revenue for each of the two years. The Excel add-ins @RISK and Crystal Ball make it easy it to generate such a large sample; it is also possible to program Excel to take the sample.

Monte Carlo simulation necessarily involves approximation that we could avoid if we could use a formula. The approximation improves as the sample becomes larger, so we could get a better estimate by taking a sample of 1 million paths. Yet the bigger the sample, the longer it takes a computer to do the calculations. Thus, speed must be traded off against accuracy. It doesn't pay to get obsessed about the approximation error in the simulation, though; with a sample of, say, 100,000, uncertainty about how the main risk factors evolve is likely to introduce larger errors.

Now consider the guarantee of revenue of $100 million in year 1. We can estimate the probability distribution for payments under this guarantee

Figure 7.4. A Forecast and Three Possible Paths for Revenue

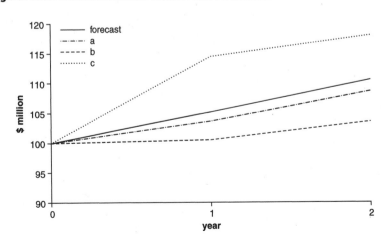

Source: Author's calculations.

Table 7.1. Measures of Risk for the Revenue Guarantee for Year 1

Measure	Estimate ($ million unless otherwise noted)	Comment
Minimum payment	0	Equation 7.1
Maximum payment	100	The amount of the guarantee
Expected payment	0.43	Average payment in the sample
Probability of payment more than $5 million	2 percent	Number of payment in the sample greater than $5 million, divided by the sample size
Cash flow at risk at the 99 percent confidence level	6.6	Calculated from the sample by ordering the payment by size and recording the 1,000th largest payment
Standard deviation of payment	1.3	Calculated from the sample in the usual way

Source: Author's calculations.

by using equation 7.1, where $k = 100$ and revenue follows a geometric Brownian motion, as in equation 7.3. Doing this, we get the histogram shown in panel a of figure 7.2. We can also estimate the other measures of risk or, for minimum and maximum payments, infer them directly from our knowledge of the guarantee (table 7.1).

Portfolios and Correlations

If there are two risk factors, we need to consider the correlation between them in the Monte Carlo simulation. For example, we might be interested in revenue and construction costs and expect them to be positively correlated because of their common dependence on economic growth. We need then to generate correlated random variables. This is possible using a technique known as Cholesky factorization (see, for example, Dowd 1998; Jorion 1997; Marrison 2002). Alternatively, we can use @RISK or Crystal Ball to generate correlated random variables.

Valuing Exposure

Analysis of the sort presented so far is useful, but it doesn't allow the government to compare the cost of a guarantee with the cost of other policies. To do that, we need to value the guarantee, accounting for the risk and the timing of the government's possible payments.

Though one could try to make a government-specific estimate of the value of a guarantee, the approach taken here is to estimate the guarantee's market value: that is, the amount it would trade for if it were traded. In the language of accounting, the approach is to estimate the guarantee's fair value, or "the amount for which an asset could be exchanged, or a liability settled, between knowledgeable, willing parties in an arm's length transaction" (International Accounting Standards Board 2004, 2169).

This approach to valuation has advantages: estimates of market values are simpler and less vulnerable to manipulation than government-specific estimates. But the approach also has limitations. In particular, it doesn't allow any distinction between cost and value: the cost to the government of granting a guarantee is assumed to be the market value of the guarantee. Thus, the approach does not mesh as well as one might like with our discussion of allocating risk. There, our aim was to judge how total value changed with different allocations of risk. Our approach to valuation is too simple to do that. It cannot tell the government whether a guarantee increases total project value. It can at best supplement qualitative analysis of the appropriate allocation of risk.

Considering Time but Ignoring the Price of Risk

Start with the timing of payments. If interest rates are positive, a sum of money paid today is more costly than an equal sum of money to be paid later. If we ignore the premium normally demanded as compensation for bearing risk, we can value exposure to the risk of a possible payment by estimating the expected value of the payment and discounting the expected value at the interest rate applicable to the period in question. If the possible payment is to be made in a year's time, for example, we discount the expected payment at the rate of interest applicable to borrowing for one year. Because we are ignoring the cost of risk, the relevant interest rate is the riskless rate, the rate at which a perfectly creditworthy borrower could borrow.

A single payment—We consider four examples, starting with a simple one. Suppose the government has agreed to make a payment of an amount that depends on the outcome of a risk factor but whose expected value is known to be $100. If the riskless rate of interest is 5 percent, the value of the obligation to make the payment, ignoring any risk premium, is about $95. In discrete time, assuming annually compounded interest, we have $100/(1 + 0.05) \approx 95$. In continuous time, assuming continuously compounded interest, we have $100 \exp(-0.05) \approx 95$.

A European put—To take a second example, suppose that the government has given an investor the right to sell a firm back to the government at a predetermined price and time. In the language of options, the government has given the investor a European put on the firm. Suppose that the firm is worth $1 billion now and that the investor can sell it back to the government for the same amount in 10 years. The loss to the government in billions of dollars in 10 years is thus equal to $\max\{0, 1 - x_{10}\}$, where x, the risk factor, is the value of the firm. Suppose that the value of the firm follows a geometric Brownian motion, as given by equation 7.4, where μ is now the expected rate of growth of the value of the firm and σ is its volatility. And suppose that μ is 0.07 and that σ is 0.1.

The government's expected loss is given by $E(\max\{0, 1 - x_{10}\})$. We know that x_{10} is given by equation 7.4, but it is not obvious how to evaluate the expectation of the maximum expression. To approximate it, we could use Monte Carlo simulation to sample x_{10} and hence the expected value of the maximum. However, the exact answer can be found with a formula, variants of which we will use several times:[6]

$$E_t \max\{0, k - x_T\} = kN(-d_2) - x_t e^{\mu(T-t)} N(-d_1), \qquad (7.5)$$

where k is the strike price of the option, $N(\cdot)$ is the cumulative distribution function for a risk factor with a standard normal distribution, and d_1 and d_2 are given by

$$d_1 = \frac{\ln(x_t / k) + (\mu + \sigma^2/2)(T - t)}{\sigma\sqrt{T - t}}$$

$$d_2 = d_1 - \sigma\sqrt{T - t}.$$

(We shall see later that this equation is similar to the Black-Scholes.)

In our example, the value of the put at the time it is granted ($t = 0$) can be found by noting that $k = 1$, $x_t = x_0 = 1$, $\mu = 0.07$, $T = 10$, and $\sigma = 0.1$. Plugging in the numbers, we see that the government's expected loss is about $2.1 million. We can then discount this amount at the riskless rate of interest to find the value, ignoring any risk premium, of the government's undertaking. If the riskless rate is 5 percent, the value of the undertaking at the time it is made is about $1.3 million: $2.1e^{-0.05 \cdot 10} \approx 1.3$.

A subsidy—As a third example, consider a government subsidy that generates a stream of payments. Suppose that the government subsidizes a service by paying a rate of $1 per unit consumed for three years. Suppose that initial consumption x_0 is 100 million units a year and that consumption is

---

6 See Hull (2003, 262–63) for the derivation of a similar result.

forecast to grow at a rate μ of 7 percent a year. Suppose further that estimation or guesswork suggests that consumption will follow a geometric Brownian motion with a volatility σ of 15 percent a year. According to equation 7.4, this means that the rate of the government's payment p at time t is given by

$$p_t = x_0 \exp\left(\left(\mu - \frac{\sigma^2}{2}\right)t + \sigma\sqrt{t}z\right).\qquad(7.6)$$

If we were considering a more complicated subsidy, we might have to use Monte Carlo simulation to estimate the government's expected payments and hence the value of its obligation. Because the scheme of this example is simple, we can use formulas. The government's expected rate of payment in dollars at time t is given by

$$E(p_t) = x_0 e^{\mu t}.\qquad(7.7)$$

(See "The Expected Value of the Exponential Function" in appendix A.) Expected payments from the beginning of the scheme at $t = 0$ to its end at $t = T$ can then be found by integration:

$$\int_{t=0}^{t=T} x_0 e^{\mu t}\, dt = \frac{x_0}{\mu} e^{\mu t}\Big|_{t=0}^{t=T}.$$

By plugging in the parameter values that describe the subsidy, we can calculate that the government can expect to spend about $334 million over the course of the scheme. To value the subsidy without taking account of any risk premium, we discount the stream of expected payments at the riskless discount factor, which in continuous time is $\exp(-rt)$. The value of a payment made at time t would be given by

$$V(p_t) = \frac{x_0 e^{\mu t}}{e^{rt}} = x_0 e^{(\mu - r)t}.$$

The total value V of the subsidy payments is then given by

$$V = \int_{t=0}^{t=T} x_0 e^{(\mu - r)t}\, dt = \frac{x_0}{\mu - r} e^{(\mu - r)t}\Big|_{t=0}^{t=T}.\qquad(7.8)$$

Thus, the value of this subsidy, ignoring any risk premium, is about $309 million.

The revenue guarantee—Last, recall the example of the revenue guarantee that created an expected payment of $0.43 million (table 7.1). If any guarantee payment must be made in exactly one year, the value of the guarantee, ignoring any risk premium, is this expected payment discounted by the one-year riskless rate of interest. If that is 5 percent, continuously compounded, the value of the guarantee is $0.41 million.

All these valuations have the disadvantage of ignoring the cost of bearing risk. The revenue guarantee, for example, exposes the government to a risk that, other things being equal, it would prefer to avoid: payments will tend to be required just when the economy and public finances are weak. But the cost of bearing this risk is not incorporated in the valuation. Offered a choice of paying $0.41 million in cash or giving the guarantee, a rational government would probably choose to pay the cash (though for the reasons discussed in chapter 3 a real government might be tempted by the guarantee). Likewise, if the government wanted to pay someone to take the guarantee off its hands, it would probably have to offer more than $0.41 million to the new guarantor. Put differently, the guarantee is probably worth more than $0.41 million.

Despite this problem, this risk-ignoring approach to valuation shouldn't be dismissed. It is simpler than approaches that incorporate a risk premium, and the error caused by ignoring the risk premium may be small compared with the error caused by overlooking important risk factors and incorrectly specifying the stochastic processes followed by other risk factors—from not knowing, for example, whether a risk factor really follows a geometric Brownian motion and, if it does, what the rates of growth and volatility are. Nonetheless, ignoring the risk premium will usually lead to an underestimate of the value of a guarantee. By contrast, ignoring the risk premium may lead to overestimates of the value of some other obligations, such as an agreement to pay shadow tolls or a consumption-based subsidy, for which risk works in the government's favor. When the stakes are high, more sophisticated approaches to valuation may therefore be justified. In the next two sections, we discuss such approaches.

Explicitly Estimating the Price of Risk

Some techniques for incorporating a risk premium in the valuation of a guarantee estimate a price of risk explicitly. Others do so implicitly. We consider the two techniques in turn, starting with the explicit estimate.

Explicitly estimating the price of risk requires a theory. Unfortunately, no theory of the price of risk is universally accepted by experts. For a while, the capital-asset pricing model, or CAPM, was widely accepted by academics and practitioners alike.[7] But in recent years, it has performed poorly in empirical tests. Confidence in it has waned, and other theories have been proposed. Yet the other theories are controversial, too, and usually more difficult to use because they require data that are hard to come by.[8] Hence, many practitioners continue to use the CAPM to value projects, businesses, and securities issued by businesses.[9] We will use it too.

In the most common version, the value of a project is calculated by discounting a stream of expected cash flows by a risk-adjusted discount rate that depends on the project's beta, which is found using the CAPM. We can also apply this approach to the valuation of a single risky payment. According to the model, the present value V of a payment p to be received one period from now is given by

$$V = \frac{E(p)}{1+r+\beta\left(E(r_m)-r\right)},$$

(7.9)

where $E(p)$ is the expected value of the payment, r is still the riskless rate of interest, β is a measure of the way the payment varies with the rate of return on the market portfolio of risky assets, and r_m is the rate of return on the market portfolio of risky assets.

The expression $r + \beta\left(E(r_m)-r\right)$ is the risk-adjusted discount rate of the CAPM. According to the model, it is equal to the expectation of the return r_p on the payment:

$$E\left(r_p\right) = r + \beta\left(E(r_m)-r\right).$$

(7.10)

The idea of a rate of return on a payment may sound a little strange, but it can be interpreted in the same way as any rate of return: it is the difference between the value of the payment in one period and its value now, all divided by its value now: $r_p = (p - V)/V$.

The crucial coefficient β is given by

$$\beta = \frac{\text{cov}\left(r_p, r_m\right)}{\sigma_m^2},$$

(7.11)

---

7 The CAPM was developed by, among others, Sharpe (1964).
8 The controversy over the CAPM is described in Cochrane (2001). New approaches include one developed by Eugene Fama and Kenneth French (1993) and several developed by researchers in behavioral finance inspired by the work on judgment and decision-making discussed in chapter 3.
9 See, for example, Benninga (2000), Graham and Harvey (2001), and the Web sites of many regulators.

where σ_m is the volatility of the return on the market portfolio of risky assets (or the market, for short). Like the expected rate of return on the market, the volatility of the market is hard to measure. The problem is that the market includes all risky assets: not just stocks, but bonds, commodities, real estate, and unlisted businesses as well. Because of the limitations of the available data, it is often approximated by an index of large stocks.

The single payment—To be specific, recall the payment in a year of an uncertain amount with an expected value of $100. Suppose that the riskless rate of interest is 5 percent and that the expected rate of return on the market is 10 percent. Suppose also that the covariance of the rate of return on the payment and the rate of return on the market is 0.02 and that the standard deviation of the rate of return on the market is 0.2. Then equation 7.11 says that the payment's beta is 0.5. Given this beta, equation 7.10 says the rate for discounting the payment, to take account of its timing and its risk, is 7.5 percent. So, according to equation 7.9, the value of the payment is about $93.

By contrast, when we ignored the price of risk, and discounted the expected payment at the riskless rate of interest, we valued the payment at $95. How much might this overvaluation matter? On the one hand, we shouldn't exaggerate the accuracy of the risk-adjusted estimate. We don't know that the CAPM is accurate, and even if we did, we couldn't be confident we knew the payment's true beta. Yet if we think the payment will be correlated with the value of the government's other assets and liabilities, so the government tends to get a larger payment when it is doing well and a smaller payment when it is doing badly, we might be skeptical of a valuation that ignored this fact. The right approach depends on the circumstances: when the stakes are small and a risk-adjusted estimate is difficult to get, ignoring the risk premium is reasonable; when the stakes are high, spending some time or money to estimate the risk premium is reasonable.

Certainty equivalents—Let's assume that estimating the risk premium is worthwhile. Then we must face the problem that the approach just set out, in which the discount rate is adjusted for risk, is not always practical. It works well for many cash flows and reasonably well for many projects and securities. But it isn't practical for valuing cash flows with option-like characteristics. The problem is that, even if the beta of the risk factor on which the option is written is stable, the beta of the option will not be. It will change with the value of the risk factor and with the time until the option expires. (See "The Impracticality of Valuing a Guarantee by Adjusting the Discount Rate" in appendix A.[10])

Typical government guarantees create exposure to risk like the exposure created by options. Indeed, equation 7.1, describing the payment made by the government under a revenue guarantee, looks like an equation describing the loss to the writer of a put option on a stock: the writer of such an option must pay max{0, $k - s$}, where k is the strike price of the option and s is the value of the stock at the expiry of the option. This resemblance is typical, and guarantees can usually be analyzed as options.

We can get around the problem of unstable betas by adjusting cash flows instead of the discount rate. To find the appropriate adjustment, we can still apply the CAPM, but we must do so in a less familiar way. In particular, we determine the value of a payment to be received in one year as follows (see "Equivalency in Principle of the Certainty-Equivalent and Risk-Adjusted-Discount-Rate Methods" in appendix A):

$$V = \frac{E(p) - \lambda \sigma_p}{1 + r}, \tag{7.12}$$

where λ is the price of the risk and σ_p is the standard deviation of the payment (which can be thought of as the quantity of risk and therefore as the natural counterpart of the price of the risk). The numerator of this equation is the certainty equivalent of the payment—that is, its risk-adjusted value. The denominator then discounts the certainty equivalent for the value of time alone; no further adjustment for risk is needed.

Continuing to use the CAPM as our theory of risk, we can estimate the price of the risk λ as

$$\lambda = \rho \frac{E(r_m) - r}{\sigma_m}, \tag{7.13}$$

where ρ is the coefficient of correlation between the payment and the rate of return on the market:

$$\rho = \frac{\text{cov}(p, r_m)}{\sigma_p \, \sigma_m}. \tag{7.14}$$

For the relationship of the price of risk λ to β, see appendix A.

---

10 Another, minor problem is that getting the correct discount rate for a payment often requires subtracting an amount from the riskless rate instead of adding one to it, which may be unfamiliar.

The single payment again—Now we can return to the valuation of the uncertain payment with an expected value of $100. When we valued it using a risk-adjusted discount rate, we assumed that r was 0.05, $E(r_m)$ was 0.1, σ_m was 0.2, and cov (r_p, r_m) was 0.02. To value the payment using the certainty-equivalent method, we retain the first three of these assumptions but replace the last with assumptions about cov (p, r_m) and σ_p. Suppose σ_p is $20. Then, to be consistent with our other assumptions (again, see appendix A), the value of cov (p, r_m) must be 1.86. Equation 7.14 then implies that ρ is approximately 0.47. Together with equation 7.13, these assumptions imply that the price of the payment's risk λ is approximately 0.12. Finally, using equation 7.12, we find that the value of the payment is about $93. Thus, we can find the value of the risky payment either by discounting its expected value at an appropriately risk-adjusted rate or by finding its certainty equivalent and discounting that at the riskless rate.

The subsidy—When we work with a risk factor that changes over time (such as revenue or consumption), it is convenient to start by specifying the process followed by the risk factor. Suppose, for example, that we think that a risk factor follows a geometric Brownian motion. Then we can infer the government's payment from equation 7.2 and an equation specifying the government's payment as a function of the risk factor, such as 7.1.

Recall the subsidy scheme that we valued, accounting for the cost of time but not of risk, at about $309 million. For some purposes, such a valuation would suffice, but let's suppose that the government wanted to refine its estimate. Consider first the certainty-equivalent approach. To find the certainty equivalents, we proceed as before, except that we reduce μ by $\lambda\sigma$ to adjust the growth rate for risk (see "Valuation by Adjusting the Expected Growth Rate of the Risk Factor" in appendix A). Thus, the equation we use to project the risk-adjusted risk factor x^* is not 7.4 but

$$x_t^* = x_0 \exp\left(\left(\mu - \lambda\sigma - \frac{\sigma^2}{2}\right)t + \sigma\sqrt{t}z\right). \qquad (7.15)$$

This gives us a new, risk-adjusted risk factor. The expected payments generated by this risk-adjusted risk factor are certainty equivalents, which can be discounted at the riskless rate of interest to arrive at a value that incorporates the time value of money and a risk premium. In the case of this simple subsidy, certainty-equivalent payments are given by $x_0\,e^{(\mu-\lambda\sigma)t}$. Discounting the certainty equivalents by the riskless rate of interest gives

$$V\left(p_t\right) = x_0 e^{(\mu-\lambda\sigma-r)t}.$$

As before, the value of payments over the duration of the subsidy scheme is then given by integration. We have made assumptions about all the parameters in this equation except λ. To estimate this parameter, we need, as equation 7.13 tells us, estimates of the expected rate of return on the market, the volatility of the return on the market, the riskless rate of interest, and the coefficient of correlation between the subsidy payments and the rate of return on the market. Let us retain the previous values of the market parameters: a riskless rate of 5 percent, an expected rate of return on the market of 10 percent, and a standard deviation of the return on the market of 20 percent. Let us suppose that the correlation is 0.5. Then, using equation 7.13, we can see that $\lambda = 0.125$. With these assumptions, we find that the value of the subsidy is $301 million.

Once we take account of the risk, then, we find that the subsidy is not as costly to the government as the expected payments discounted at the riskless rate ($309 million) might have led us to expect. The reason is that subsidy payments are positively correlated with returns on the market, which means that the government tends to pay more in good times and less in bad times. In contrast to the risk of the single payment considered above and the risk of most guarantees, the risk here reduces the value of the obligation.

Because the payments in this example are not option-like, we can also value them using a risk-adjusted discount rate. To do so, we follow the procedure used in the valuation with the riskless rate of interest, but we substitute a risk-adjusted rate for the riskless rate. Given our assumptions about λ, σ, r, and $E(r_m)$, the β of the scheme must be 0.375 (see "Equivalence in Principle of the Certainty-Equivalent and Risk-Adjusted-Discount-Rate Methods" in appendix A). According to equation 7.10, the risk-adjusted discount rate is therefore 6.875 percent. If we evaluate the integral set out in equation 7.8 but substitute this risk-adjusted discount rate for the riskless rate, we find, as we expected, that the value of the subsidy is $301 million.

The European put—Now consider the example of the European put, in which the payment is option-like and the approach of the risk-adjusted discount rate is impractical. We show in the next section how we can use the Black-Scholes formula to value the put. But we can also use the certainty-equivalent approach set out above. In particular, we can find the certainty equivalent of the government's payment by reducing the actual growth rate of the value of the firm by $\lambda\sigma$ and then calculating the government's expected payment. We use the risk-adjusted process of equation 7.15, where now x_0 is the value of the firm ($1 billion), μ is its expected rate of growth (0.07), and σ is the volatility of the growth of its value (0.1). The value V of the put can then be determined by calculating $V = e^{-r(T-t)}E_t \, (\max\{0, k - x_T^*\})$. We can find the expected value of the maximum expression using equation 7.5 and replacing μ by $\mu - \lambda\sigma$.

To value the put, we need to estimate a few more parameters. Suppose first that the riskless rate of interest and the expected rate of return on the market are again 0.05 and 0.1, respectively. Suppose that observation of the share prices of listed firms otherwise similar to the firm in question suggests that the best estimate of the beta of the firm is 0.4. Using the relationship $\lambda\sigma = \beta(E(r_m)-r)$, derived in appendix A, we can infer the price of the risk of the firm's value λ from our other assumptions; it must be 0.2. We then proceed as though the value of the firm increased at a rate of 0.05 a year ($\mu - \lambda\sigma$) rather than 0.07 a year (μ). Given these assumptions, and using the equations above, the value of the put can found to be $5.9 million—much more than the risk-ignoring valuation of $1.3 million.

The revenue guarantee—For the final example in this section, we can return to the revenue guarantee. Recall that we used Monte Carlo simulation to estimate the expected payment under the guarantee at $0.43 million. Then, discounting this payment by one year at the riskless rate of interest, we got a risk-ignoring valuation of $0.41 million. To get a better valuation, we can use the certainty-equivalent approach.

Recall that revenue was initially $100 million and was expected to grow at a rate of 5 percent a year. The calculations also assumed a volatility of 5 percent. Assuming the expected rate of return on the market and the riskless rate of interest are again 0.1 and 0.05, respectively, we need to estimate, or guess, only one further parameter, namely λ. Suppose a combination of research and guesswork suggests that the coefficient of correlation between revenue and the return on the market is 0.6. Then equation 7.13 tells us that the λ of revenue risk is 0.15. To find the certainty equivalent of the government's payment, we repeat the Monte Carlo simulation, but proceed as though revenue grew at the risk-adjusted rate of $\mu - \lambda\sigma = 0.0425$. The Monte Carlo simulation of risk-adjusted revenue generates an estimate of the certainty equivalent of the government's payment of $0.62 million, instead of $0.43 million. Discounting the certainty equivalent at the riskless rate of interest of 5 percent gives us a value of about $0.59 million—rather more than the risk-ignoring estimate of $0.41 million.

Implicitly Estimating the Price of Risk: Risk-Neutral Pricing

Valuing exposure to risk is sometimes easier. In particular, there are times when we need not estimate the price of risk explicitly—when we need not estimate β or λ—yet can still find the value of the government's exposure taking account of its risk. The times we can do this are the times when the risk factor is an asset and therefore has a value that incorporates the price of risk. The price of risk bearing is therefore implicit in the analysis. For example, the value of the European put considered above can be estimated as a function of the value of the firm on which the put is written, without need of further estimates of the price of risk. The underlying risk factor is the value of the firm, and that value depends on the risk inherent in owning the firm. The government's risk in having written the put comes from the same source, and the cost of bearing the risk of the put can be derived from the cost of bearing the risk of the value of the firm.

The techniques that estimate the price of risk implicitly are those that were developed to value financial options on listed shares. The Black-Scholes equation is the most famous of them (Black and Scholes 1973; Merton 1973). Although the techniques are complex, they are by now well known. As well as being used to value financial options, they are now used to value real options, such as opportunities to defer or expand an investment.

The European put—We have already valued the European put by way of an estimate of the β and hence the λ of the underlying risk. Now we can do the valuation without reference to β or λ—at least if we continue to take the firm's value as given; we might well estimate the firm's β in order to estimate its value. Recall that the government's obligation is a European put written on the value of the firm with a strike price of $1 billion and that the volatility of the value of the firm is 0.1. Continuing to assume a riskless rate of 0.05—but no longer caring about the expected rate of return on the market—we can find the present value of the obligation to make the payment at time T using the Black-Scholes equation:

$$V = ke^{-r(T-t)}N(-d_2) - x_t N(-d_1), \qquad (7.16)$$

where $N(\cdot)$ is again the standard normal cumulative distribution function, and d_1 and d_2 are now given by

$$d_1 = \frac{\ln(x_t/k) + (r + \sigma^2/2)(T-t)}{\sigma\sqrt{(T-t)}},$$

$$d_2 = d_1 - \sigma\sqrt{(T-t)}.$$

This equation is still complex, but it is simpler than the equation we used to value the put when we estimated the price of the risk explicitly. In particular, the Black-Scholes equation makes no reference to λ, β, or r_m. (We could, however, infer the price of risk implicit in the valuation by calculating the expected payment and finding the value of β that equated the discounted expected payment with the Black-Scholes value.)

Plugging the numbers into the equation, we can find anew the value of the put. Given our assumptions, it turns out to be $5.9 million again. We got the same value because we used the CAPM to set the expected rate of growth of the value of the firm and then chose a value of λ that was consistent with our assumption about β (see "Valuation by Adjusting the Expected Growth Rate of the Risk Factor" in appendix A).

A European call—To take a second example, suppose the government has the right to purchase the assets of a concession for a fixed sum of money on a fixed future date. Now the government's exposure to risk is positive; it can't lose and it might gain. Specifically, its payoff p at time T when it can buy the assets is given by $p_T = \max\{0, x_T - k\}$, where x is the value of the assets and k is the amount it must pay to buy the assets.

Analyzed as an option, the government's right is a European call with a strike price of k. The call can be valued using another variant of the Black-Scholes formula, applicable to calls on dividend-paying stocks. The present value of the call is given by

$$V = x_t e^{-\delta(T-t)}N(d_1) - ke^{-r(T-t)}N(d_2), \qquad (7.17)$$

where δ is the rate at which dividends are paid to the concession's owners, T is the date of the option's expiry, and d_1 and d_2 are now given by

$$d_1 = \frac{\ln(x_t/k) + (r - \delta + \sigma^2/2)T}{\sigma\sqrt{T}},$$
$$d_2 = d_1 - \sigma\sqrt{T}.$$

Notice again that the formula omits mention of the price of risk: the riskless rate of interest is there, but nothing like β or λ. The trick in this approach is again to value the option in terms of the value of the underlying risk factor, here the value of the assets of the concession. Because the value of the assets takes account of the price of risk, the valuation of the right to purchase the assets implicitly incorporates a measure of the price of risk. The assets must, of course, be valued for this approach to work, but this is usually a simpler problem than valuing the guarantee and estimates are likely to be available.

Suppose we estimate that the assets are worth $1 billion and that the government has the option to purchase them in 10 years for $1.5 billion. Suppose also that the riskless rate of interest is 5 percent, the dividend yield is 5 percent, and the volatility of the value of the assets is 30 percent. Equation 7.17 then tells us that the value of the call is about $150 million.

We use similar approaches in the next chapter to show how some exchange-rate and debt guarantees can be valued.

CHAPTER 8

The Valuation of Exposure to Three Risks

In chapter 5, we discussed the allocation of exchange-rate, insolvency, and policy risk. In this chapter, we discuss the measurement and valuation of these same risks.

Exchange-Rate Risk

Consider a guarantee that applies to the foreign-currency debt-service payments of the firm and protects the firm from depreciations in the local currency of more than a certain percentage. If that percentage is 10, the guarantee ensures that, however much the local currency depreciates, the firm will be no worse off, insofar as the debt-service payment is concerned, than if the currency had depreciated by only 10 percent.

Specifically, we suppose that the government's payment p_T in local currency at the time the debt-service payment must be made is given by

$$p_T = \begin{cases} d\left(x_T - x_0\left(1+\theta\right)\right) & \text{if } x_T > x_0\left(1+\theta\right), \\ 0 & \text{otherwise,} \end{cases}$$

where d is the debt-service payment denominated in foreign currency, x is the exchange rate, defined as the price of foreign currency in local currency (so an increase in x implies a depreciation of the local currency), x_0 is the exchange rate at the time the guarantee is given, x_T is the exchange rate at the time the debt-service payment must be made, and θ is the threshold proportional depreciation in the local currency, below which the government need pay nothing.

Modeling the Exchange Rate

To measure and value the government's exposure to risk caused by the guarantee, we need a model of the process followed by the exchange rate. The model should allow for a trend and for randomness. We can get these features by assuming the exchange rate follows a geometric Brownian motion, as set out in equations 7.2, 7.3, and 7.4. Now μ is to be interpreted as the expected rate of depreciation of the exchange rate and σ as its volatility.[1]

One way to estimate the trend rate of appreciation or depreciation of μ would be to look at the history of the exchange rate and to assume the historical trend will continue. Another would be to compare forecasts of local inflation and foreign inflation and to assume that the trend rate of depreciation was the difference between the two. Thus the currency with lower inflation would be expected to appreciate against the other. A third approach, followed here, recognizes that expected appreciation should reflect the difference between the local and the foreign interest rates. Comparing riskless rates of interest in both currencies for the appropriate duration therefore gives us an estimate of the expected rate μ of depreciation in the local currency:

$$\mu = r - r^*,\tag{8.1}$$

where r is the local riskless rate of interest and r^* is the foreign riskless rate of interest.[2] If the local rate is higher than the foreign rate, x is expected to increase; that is, the local currency is expected to depreciate.

---

1 Other somewhat more complicated approaches could be considered, such as assuming that the exchange rate experiences jumps, that its volatility varies over time, and that over long periods it is mean reverting. For techniques and evidence, see Jorion (1988), Jorion and Sweeney (1996), Rogoff (1996), M. Taylor (1995), and A. Taylor and M. Taylor (2004).

2 Note that truly riskless rates of interest are unobservable, since governments' credit is never perfect. To avoid biasing the estimate, we should ensure that the two rates of interest have the same degree of credit risk. If the domestic government borrows in both the local and the foreign currency, the interest rates on these borrowings may be the best sources for estimates of r and r^*.

We can estimate the volatility of the exchange rate by reviewing the history of the exchange rate and estimating the standard deviation of changes in the rate. Then by observing the current exchange rate and noting the values of d and θ, we can measure the government's exposure to risks.

Given our assumptions, we could calculate at least some of the measures of interest using a formula. But Monte Carlo simulation generates estimates of all the measures of interest and, even when formulas can be derived, simulation is often easier in practice. Using both approaches can be helpful, because each estimate can be used to check the other. The formula should give the precise answer, given the assumptions; but if Monte Carlo simulation and the formula give quite different answers, it may be a sign that the formula is wrong. If Monte Carlo simulation and the formula give roughly the same answers, we can be more confident we've got the right formula and entered it correctly in the spreadsheet.

Measuring Exposure to the Risk of the Guarantee

Suppose the guarantee is of a single debt-service payment of $100 million to be made in five years. Call the local currency the peso and suppose that the current exchange rate is 1 peso to the dollar. Suppose the threshold θ is 20 percent, so the guarantee kicks in if the peso depreciates by more than 20 percent—that is, if it falls below 1.2 pesos to the dollar. Suppose the riskless rates of interest are 5 percent a year for dollars and 8 percent a year for pesos and that the measured volatility of the peso-dollar exchange rate is 10 percent a year.

The minimum payment the government can be required to make is zero, which happens unless the peso depreciates by more than 20 percent. The maximum payment the government might have to make, denominated in pesos, is unlimited. It won't ever have to pay more than $100 million, but there is no upper limit to the cost in pesos of buying a dollar.

Monte Carlo simulation gives an estimate of the probability distribution of payments (figure 8.1). The most common outcome is that the government pays nothing. This happens in about 6,000 of 10,000 trials or about 60 percent of the time. Payments of between 0 and 10 million pesos happen about 13 percent of the time. The expected payment, according to the simulation, is about 8.76 million pesos.

The expected payment, however, can also be calculated by a formula. Because we have assumed that the exchange rate follows a geometric Brownian motion, we know that the expected value of the exchange rate

Figure 8.1. Histogram of Guarantee Payments

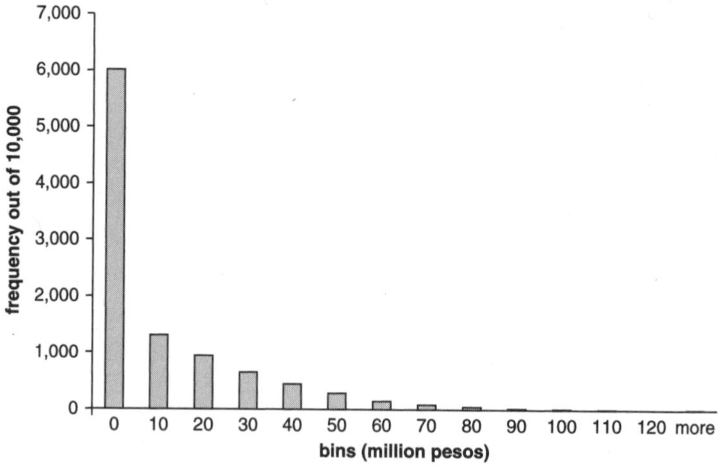

Source: Author's calculations.
Note: The first bar on the left shows the frequency of payments of 0, the second of payments between 0 and 10 million pesos, the third of payments between 10 million and 20 million pesos, and so on.

at T is $x_0 \exp((r - r^*)T)$. If we let $k = x_0(1 + \theta)$, we can express the government's payment as follows:

$$p_T = \max\{0, dx_T - dk\} = d\max\{0, x_T - k\}. \tag{8.2}$$

The government's expected payment per dollar of guaranteed debt-service payment is therefore $E(\max\{0, x_T - k\})$. We can calculate this value using equation 7.5, as long as we substitute $r - r^*$ for μ. Doing this, we find that the expected value of the government's payment, given our assumptions, is 8.71 million pesos. Thus, the estimate from the Monte Carlo simulation was a little too high.

We can estimate the roughness of a simulation from the simulation itself. The standard error of the estimate se can be calculated as

$$se = N^{-1/2}\hat{\sigma}, \tag{8.3}$$

where N is the number of trials (10,000 in the example) and $\hat{\sigma}$ is the sample standard deviation of the payments. The formula for the sample standard deviation is

$$\hat{\sigma} = (N-1)^{-1} \sum_{i=1}^{N} (x_i - \bar{x})^2,$$

where the x_i are the individual estimates of the government payment and $\bar{x}$ is the average payment from the Monte Carlo simulation.

In the example, the standard error of the Monte Carlo estimate of the expected payment is 0.16. The estimated expected payment should be approximately normally distributed, with a mean equal to the true mean 8.71 million pesos and a standard deviation equal to 0.16. If our assumptions are correct, therefore, we can be about 95 confident that our estimate lies in an interval equal to the true mean plus or minus about 0.32 (0.16 × 2). So we should not express our estimate of 8.76 million pesos to two decimal places. We might say instead that the expected payment is about 9 million pesos or we might use a range, such as 8.5–9.0 million pesos.

We could improve the expected accuracy of the Monte Carlo estimate by taking more than 10,000 trials. Equation 8.3 shows the relationship between the standard error and the number of trials: the error declines with the square root of the number. So by taking a sample 10 times as large (100,000), we could reduce the 95 percent confidence interval by a factor equal to the square root of 10 (about 3.16).

We said we could be 95 percent confident, given our assumptions. The qualification is important. By increasing the number of trials in the Monte Carlo simulation, we can get an estimate that, given the assumptions, is as accurate as we might reasonably want. But errors in our assumptions—about the process followed by the exchange rate and about the parameters of that process—remain, and those errors may well be larger than the errors introduced by approximation in the Monte Carlo simulation. We should treat the confidence interval as an indication of the minimum amount of uncertainty about the estimate.

We can also use the Monte Carlo simulation to estimate the other risk measures. According to the simulation, cash flow at risk at the 99 percent confidence interval is about 70 million pesos. And the estimated probability of a payment of more than 100 million pesos is 0.2 percent.

Valuing Exposure to the Risk of the Guarantee

To value the guarantee, we can simply discount the estimated expected payment of 8.76 million pesos at the local riskless rate of interest (8 percent) over five years. The value is thus $5.9 million (8.76 exp(–0.08·5)).

We can also use a variant of the Black-Scholes formula to value this option (Garman and Kohlhagen 1983; see also Hull 2003). To see this, recall that the government's payment can be rewritten in terms of the payoff to a put option, as in equation (8.2). That is, the guarantee can be interpreted as the government's being short d call options on the foreign currency with a strike price of k.

In "Valuing Exposure" in chapter 7, we saw how an option on a dividend-paying stock could be valued by assuming the stock pays a continuous dividend that slows its expected rate of price appreciation (equation 7.17). Likewise, an option on a foreign currency can be analyzed by assuming that the interest paid on the foreign currency slows its expected rate of appreciation. In fact, the risk-adjusted rate of expected appreciation in the price of foreign currency in local currency equals the local riskless rate less the foreign riskless rate—as set out in equation (8.1). Thus the value of the guarantee per dollar of guaranteed foreign currency can be found using equation (7.17) if we substitute r^* for δ.

Doing this and multiplying by the debt-service payment of $100 million, we get a guarantee value of 5.8 million pesos—slightly less than the estimate from the Monte Carlo simulation, again because the Monte Carlo estimate was slightly too high.

Insolvency Risk

In thinking about the allocation of insolvency risk and how to prevent or mitigate undesired allocation to governments and customers, it's useful to have an idea of the size of the risks and transfers involved. We set out some estimation techniques here, considering a debt guarantee, which could be explicit or implicit, and a guarantee of a long-term power-purchase agreement.

A Debt Guarantee

We noted in chapter 5 that insolvency risk depends on uncertainty in the value of the firm and on the firm's leverage. One approach to the measurement and valuation of exposure to insolvency risk focuses on these two things (Black and Scholes 1973).[3] We consider a firm financed by creditors and shareholders. It is natural to suppose that the firm's value x follows a geometric Brownian motion, as set out in equations 7.2, 7.3, and 7.4, where μ is now the expected growth rate of the value of the firm's assets and σ is the volatility of the growth rate.

---

3 Another approach is to develop a statistical model of default that doesn't try to explain default in terms of the value of the firm's assets and liabilities (see Duffie and Singleton 2003; Hull 2003, chapters 26 and 27). On the valuation of debt guarantees, see also Baldwin, Lessard, and Mason (1983); Chen, Chen, and Sears (1986); Jones and Mason (1980); Merton (1977); Mody and Patro (1996); and Sosin (1980).

The expected rate of growth of the value of the firm's assets is the expected rate of return on the assets, assuming no cash returns to the providers of capital. Estimates may be available, and if they are not, they can easily be made. Since x is the actual value of the firm, not just an accounting estimate, the expected rate of price appreciation μ should normally equal the firm's estimated cost of capital less the rate of cash returns. It might be estimated by means of the capital-asset pricing model (equation 7.10).

The volatility of returns is less familiar. It depends partly on the size of total-project-value risk, which depends on such risk factors as demand, construction costs, and operating costs, and partly on the allocation of total-project-value risk between the firm and other parties—for example, on whether pricing rules cause prices to change in response to changes in costs and demand. It also depends on the extent of distributional risk and, in particular, on whether pricing rules are implemented as written.

Suppose the firm takes out a government-guaranteed loan. To be concrete, suppose the firm's initial value is $100 million and that the loan is for $66.6 million, to be repaid in one year. The firm's leverage is thus high but not unusual for a project-financed infrastructure firm.[4] Suppose also that the riskless rate of interest for one-year loans is 5 percent continuously compounded. With the guarantee, the firm pays only the riskless rate of interest on the debt. (We assume that the chance of the government's reneging on its guarantee is the same as the chance of its defaulting on its own debt.) So the repayment in one year that the firm must make and that the government has guaranteed is $70 million ($66.6\exp(0.005\cdot1)$).

We assume that whether the firm repays the debt depends only on the value of its assets in one year. We assume that if the firm is solvent—if the value of its assets exceeds the value of its debt—it can borrow to make the payment. If the firm's assets exceed its liabilities, it makes the full payment. If they are less than the liabilities, the firm effectively pays its entire value to the creditors. The government, however, makes a payment equal to the difference between the required debt payment and the value of the firm. Specifically, its payment at maturity is equal to

$$\max\{0, k - x_T\}, \tag{8.4}$$

---

4 For information on typical leverage in infrastructure projects, see Correia da Silva, Estache, and Järvelä (2004) and Ehrhardt and Irwin (2004).

where k is the required debt repayment ($70 million) and x_T is the value of the firm at time of the debt repayment at $T = 1$.

Measurement—Given the nature of the guarantee and our assumptions about the way the value of the firm changes, we can measure and value the government's exposure to risk from this debt guarantee.

We can ascertain the minimum and maximum payments by inspecting expression 8.4, which gives the government's payment. The government's minimum payment is zero. Its maximum payment is k, the full amount of the required repayment ($70 million), which it pays if the firm's assets lose all value and the government must make the entire payment.

As for the exchange-rate guarantee, we can use formulas to derive some of the other measures and the value of this guarantee, but Monte Carlo simulation is the easiest (and perhaps the only) way to derive others. As before, it also allows us to check whether we've used the formulas correctly. For complex debt guarantees, it may be needed for all the estimates.

As with the revenue and exchange-rate guarantees, we start by taking a large number of samples of the risk factor of interest—here the value of the firm. To do that, we need to estimate the parameters of the geometric Brownian motion, μ and σ, or the expected rate of return on the firm's assets and the volatility of those returns. Let's suppose that financial analysts have a sufficiently reliable estimate of the expected rate of return. Suppose it is 10 percent.

Estimates of volatility are less likely to be available. If the firm's shares have been listed on a stock exchange for a few years, we can measure the volatility of the value of the firm's equity. Then, taking account of the firm's leverage, we can infer an estimate of the volatility of the value of the firm.[5] Otherwise, the best option may be to estimate the equity volatility of listed firms subject to similar risks. Judging similarity is difficult and the estimates will be rough at best, but a rough estimate is better than none. Suppose our estimate is 30 percent.

---

5 See Aswath Damodaran's Web site (http://pages.stern.nyu.edu/~adamodar/) for data and a method for estimating firm volatilities with data on equity volatilities. Damodaran notes that the volatility of the firm's assets σ_f is given by

$$\sigma_f = \sqrt{\left(\frac{D}{V}\right)^2 \sigma_d^2 + \left(\frac{E}{V}\right)^2 \sigma_e^2 + 2\frac{DE}{V^2} \rho \sigma_d \sigma_e},$$

where D is the value of debt, E is the value of equity, V is the value of the firm, σ_d is the volatility of the firm's debt, σ_e is the volatility of the firm's equity, and ρ is the correlation of returns on debt and returns on equity. The parameter σ_e is observable, but σ_d and ρ usually aren't. Damodaran suggests using estimates of $1/3\sigma_e$ and 0.3.

With these assumptions and equation 7.3, we can simulate possible values of the firm in a year and estimate the probability of the value being less than the required debt payment ($70 million). With this and equation 8.4 we can simulate the possible values of the government's payment (figure 8.2).

Figure 8.2. The Value of the Firm and Guarantee Payments

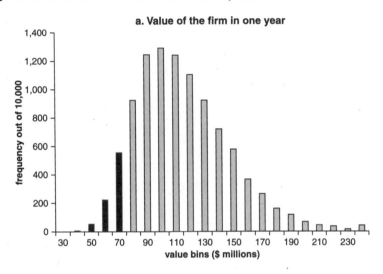

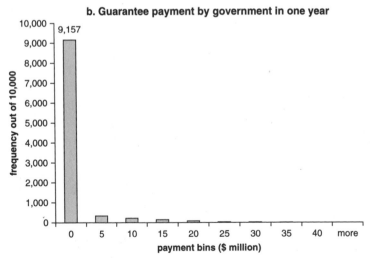

The simulation implies the firm can pay its debt with about 92 percent probability (the government pays nothing in 9,157 of the 10,000 trials—panel b of figure 8.2). In other words, the probability of bankruptcy is about 8 percent. The expected payment by the government is $0.72 million, but let's round to 0.7 million, given the approximation in the estimate. Other measures of the government's exposure to risk are shown in table 8.1.

We can check some of these measures against formulas. The expected payment is given by $E(\max\{0, k - x_T\})$, which we can calculate using equation 7.5. In this case, with $x_0 = 100$, $k = 70$, $\mu = 0.1$, $\sigma = 0.3$, and $T = 1$, the expected payment at $t = 0$ is $0.73 million—so the Monte Carlo simulation underestimated the payment slightly. Again, however, the uncertainty created by not knowing the true stochastic process (geometric Brownian motion or something else?) and its parameters (expected returns and volatility) may well exceed the uncertainty created by the simulation.

Valuation—Ignoring the price of bearing risk, we could value the government's debt guarantee by discounting the expected payment ($0.73 million) by the riskless rate of interest, which we assumed was 5 percent. The value would thus be $0.69 million—or, rounding to the nearest hundred thousand, $0.7 million. But we can easily apply option-pricing methods that incorporate the price of risk embedded (explicitly or implicitly) in the estimate of the value of the firm.

The payments the government makes have the same form as those made by the writer of a European put. The government is, in effect, short a European put written on the value of the firm with a strike price of the debt repayment, maturing on the date of the debt repayment. We can therefore value the debt guarantee using the Black-Scholes formula for

Table 8.1. Summary Measures of Risk

Measure	Amount ($ million, except for probability)
Minimum payment	0.0
Maximum payment	70.0
Expected value	0.7
Probability of payment	8 percent
Cash flow at risk at 99 percent	17.1

Source: Author's calculations.

valuing a European put given in equation 7.16 of chapter 7. Note again the similarity of this formula to the formula for estimating the expected payment: this formula differs because we discount at the riskless rate of interest and assume that the firm's value is expected to increase at the riskless rate.

Given the parameters in our example, the estimated value of the debt guarantee is $0.98 million. The value is higher than the amount obtained by discounting the expected payment by the riskless rate of interest because now we are including a risk premium. The put exposes the government to risk that is costly to bear, and the option-pricing valuation captures that cost.

The cost of providing the debt guarantee varies with the firm's insolvency risk. Thus, it varies with the volatility of the value of the firm and with the firm's leverage (figure 8.3). Low volatility and low leverage make the guarantee cheap. High volatility and high leverage make it expensive.

Although we have illustrated the valuation of an explicit government guarantee, the same approach can give an idea of implicit government guarantees and customer guarantees. A customer guarantee could be valued identically, as could an implicit government guarantee if it were

Figure 8.3. Value of the Debt Guarantee as a Function of Changes in Leverage and Volatility

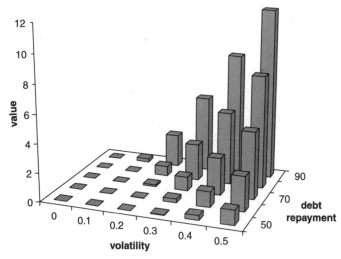

Source: Author's calculations.

as firm as an explicit guarantee. Yet an implicit guarantee is usually not firm: indeed it is not a guarantee in any precise sense. The government may be likely to bail out the firm, but it doesn't have to. Thus, the value of the explicit guarantee provides an upper bound on the value of the government's liability.

A Guarantee of a Utility's Long-Term Purchase Contract
In the power and water sectors, governments sometimes guarantee the purchase obligations of a publicly owned utility (see chapter 5). The utility may, for example, sign a contract with a private power generator under which the generator will construct a power plant and make available a certain amount of power over the life of the plant, in return for which the utility agrees to pay certain sums whether it uses the power or not, so long as the power is available. The contract might stipulate that, so long as the plant was working, a certain amount would be paid each month. Additional amounts would be paid if the government asked for power, these additional amounts being set to allow the private generator to recoup the variable costs of producing power, including the cost of fuel used to run the plant. In developing countries, where such contracts are common, state-owned utilities often have poor credit, and the government often guarantees their purchase obligations.

To be concrete, suppose that the utility contracts a private company to construct a 100-megawatt plant, at a cost of $100 million, and run it for 20 years. In return, the government agrees to pay $13.4 million at the end of each of the 20 years, as long as power is available. The value of those payments, at a discount rate of 12 percent, is $100 million. So if the project's cost of capital is 12 percent, the 20 annual payments cover the private generator's costs. If the utility requests the power, it pays more, but these payments are not obligations: the utility can decide whether to take power from the plant. So we can ignore these payments. To simplify, we assume the power plant is always available.

Such a power plant is said to be privately financed, since a private company finances the construction of the plant using some of its equity and some borrowed money. The utility's rights and obligations are similar, however, to the rights and obligations it would have had if it had financed the power plant itself. For example, it might have borrowed $100 million, contracted separately with two firms for the construction and operation of the plant, and paid back the loan in equal annual installments of $13.4 million over the same 20-year term. In both cases, the utility has the right to use the plant to generate power as it wants but must make the payments whether or not it needs the plant.[6]

The rights and obligations of the utility are not identical to the rights and obligations it would have if it were the legal owner of the power plant and had contracted the debt itself. In particular, its obligation to repay the loan would not be contingent on the plant's being available. But the utility's rights and obligations under a power-purchase agreement are similar enough for our purposes for us to treat the obligations as debt and the corresponding rights to purchase power as an asset.[7]

How should the government analyze, measure, and value its obligations? We consider two approaches, one treating the utility's obligations as the government's, the other treating them as separate.

Consolidation—A state-owned utility is legally separate from the government, and the obligations of the utility are not legally the obligations of the government. Yet governments rarely allow a state-owned utility to go bankrupt; they rarely allow its creditors to take it over. As long as they themselves are solvent, they usually step in to ensure that the utility meets its obligations—its ordinary debts as well as any obligations under long-term purchase agreements. So it may be reasonable to analyze the utility's obligations as though the utility were just part of the government.

---

6 Some analysts do treat such contracts as creating debt. Standard and Poor's (2003) says it "views these contracts as a form of long-term financing, and adds the net present value (NPV) of the fixed payments under the contracts, adjusted for risk, to the calculations of . . . total debt." Discussing two particular types of long-term purchase agreement in a guide to the analysis of financial statements, White, Sondhi, and Fried (1998, 548) note that "As take-or-pay contracts and throughput agreements effectively keep some operating assets and liabilities off the balance sheet, the analyst should add the present value of minimum future commitments to both property and debt."

7 Recall that we have assumed that the government contracts with firms to construct and operate the plant. If the plant weren't available because of negligence on the part of the construction or operating company, the government would likely be able to recover damages from that company that might offset its debt-service obligations. An advantage of a typical power-purchase contract over the publicly financed project (with construction and operations contracted out to two private firms) is that the power-purchase contract doesn't require the government to determine whether the fault, if any, lies with the construction company or the operating company. More generally, the power-purchase contract can help the government delegate tradeoffs between operating costs and construction costs. For a general discussion of when governments should contract with one firm for both construction and operations rather than two firms, see Quiggin (2004).

In accounting terms, this approach amounts to consolidating the utility's accounts with those of the government. It means treating the assets and liabilities of the utility as assets and liabilities of the government. And if we treat the rights and obligations created by the power-purchase agreement as assets and liabilities of the utility, it means treating those rights and obligations as assets and liabilities of the government.

This simplifies the analysis of the government's guarantee. Indeed, the guarantee drops out. The analysis treats the obligations of the utility as the obligations of the government, so the guarantee adds nothing to the government's obligations. The government's risks are the risks of its consolidated assets and liabilities (including power plants effectively purchased under power-purchase agreements and obligations to make payments under the power-purchase agreements). These risks are important but not substantially different from those the government is exposed to in all its businesses. They don't need any special analysis.

No Consolidation—The consolidated treatment of power-purchase obligations is simple and not unrealistic. A government that adopted this approach would probably be doing everything that was warranted. Yet most governments do not consolidate utilities in their accounts, and many would like to treat the utility's obligations as different from their own. They don't guarantee all their utilities' obligations and don't want to imply that they do. Thus, a case can be made for not consolidating the subsidiary (the utility) in the accounts of the parent (the government). And if the government really would let the utility go bankrupt in the absence of any explicit guarantees, the unconsolidated analysis is better. If this approach is taken, the guarantee must be analyzed separately.[8]

For the reasons set out earlier, the government's guarantee of the utility's purchase obligations can be analyzed as a debt guarantee. For analytical purposes, we could consider the guarantee as being in fact 20 separate guarantees, each corresponding to one of the 20 required payments. We could then apply the techniques set out earlier to measure and value the government's exposure to risks created by debt guarantees.

That approach doesn't model the firm's cash flows, just its value; it assumes that default occurs when the firm's value falls below the value of the liabilities. An alternative is to model the debt payments and the

---

8 The government might reasonably report a consolidated analysis for external use but use an unconsolidated analysis for managing the public enterprise (see Merton and Bodie 1992, 101–2).

cash flows available to meet those payments. Assuming the debt cash flows (the availability payments under the power-purchase obligations) are fixed, all we need is the stochastic process followed by cash flows that are available for meeting those payments.

Such a model might be complex, like a standard deterministic financial model of the utility, with many inputs made random—prices, demand, costs, other debt payments, and so on. Such an analysis might be helpful, but in line with the approach we have taken so far, we prefer a simpler model that collects all the sources of uncertainty into just two risk factors that matter directly—cash revenues and cash operating costs, whose difference is available for meeting the obligations.

In choosing the stochastic model for these cash flows, however, we can consider the determinants of the cash flows. Does price control mean that cash flows are mean reverting? That is, do prices tend to rise when cash flows are low and fall when they are high? If so, we could choose a mean-reverting stochastic process for the difference (see "Policy Risk" below). Consideration of the underlying causes of operating cash flows may also help choose the parameters of the process—the μ and the σ in a geometric Brownian motion, for example.

To be concrete, suppose that the utility has no other debt, so that all operating cash flows (cash revenues less cash operating costs) can be used to make availability payments under the power-purchase agreement. Suppose also that data on past cash revenues and cash operating costs give us no reason to choose a stochastic process more complex for either than geometric Brownian motion. We can then model operating cash flows as the difference between two processes that individually follow geometric Brownian motions. (The difference won't itself follow a geometric Brownian motion.)

Suppose that we have found that cash revenues and operating costs have tended to increase with inflation, which is forecast to be 3 percent a year. Suppose our estimate of the volatility of each process is 15 percent. Last year's operating cash flows were $15 million, only a little above next year's required availability payment of $13.4 million. If we assume the government's payments are equal to the difference between the utility's operating cash flow and the required availability payments, we can use Monte Carlo simulation as before to estimate the frequency distribution of the government's payments. Figure 8.4 shows two possible paths.

Given this analysis, we can go on to estimate, for each year, the probability distribution of the government's payments and derive from

Figure 8.4. Two Possible Paths of Operating Cash Flows and Government Payments under a Guarantee of Power-Purchase Agreement

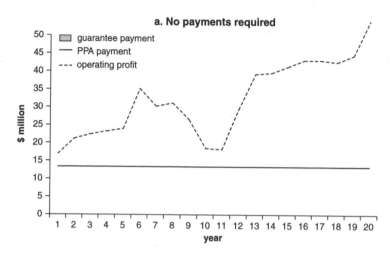

a. No payments required

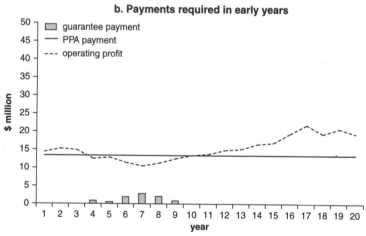

b. Payments required in early years

Source: Author's calculations.
Note: PPA = power-purchase agreement.

that distribution the expected payments, cash flow at risk, and other measures of interest. To value the guarantees, we could discount the expected payments at the riskless rate of interest. Or we could estimate the price of bearing operating-cash-flow risk, using an approach similar to that set out in "Valuing Exposure" in chapter 7 for valuing a revenue guarantee. That is, we would estimate the correlation between operating cash flows and the return on the market and, hence, the λ of operating-cash-flow risk.

Policy Risk

Consider finally a rather different issue: policy risk. Bearing policy risk has a fiscal cost, since if governments bear policy risk and change policies, they must compensate, as the examples of Singapore and Malaysia in "Policy Risk" in chapter 5 show. The argument of this book might seem to imply, therefore, that governments should measure and value their prospective exposure to policy risk before agreeing to bear it.[9]

Should Governments Value Their Exposure to Policy Risk?

Governments could value their exposure to policy risk, but whether they should is less clear. The difference is that governments control policy risks; they decide whether to incur any fiscal cost. They may have to choose among unpleasant options (losing their reputation with investors or with customers), but they choose nonetheless. By contrast, the other risk factors we've discussed are sometimes influenced by governments but are never under their control.

The obligations created by guarantees are sometimes described as contingent liabilities. An accounting definition of a contingent liability illustrates the difference between policy and other risks. The International Accounting Standards Board's definition of a contingent liability, quoted in "Reporting According to Modern Accounting Standards" in chapter 6, stipulates that it must be related to "the occurrence or nonoccurrence of one or more uncertain future events *not wholly within the control of the entity* [emphasis added]" (International Accounting Standards Board 2004, 2159).[10] Thus, policy risk does not seem to create a contingent liability for accounting purposes.

Moreover, there are innumerable ways that a government could incur costs by changing its behavior. Every contract it signs—every employment contract, every procurement contract, every sales contract—entails the possibility of the government breaching the contract and being

---

9   Note also that people often underestimate downside risks to which they are exposed, and the underestimation is greater if they have some control over the risk (Weinstein 1989; Zeckhauser and Viscusi 1990).

10 See also Bedford and Cooke (2001), who argue that people cannot measure uncertainty related to their own actions.

required by a court to pay damages. Even in the absence of contracts, the possibility of the government acting negligently creates fiscal risk. Measuring and valuing all these risks would be impossible. Perhaps partly for these reasons, Colombia, which generally requires the government's contingent contractual obligations to be quantified, makes an exception for risks relating to changes in regulations governing prices and subsidies (Government of Colombia, Department of National Planning 2001b).[11]

Yet a government that recognizes that it may come under pressure to renege on a large commitment may want to know in advance the expected value of its payment. And even if a government doesn't want to value its exposure to policy risks, investors, credit-rating analysts, and others may. To illustrate the possibilities, we consider two policy risks: expropriation risk and regulated-price risk. We don't assume that the government would want to publish the results of such analyses.

Expropriation Risk

One possible source of expenditure is a requirement to compensate for expropriation. Nowadays, governments nearly always bear this risk, at least on paper, if not because of a contract then because of a law, the constitution, or an international treaty. Expropriation risk can be thought of as unpredictable variation in the distribution of value arising from unpredictability in whether the government will expropriate the assets of the firm. As with other policy risks, if it is truly borne by the government, it disappears. If the government truly bears the risk, it must fairly compensate the shareholders and creditors of the firm if it expropriates, so the shareholders and creditors lose nothing.

Likewise, if the compensation is fair—that is, equal to the value of the expropriated assets—the government neither gains nor loses when it expropriates the assets. But the government might nevertheless care about the cash-flow risks: though it may get the firm, it doesn't necessarily get any cash or other liquid assets with which to help pay the compensation. (An infrastructure investor doing the analysis might want to assume, however, that compensation was less than fair.)

How might we measure this cash-flow risk? One way would be to assume that the timing of expropriation is exponentially distributed.

---

11 See Foster and Hendrick (2004), however, who say the exception was made because of the difficulty of measuring these liabilities and note that liabilities associated with "uninsurable force majeure" and the early termination of a concession contract are also excepted.

This implies that expropriation will eventually occur, the only question being when; it may not happen for a hundred years, but it will happen. A random variable t with an exponential distribution has the following probability distribution:[12]

$$f(t) = \begin{cases} \alpha e^{-\alpha t} & \text{for } t > 0, \\ 0 & \text{otherwise,} \end{cases}$$

where α is a parameter greater than zero. The random variable can be interpreted as the life of something in years or, equivalently, the date of its death. It could be the life of private ownership or, equivalently, the date of expropriation.

If we assume that t is greater than zero, the cumulative distribution function of the exponential function is

$$F(t) = \int_{s=0}^{s=t} f(s)\,ds = \int_{s=0}^{s=t} \alpha e^{-\alpha s}\,ds = 1 - e^{-\alpha t}.$$

The hazard function, interpreted as the probability of expropriation given private ownership until t, is defined as

$$h(t) = \frac{f(t)}{1 - F(t)}.$$

For the exponential distribution, the hazard rate is constant and equal to α:

$$h(t) = \frac{\alpha e^{-\alpha t}}{1 - \left(1 - e^{-\alpha t}\right)} = \alpha.$$

Suppose that the government must pay an amount V if it expropriates; to simplify, we assume V is the constant value of the firm. The expected payment by the government, discounted at the riskless rate of interest r, is given by

$$\int_0^\infty V e^{-rt} f(t)\,dt = \alpha V \int_0^\infty e^{-(\alpha + r)t}\,dt = \frac{\alpha V}{\alpha + r}.$$

To illustrate, suppose the firm's value is $1 billion, the riskless rate of interest is 10 percent, and the hazard rate of expropriation is 5 percent. That is, the probability of the government's expropriating in any given

---

12 See, for example, DeGroot and Schervish (2002, 298).

year, assuming it has not done so already, is 5 percent. Then, by plugging the numbers in the equation above, we see that the value of the government's exposure to the risk, ignoring any risk premium, is $333 million.

Regulated-Price Risk

Suppose the government agrees to increase a regulated price with inflation and therefore to compensate the firm if it fails to increase the price. Suppose that the required compensation is equal to the firm's lost revenue. How might we model the possible payments by the government? How might we estimate the value of the government's undertaking?

One option is to assume that there is a maximum politically acceptable nominal price increase, caused perhaps by money illusion (Shafir, Diamond, and Tversky 1997). Increases greater than this are, we assume, vigorously opposed, even though they merely maintain the real price. Fearing this opposition, the government limits the price increase to the maximum acceptable amount. But then it must pay the firm an amount equal to the difference between the revenue the firm would have earned with the contractually permitted price and the revenue it will actually earn. To simplify, we can assume the firm sells a constant quantity of output, so that the only variable is the price. We assume that later the government increases the nominal price at the maximum politically acceptable rate until the price catches up with the contractually agreed rate.

We assume, that is, that the contractually permitted price P^c is constant in real terms:

$$P_t^c = P_{t-1}^c \left(1 + x_{t-1}\right),$$

where x is the rate of inflation. The actual price P^a, however, depends as follows on the maximum politically acceptable increase $\hat{x}$:

$$P_t^a = \begin{cases} P_{t-1}^a \left(1 + \min\left(x_{t-1}, \hat{x}\right)\right) & \text{if } P_{t-1}^a = P_{t-1}^c, \\ \min\left(P_t^c, P_{t-1}^a \left(1 + \hat{x}\right)\right) & \text{if } P_{t-1}^a < P_{t-1}^c. \end{cases}$$

The risk factor here is inflation. How do we model it? One possibility is to assume that it follows a mean-reverting process, such as the following Ornstein-Uhlenbeck process (Dixit and Pindyck 1994, chapter 3):

$$dx = \eta\left(\bar{x} - x\right)dt + \sigma dz,$$

where $\bar{x}$ is the level to which inflation has a tendency to revert and η is a parameter, between 0 and 1, that determines how quickly it tends to revert to this level. This process is the limiting case of the following discrete-time process that can be used in a spreadsheet (Dixit and Pindyck 1994, 76):

$$x_t = \bar{x}\left(1 - e^{-\eta}\right) + x_{t-1} e^{-\eta} + \sigma z_t.$$

We can now estimate the government's payments using Monte Carlo simulation. Suppose that the initial price is $10 and that the firm sells 10 million units a year, irrespective of price. The contract and our assumptions therefore guarantee the firm annual revenue of $100 million a year in real terms. Suppose that inflation is currently equal to its long-term average of 10 percent, that the maximum politically acceptable nominal increase is 15 percent, and that $\eta = 0.5$ and $\sigma = 0.03$.

Figure 8.5 shows one possible path of contractual and actual prices. In this trial, inflation remains below 15 percent until year 3, when it rises above that level. The government does not allow the contractually permitted increase, so it must compensate. It is five years until the maximum possible price increases catch up with inflation and bring the actual price back to the contractual price. Until then the government continues to pay the firm. Thereafter, inflation remains below 10 percent, and no compensation is required.

If we take a sample of many such outcomes, we get an estimate of the probability distribution of the value of the government's payments. For

Figure 8.5. Contractual and Actual Prices and Consequent Government Compensation: One Trial

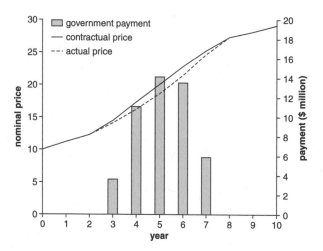

Source: Author's calculations.

Figure 8.6. Relative Frequency of Possible Values of Pricing Undertaking

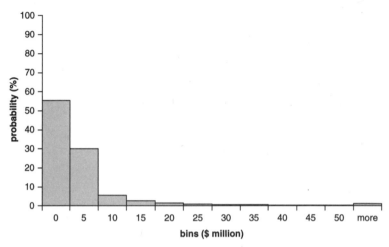

Source: Author's calculations.
Note: The bins have a width of $5 million. The first shows payments of $0, the second payments between $0 and $5 million, the third payments between $5 million and $10 million, and so on.

the sake of simplicity, we ignore any risk premium related to inflation risk and assume the nominal riskless rate of interest is a constant 10 percent. Then, taking a sample of 100,000 trials, we get an estimate of the value of the government's pricing commitment of $3.5 million. The histogram of the value is shown in figure 8.6, which indicates that there is a small chance of payments with a much higher present value.

Appendix A

Equations for Geometric Brownian Motion

In chapter 7, we show three equations, 7.2, 7.3, and 7.4, that describe geometric Brownian motion. Here, we show how equations 7.3 and 7.4 follow from 7.2 by means of Itô's Lemma.[1] Itô's Lemma applies to Itô processes, a class of stochastic processes that includes geometric Brownian motion. The change in a variable x that follows an Itô process is given by

$$dx = a(x,t)dt + b(x,t)\sqrt{dt}z,$$

where a and b are functions of x and t. Itô's Lemma states that, if x follows an Itô process and v is a function of x and t, the change in v is given by

$$dv = \left(\frac{\partial v}{\partial t} + a(x,t)\frac{\partial v}{\partial x} + \frac{b(x,t)^2}{2}\frac{\partial^2 v}{\partial x^2} \right)dt + b(x,t)\frac{\partial v}{\partial x}\sqrt{dt}z. \qquad (A.1)$$

---

1 For more on Itô's Lemma, see, for example, Dixit and Pindyck (1994, chapter 3) and Hull (2003, chapter 11).

If we assume x follows a geometric Brownian motion as in equation 7.2, then $a(x,t) = \mu x$ and $b(x,t) = \sigma x$. If we let $v = \ln x$, then $\partial v/\partial x = 1/x$, $\partial^2 v/\partial x^2 = -1/x^2$, and $\partial v/\partial t = 0$. Applying Itô's Lemma, we get

$$d\ln x = \left(\mu x \frac{1}{x} + \frac{(\sigma x)^2}{2} \frac{(-1)}{x^2} \right) dt + \sigma x \frac{1}{x} \sqrt{dt}\, z,$$

or

$$d\ln x = \left(\mu - \frac{\sigma^2}{2} \right) dt + \sigma \sqrt{dt}\, z.$$

For $dt = 1$, we get

$$\ln x_t - \ln x_{t-1} = \left(\mu - \frac{\sigma^2}{2} \right) + \sigma z.$$

If we add $\ln x_{t-1}$ to both sides of this equation and then exponentiate both sides, we get equation 7.3. If we let $dt = t$, and go through the same steps, we get equation 7.4.

The Expected Value of the Exponential Function

In writing equation 7.7 for the expected value of the subsidy payment, we made use of the fact that, if a variable x is normally distributed,

$$E\left(e^x \right) = e^{E(x) + \text{var}(x)/2}.$$

The expected value of the exponent in equation 7.6 is

$$E\left(\left(\mu - \frac{\sigma^2}{2} \right) t + \sigma \sqrt{t}\, z \right) = \left(\mu - \frac{\sigma^2}{2} \right) t,$$

and its variance is

$$\text{var}\left(\left(\mu - \frac{\sigma^2}{2} \right) t + \sigma \sqrt{t}\, z \right) = \text{var}\left(\sigma \sqrt{t}\, z \right) = \sigma^2 t.$$

Thus,

$$E\left(e^{\left(\mu-\sigma^2/2\right)t+\sigma\sqrt{t}z}\right) = e^{\left(\mu-\sigma^2/2\right)t+\left(\sigma^2t\right)/2} = e^{\mu t}.$$

The Impracticality of Valuing a Guarantee by Adjusting the Discount Rate

To see why it is easier to value a guarantee by finding a certainty equivalent than by adjusting the discount rate, consider a guarantee that can be analyzed as a put option. Let the strike price be k and let the risk factor x follow a geometric Brownian motion. Assume the other assumptions underlying the Black-Scholes model are satisfied. Then we know that the guarantee's true value can be found using the Black-Scholes formula, equation 7.16. To value the guarantee using a CAPM risk-adjusted discount rate, we have to find

$$V = \frac{E_t\left(\max\{0, k - x_T\}\right)}{1 + r + \beta\left(E(r_m) - r\right)}. \tag{A.2}$$

The numerator of equation A.2 can be found using equation 7.5. So we can calculate the value as long as we know the values of k, r, β, $E(r_m)$, μ, and σ, as well as the current value of the risk factor x_t and the time until the expiry of the option $T-t$. Assume we know these values apart from β and that r, $E(r_m)$, μ, and σ are constant.

To illustrate, suppose that x_0 and k are both \$100, that the guarantee expires at $t=1$, and that $\sigma=0.2$ and $r=0.05$. Using the Black-Scholes equation (7.16), we calculate that the guarantee is worth \$5.57 at $t=0$. If we suppose further that $\mu=0.1$, we find, using equation 7.5, that the expected payment is \$4.15. Setting equation 7.16 equal to equation A.2, we can then infer that $\beta(x_t, T-t)=\beta(100,1)=-6.1$.

So far, so good. Suppose, though, that six months pass, so that t is now 0.5. Suppose further that nothing else changes and that x in particular is still \$100. If we revalue the guarantee using equation A.2 and our old estimate of β, we conclude that it is now worth \$4.80. But the Black-Scholes formula tells us that the true value is now \$4.42. To get the right answer using equation A.2, we would have to use a β of -4.8. To make matters worse, the true value of β also changes when x changes.

Note that β varies even if the risk of the underlying risk factor is constant—that is, if its volatility σ, its correlation ρ with the return on the market, and the market parameters r and $E(r_m)$ are constant. By contrast, unless these factors change, the certainty-equivalent adjustment for risk, which involves subtracting $\lambda\sigma$, remains constant.

Equivalence in Principle of the Certainty-Equivalent and Risk-Adjusted Discount-Rate Methods

We can, however, show that the certainty-equivalent and risk-adjusted discount-rate methods give the same answer. In particular, following Brealey and Myers (2000), we can derive the certainty-equivalent version of the CAPM from its more familiar counterpart. First, by rearranging equation 7.9, we can get

$$\frac{E(p)}{V}=1+r+\beta\left(E(r_m)-r\right). \tag{A.3}$$

Next we can rewrite the covariance term in equation 7.11 for β as

$$\operatorname{cov}\left(r_p,r_m\right)=\operatorname{cov}\left(\frac{p}{V}-1,r_m\right)=\frac{\operatorname{cov}\left(p,r_m\right)}{V}$$

and express β as

$$\beta=\frac{\operatorname{cov}\left(p,r_m\right)}{V\sigma_m^2}. \tag{A.4}$$

Substituting the right-hand side of equation A.4 for β in equation A.3, we get

$$\frac{E(p)}{V}=1+r+\frac{\operatorname{cov}\left(p,r_m\right)}{V\sigma_m^2}\left(E(r_m)-r\right).$$

Then, multiplying both sides of this equation by V and rearranging terms, we get

$$E(p)=V(1+r)+\frac{\operatorname{cov}\left(p,r_m\right)}{\sigma_m^2}\left(E(r_m)-r\right),$$

or

$$V=\frac{E(p)-\operatorname{cov}\left(p,r_m\right)\left(E(r_m)-r\right)/\sigma_m^2}{1+r}.$$

Using the definition of λ in equation 7.13, we can write this more concisely as equation 7.12 in the text.

To see the relationship between β and λ, we can combine equation A.4 with equation 7.13 for λ and equation 7.14 for ρ, to get

$$\lambda = \beta V \frac{E(r_m) - r}{\sigma_\rho}.$$

The equivalence of the certainty-equivalent and risk-adjusted discount-rate versions of the CAPM can also be seen in continuous time. Consider a payment tied to a risk factor that follows a geometric Brownian motion and whose expected value is therefore of the form just considered. For simplicity, suppose that the expected payment is $\exp(\mu t)$. The value V of such a payment can be found using a risk-adjusted discount rate:

$$V = \frac{e^{\mu t}}{e^{(r + \beta(E(r_m) - r))t}}.$$

Given the properties of exponents, this equation can be rearranged to give the certainty-equivalent version

$$V = \frac{e^{(\mu - \beta(E(r_m) - r))t}}{e^{rt}}.$$

The numerator now adjusts the expected payment for risk, and the denominator discounts the resulting certainty-equivalent payment at the riskless rate of interest.

If instead we replaced the true expected value of the payment with a risk-adjusted payment derived from equation 7.15, we would get

$$V = \frac{e^{(\mu - \lambda \sigma)t}}{e^{rt}}.$$

Comparison of this equation with the one immediately above reveals another way of expressing the relationship between λ and β:

$$\lambda \sigma = \beta (E(r_m) - r). \qquad (A.5)$$

Valuation by Adjusting the Expected Growth Rate of the Risk Factor

This section explains why we can value a guarantee by assuming that the risk factor's expected growth rate is equal to its actual expected growth rate less $\lambda\sigma$, where σ is the volatility of the risk factor and λ is the price of risk, given by equation 7.13. The explanation is a special case of a more general approach set out by George Constantinides.[2]

Consider a guarantee with value V given by $V = V(x, t)$, where t is time and x is a risk factor that follows a geometric Brownian motion (equation 7.2). Applying Itô's Lemma (equation A.1), we get

$$dV = \left(\frac{\partial V}{\partial t} + \mu x \frac{\partial V}{\partial x} + \frac{\sigma^2 x^2}{2} \frac{\partial^2 V}{\partial x^2} \right) dt + \sigma x \frac{\partial V}{\partial x} \sqrt{dt} z. \qquad \text{(A.6)}$$

The rate of return on the guarantee r_p is given by

$$r_p = \frac{dV}{V} = \frac{1}{V} \left(\frac{\partial V}{\partial t} + \mu x \frac{\partial V}{\partial x} + \frac{\sigma^2 x^2}{2} \frac{\partial^2 V}{\partial x^2} \right) dt + \frac{\sigma x}{V} \frac{\partial V}{\partial x} \sqrt{dt} z.$$

The expected rate of return on the guarantee is given by

$$E\left(r_p \right) = \frac{1}{V} \left(\frac{\partial V}{\partial t} + \mu x \frac{\partial V}{\partial x} + \frac{\sigma^2 x^2}{2} \frac{\partial^2 V}{\partial x^2} \right). \qquad \text{(A.7)}$$

The covariance of the return on the guarantee with the return on the market is given by

$$\text{cov}\left(r_p, r_m \right) = \rho \sigma_m \frac{\sigma x}{V} \frac{\partial V}{\partial x}, \qquad \text{(A.8)}$$

where ρ is the correlation coefficient between z and the return on the market and σ_m is, as before, the volatility of the return on the market.

---

2   Constantinides's (1978) approach is more general in that it applies to any sort of project, and the risk factor can follow any sort of Itô process, not necessarily a geometric Brownian motion. Constantinides further generalizes the approach to the case in which there is a vector of state variables and the project pays a dividend.

If we assume that the CAPM is true, the rate of return on the guarantee is given by equation 7.10. If we substitute into equation 7.10 the definition of β using equation 7.11, we get

$$E\left(r_p\right) = r + \frac{\mathrm{cov}\left(r_p, r_m\right)}{\sigma_m^2}\left(E\left(r_m\right) - r\right). \qquad (A.9)$$

Substituting equations A.7 and A.8 into equation A.9, and simplifying, we get

$$\frac{1}{V}\left(\frac{\partial V}{\partial t} + \mu x\frac{\partial V}{\partial x} + \frac{\sigma^2 x^2}{2}\frac{\partial^2 V}{\partial x^2}\right) = r + \frac{1}{V}\frac{\partial V}{\partial x}\sigma x\frac{\rho\left(E\left(r_m\right) - r\right)}{\sigma_m}.$$

We can now substitute λ in to this equation using equation 7.13 to get

$$\frac{1}{V}\left(\frac{\partial V}{\partial t} + \mu x\frac{\partial V}{\partial x} + \frac{\sigma^2 x^2}{2}\frac{\partial^2 V}{\partial x^2}\right) = r + \frac{1}{V}\frac{\partial V}{\partial x}\sigma x\,\lambda.$$

Simplified, this becomes

$$\frac{\partial V}{\partial t} + \left(\mu - \lambda\,\sigma\right)x\frac{\partial V}{\partial x} + \frac{\sigma^2 x^2}{2}\frac{\partial^2 V}{\partial x^2} = rV. \qquad (A.10)$$

The solution to this partial differential equation that also satisfies the relevant boundary condition, such as $V_T = \max\{0, k - x_T\}$, gives the market value of the guarantee.

Now imagine all investors were risk neutral, so that $E(r_p) = r$. Substituting this into equation A.7, we get

$$\frac{\partial V}{\partial t} + \mu x\frac{\partial V}{\partial x} + \frac{\sigma^2 x^2}{2}\frac{\partial^2 V}{\partial x^2} = rV. \qquad (A.11)$$

Equations A.10 and A.11 are alike except that in equation A.11 the coefficient on $\partial V/\partial x$ is μx instead of $(\mu - \lambda\sigma)x$. That implies that we can find the value of the guarantee by assuming that the required rate of return on the guarantee—that is, the expected rate of growth of its value, assuming it pays no dividends—is equal to $\mu - \lambda\sigma$ instead of μ.

We can also see how this approach relates to the Black-Scholes formula. The Black-Scholes formula is derived from the following partial differential equation:

$$\frac{\partial V}{\partial t} + rx\frac{\partial V}{\partial x} + \frac{\sigma^2 x^2}{2}\frac{\partial^2 V}{\partial x^2} - rV = 0. \tag{A.12}$$

Equations A.10 and A.12 are alike except than in equation A.10 $\mu - \lambda\sigma$ takes the place of r in the second term on the left-hand side of the equation. So when the risk factor follows a geometric Brownian motion, we can use the Black-Scholes approach to value the guarantee, substituting $\mu - \lambda\sigma$ for the drift rate r. If the guarantee is like a European option on the value of the risk factor at maturity, we can use the Black-Scholes equation with the appropriate substitution to value the guarantee—as we did when we valued the European put in chapter 7, estimating the price of risk explicitly.

If the risk factor and the guarantee are tradable, we can simply apply the standard Black-Scholes approach and avoid having to estimate λ by making the standard arbitrage argument. Specifically, we could form a portfolio, with value Π, that is long one unit of the guarantee and short $\partial V/\partial x$ units of the risk factor:

$$\Pi = V - \frac{\partial V}{\partial x}x. \tag{A.13}$$

Then

$$d\Pi = dV - \frac{\partial V}{\partial x}dx. \tag{A.14}$$

Substituting equations A.6 and 7.2 into equation A.14, we get

$$d\Pi = \left(\frac{\partial V}{\partial t} + \mu x\frac{\partial V}{\partial x} + \frac{\sigma^2 x^2}{2}\frac{\partial^2 V}{\partial x^2}\right)dt + \sigma x\frac{\partial V}{\partial x}\sqrt{dt}z - \frac{\partial V}{\partial x}\left(\mu x dt + \sigma x\sqrt{dt}z\right),$$

which simplifies to

$$d\Pi = \left(\frac{\partial V}{\partial t} + \frac{\sigma^2 x^2}{2}\frac{\partial^2 V}{\partial x^2}\right)dt. \tag{A.15}$$

The portfolio is thus riskless and its value increases at the riskless rate of interest:

$$d\Pi = r\Pi dt. \tag{A.16}$$

Substituting equations A.14 and A.15 into this equation, we get

$$\left(\frac{\partial V}{\partial t} + \frac{\sigma^2 x^2}{2} \frac{\partial^2 V}{\partial x^2}\right) dt = r\left(V - \frac{\partial V}{\partial x} x\right) dt,$$

which simplifies to the Black-Scholes partial differential equation (A.12).

When the risk factor and the guarantee are tradable and the arbitrage argument is available, we do not need to assume the CAPM. We can simply apply the Black-Scholes equation. But if we do assume the CAPM and the risk factor x is the price of an asset, traded or not, we can infer that the expected rate of increase r_p of the value of the asset (assuming it pays no dividends) is given by the CAPM equation 7.10: $E(r_p) = r + \beta(E(r_m) - r)$. Recalling equation A.5, we know that $\beta(E(r_m) - r) = \lambda\sigma$. Thus, we can infer that the expected growth rate of the value of the asset is $r + \lambda\sigma$. If we follow the approach set out above, in which we adjust for risk by subtracting $\lambda\sigma$ from the growth rate of the risk factor, we get a risk-adjusted growth rate of r, as in the Black-Scholes approach. Even if we cannot hedge then, we can apply the Black-Scholes equation when the risk factor is an asset. We can therefore use the Black-Scholes equation to value a guarantee written on the value of an asset if we assume either that the CAPM holds or that hedging is possible.

If the risk factor x is not the price of an asset, however, we can make no such assumption. Hedging isn't possible, and the CAPM tells us nothing about the rate of growth of the value of the risk factor. Then we must proceed as described earlier and adjust the growth rate by subtracting $\lambda\sigma$—or by ignoring the price of risk and discounting expected payments at the riskless rate of interest.

References

Adler, Matthew D., and Eric A. Posner, eds. 2001. *Cost-Benefit Analysis: Legal, Economic, and Philosophical Perspectives*. Chicago: University of Chicago Press.

Ajzen, Icek. 1996. "The Social Psychology of Decision Making." In *Social Psychology: Handbook of Basic Principles*, ed. E. Tory Higgins and Arie W. Kruglanski, 297–325. New York: Guildford Press.

Akerlof, George. 1970. "The Market for 'Lemons': Qualitative Uncertainty and the Market Mechanism." *Quarterly Journal of Economics* 84 (3): 488–500.

Albouy, Yves, and Reda Bousba. 1998. "The Impact of IPPs in Developing Countries—Out of the Crisis and into the Future." *Public Policy for the Private Sector*. Note 162, World Bank, Washington, DC.

Arrow, Kenneth J. 1971. *Essays in the Theory of Risk-Bearing*. Amsterdam: North-Holland.

Arrow, Kenneth J., and Robert C. Lind. 1970. "Uncertainty and the Evaluation of Public Investment Decisions." *American Economic Review* 60 (3): 364–78.

Australian Heritage Commission. 2003. *Linking a Nation: Australia's Transport and Communications, 1788–1970*. Canberra: Commonwealth of Australia. http://www.ahc.gov.au/publications/national-stories/transport/.

Babbar, Suman, and John Schuster. 1998. "Power Project Finance: Experience in Developing Countries." Resource Mobilization and Cofinancing Discussion Paper 119, Project Finance and Guarantee Department, World Bank, Washington, DC.

Baldwin, Carliss, Donald Lessard, and Scott Mason. 1983. "Budgetary Time Bombs: Controlling Government Loan Guarantees." *Canadian Public Policy* 9 (3): 338–46.

Baumol, William J. 1963. "An Expected Gain-Confidence Limit Criterion for Portfolio Selection." *Management Science* 10 (1): 174–82.

Becquey, François Louis. 1820. *Rapport au roi sur la navigation intérieure de la France*. Extrait par Héricart de Thury. Paris: Imprimerie de Madame Huzard.

Bedford, Tim, and Roger Cooke. 2001. *Probabilistic Risk Analysis: Foundations and Methods*. Cambridge, U.K.: Cambridge University Press.

Benninga, Simon. 2000. *Financial Modeling*. 2nd ed. Cambridge, MA: MIT Press.

Bertolini, Lorenzo. 2004. "Contracting Out Regulatory Functions." *Public Policy for the Private Sector*, Note 269, World Bank, Washington, DC.

Bezançon, Xavier. 2004. *2000 ans d'histoire du partenariat public–privé pour la réalisation des équipements et services collectifs*. Paris: Presses de l'École Nationale des Ponts et Chaussées.

Birmingham, David. 2003. *A Concise History of Portugal*. 2nd ed. Cambridge, U.K.: Cambridge University Press.

Black, Fischer, and Myron Scholes. 1973. "The Pricing of Options and Corporate Liabilities." *Journal of Political Economy* 81 (3): 637–54.

Boyle, Glenn, and Timothy Irwin. 2005. "Techniques for Estimating the Fiscal Costs and Risks of Long-Term Output-Based Payments." Output-Based Aid Working Paper 5. Global Partnership on Output-Based Aid, World Bank, Washington, DC.

Boyle, Phelim. 1977. "Options: A Monte Carlo Approach." *Journal of Financial Economics* 4 (4): 323–38.

Brailsford, Henry N. 1918 [1914]. "Real Politics." In *The War of Steel and Gold: A Study of the Armed Peace*, 10th ed. London: G. Bell & Sons.

Brealey, Richard A., Ian A. Cooper, and Michel A. Habib. 1997. "Investment Appraisal in the Public Sector." *Oxford Review of Economic Policy* 13 (4): 12–28.

Brealey, Richard A., and Stewart C. Myers. 2000. *Principles of Corporate Finance*. 6th ed. New York: McGraw-Hill.

Breyer, Stephen. 1993. *Breaking the Vicious Circle: Toward Effective Risk Regulation*. Cambridge, MA: Harvard University Press.

Brixi, Hana Polackova, and Ashoka Mody. 2002. "Dealing with Government Fiscal Risk: An Overview." In *Government at Risk: Contingent Liabilities and Fiscal Risk*, ed. Hana Polackova Brixi and Allen Schick, 21–58. Washington, DC: World Bank.

Brixi, Hana Polackova, and Allen Schick, eds. 2002. *Government at Risk: Contingent Liabilities and Fiscal Risk*. Washington, DC: World Bank.

Brixi, Hana Polackova, Allen Schick, and Leila Zlaoui. 2002. "The Challenges of Fiscal Risks in Transition: Czech Republic, Hungary, and Bulgaria." In *Government at Risk: Contingent Liabilities and Fiscal Risk*, ed. Hana Polackova Brixi and Allen Schick, 203–34. Washington, DC: World Bank.

Burton, Anthony. 1994. *The Railway Empire*. London: John Murray.

Camerer, Colin F. 1995. "Individual Decision Making." In *The Handbook of Experimental Economics*, ed. John H. Kagel and Alvin E. Roth, 587–704. Princeton, NJ: Princeton University Press.

Caron, François. 1983. "France." In *Railways and the Economic Development of Western Europe, 1830–1914*, ed. Patrick O'Brien. London: MacMillan.

Chen, Andrew H., K. C. Chen, and R. Stephen Sears. 1986. "The Value of Loan Guarantees: The Case of Chrysler Corporation." *Research in Finance* 6: 101–17.

Cialdini, Robert B. 1998. *Influence: The Psychology of Persuasion*. Rev. ed. New York: Collins.

Cochrane, John. 2001. *Asset Pricing*. Princeton, NJ: Princeton University Press.

Cohen, Daniel. 2002. "Fiscal Sustainability and a Contingency Trust Fund." In *Government at Risk: Contingent Liabilities and Fiscal Risk*, ed. Hana Polackova Brixi and Allen Schick, 143–58. Washington, DC: World Bank.

Constantinides, George M. 1978. "Market Risk Adjustment in Project Valuation." *Journal of Finance* 33 (2): 603–16.

Copeland, Thomas E., and Vladimir Antikarov. 2001. *Real Options: A Practitioner's Guide*. New York: Texere.

Correia da Silva, Luis, Antonio Estache, and Sakari Järvelä. 2004. "Is Debt Replacing Equity in Regulated Privatized Infrastructure in Developing Countries?" Policy Research Working Paper 3374, World Bank, Washington, DC.

Currie, A. W. 1957. *Grand Trunk Railway of Canada*. Toronto: University of Toronto Press.

Currie, Elizabeth. n.d. "The Potential Role of Government Debt Management Offices in Monitoring and Managing Contingent Liabilities." World Bank, Washington, DC.

Dawes, Robin M., David Faust, and Paul E. Meehl. 1989. "Clinical versus Actuarial Judgment." *Science* 243 (4899): 1668–74.

DeGroot, Morris H., and Mark J. Schervish. 2002. *Probability and Statistics*. 3rd ed. Boston: Addison-Wesley.

de Meza, David, and David Webb. 2000. "Does Credit Rationing Imply Insufficient Lending?" *Journal of Public Economics* 78 (3): 215–34.

Dixit, Avinash K., and Robert S. Pindyck. 1994. *Investment under Uncertainty*. Princeton, NJ: Princeton University Press.

Dobbin, Frank. 1994. *Forging Industrial Policy: The United States, Britain, and France in the Railway Age.* Cambridge, U.K.: Cambridge University Press.

Doukas, Kimon A. 1945. *The French Railroads and the State.* New York: Columbia University Press.

Dowd, Kevin. 1998. *Beyond Value at Risk: The New Science of Risk Management.* Chichester, U.K.: John Wiley & Sons.

Duffie, Darrell, and Kenneth J. Singleton. 2003. *Credit Risk: Pricing, Measurement, and Management.* Princeton, NJ: Princeton University Press.

du Marais, Bertrand. 2004. *Droit publique de la régulation économique.* Paris: Presses de Science Po et Dalloz.

Dunham, Arthur L. 1941. "How the French Railways Were Planned." *Journal of Economic History* 1 (1): 12–25.

Dunlavy, Colleen A. 1994. *Politics and Industrialization: Early Railroads in the United States and Prussia.* Princeton, NJ: Princeton University Press.

Duvergier, J. B. Various years. *Collection complète des lois, décrets, ordonnances, réglemens, avis du conseil d'état.* Various vols. Paris: Guyot.

Earle, Edward Mead. 1923. *Turkey, the Great Powers, and the Bagdad Railway: A Study in Imperialism.* New York: Macmillan.

Easterly, William, and Luis Servén. 2003. *The Limits of Stabilization: Infrastructure, Public Deficits, and Growth in Latin America.* Washington, DC: World Bank.

Echeverry, Juan Carlos, Verónica Navas, Juan Camilo Gutierrez, and Jorge Enrique Cardona. 2002. "Dealing with Contingent Liabilities in Colombia." In *Government at Risk: Contingent Liabilities and Fiscal Risk*, ed. Hana Polackova Brixi and Allen Schick, 269–80. Washington, DC: World Bank.

Ehrhardt, David, and Timothy Irwin. 2004. "Avoiding Customer and Taxpayer Bailouts in Private Infrastructure Projects: Policy toward Leverage, Risk Allocation, and Bankruptcy." Policy Research Working Paper 3274, World Bank, Washington, DC.

Eichengreen, Barry. 1996. "Financing Infrastructure in Developing Countries: Lessons from the Railway Age." In *Infrastructure Delivery: Private Initiative and the Public Good*, ed. Ashoka Mody. Washington, DC: World Bank.

Engel, Eduardo, Ronald Fischer, and Alexander Galetovic. 1997. Infrastructure franchising and government guarantees. In *Dealing with Public Risk in Private Infrastructure*, ed. Timothy Irwin, Michael Klein, Guillermo E. Perry, and Mateen Thobani, 89–105. Washington, DC: World Bank.

———. 2001. "Least-Present-Value-Revenue Auctions and Highway Franchising." *Journal of Political Economy* 109 (5): 993–1020.

Ericson, Steven J. 1996. *The Sound of the Whistle: Railroads and the State in Meiji Japan*. Harvard East Asian Monograph 168. Cambridge, MA: Council on East Asian Studies, Harvard University.

Estache, Antonio. 2002. "Argentina 1990s' Utility Privatization: A Cure or a Disease?" World Bank, Washington, DC.

Esty, Benjamin C. 2004. *Modern Project Finance: A Casebook*. World Bank: John Wiley & Sons.

European Commission. 2004. *Resource Book on PPP Case Studies*. Directorate-General, Regional Policy, European Commission, Brussels. http://europa.eu. int/comm/regional_policy/sources/docgener/guides/pppresourcebook.pdf.

Faith, Nicholas. 1990. *The World the Railways Made*. London: Pimlico.

Fama, Eugene F., and Kenneth R. French. 1993. "Common Risk Factors in the Returns on Stocks and Bonds." *Journal of Financial Economics* 33 (1): 3–56.

Fishbein, Gregory, and Suman Babbar. 1996. "Private Financing of Toll Roads." Resource Mobilization and Cofinancing Discussion Paper 117. Project Finance and Guarantee Department, World Bank.

Flemming, John, and Colin Mayer. 1997. "The Assessment: Public-Sector Investment." *Oxford Review of Economic Policy* 13 (4): 1–11.

Flyvbjerg, Bent, Mette Skamris Holm, and Soren Buhl. 2002. "Underestimating Costs in Public Works Projects: Error or Lie?" *APA Journal* 68 (3): 279–295.

Fogel, Robert William. 1960. *The Union Pacific Railroad: A Case in Premature Enterprise*. Baltimore, MD: Johns Hopkins Press.

Foster, Vivien, and Oscar Hendrick. 2004. "Pilot Study on Public Investment and Fiscal Policy: Private-Public Partnerships." World Bank and International Monetary Fund, Washington, DC.

Fox, Craig R., and Amos Tversky. 1998. "A Belief-Based Account of Decision under Uncertainty." *Management Science* 44 (7): 879–95.

Gale, William G. 1991. "Economic Effects of Federal Credit Programs." *American Economic Review* 81 (1): 133–52.

Garman, Mark B., and Steven W. Kohlhagen. 1983. "Foreign Currency Option Values." *Journal of International Money and Finance* 2: 231–37.

Geiger, Reed G. 1984. "Planning the French Canals: The 'Becquey Plan' of 1820–1822." *Journal of Transport History* 44 (2): 329–39.

———. 1994. *Planning the French Canals: Bureaucracy, Politics, and Enterprise under the Restoration*. Newark, DE: University of Delaware Press.

Gigerenzer, Gerd, Peter M. Todd, and the ABC Research Group. 1999. *Simple Heuristics That Make Us Smart*. New York: Oxford University Press.

Gilovich, Thomas, Dale Griffin, and Daniel Kahneman. 2002. *Heuristics and Biases: The Psychology of Intuitive Judgment.* Cambridge, U.K: Cambridge University Press.

Goldberger, Arthur S. 1991. *A Course in Econometrics.* Cambridge, MA: Harvard University Press.

Gómez-Ibáñez, José A. 1997. *Mexico's Private Toll Road Program.* Cambridge, MA: Kennedy School of Government Case Program, Harvard University.

————. 2003. *Regulating Infrastructure: Monopoly, Contracts, and Discretion.* Cambridge, MA: Harvard University Press.

Gómez-Ibáñez, José A., and John R. Meyer. 1993. *Going Private: The International Experience with Transport Privatization.* Washington, DC: Brookings Institution.

Gómez Lobo, Andrés, and Sergio Hinojosa. 2000. "Broad Roads in a Thin Country." Policy Research Working Paper 2279, World Bank, Washington, DC.

Goode, Roy. 2004. *Commercial Law.* 3rd ed. London: Penguin.

Goodrich, Carter. 1950. "The Revulsion against Internal Improvements." *Journal of Economic History* 10 (2): 145–69.

————. 1974 [1960]. *Government Promotion of American Canals and Railroads, 1800–1890.* London: Greenwood Press.

Government of Chile. 2003. "Report on Public Finances: Government Budget Bill for 2004." Presented by Mario Marcel Cullel, Budget Director, to the Special Joint Committee on the Budget of the National Congress, Santiago. http://www.dipres.cl/fr_news_english.html.

Government of Colombia, Department of National Planning. 2001a. "Modificaciones a la política de maneje de riesgo contractual del estado para procesos de participación privada en infraestructura establecida en el documento Conpes 3107 de abril de 2001." Conpes 3133, Department of National Planning, Bogotá.

————. 2001b. "Política de manejo de riesgo contractual del estado para procesos de participación privada en infraestructura." Conpes 3107, Department of National Planning, Bogotá.

Government of Colombia, Ministerio de Hacienda y Crédito Público, Dirección General de Crédito Público, División de Pasivos Contingentes. n.d. *Manual para la valoración de pasivos contingentes: Proyectos de infraestructura.* Ministerio de Hacienda y Crédito Público, Dirección General de Crédito Público, División de Pasivos Contingentes, Bogotá.

Government of Indonesia. 2006. "Directive for Controlling and Managing Risks of Infrastructure Provision." Regulation of the Minister of Finance 38, Jakarta, Government of Indonesia.

Government of Mexico, Secretaría de Comunicaciones y Transportes and Banco Nacional de Obras y Servicios Públicos. 2003. "New Model for the Concession of Toll Roads." Secretaría de Comunicaciones y Transportes and Banco Nacional de Obras y Servicios Públicos, Mexico City.

Government of New South Wales, Australia, Auditor-General's Office. 1994. *Private Participation in the Provision of Public Infrastructure: The Roads and Traffic Industry*. Sydney: Auditor-General's Office.

Government of South Africa, National Treasury. 2002. "Demand Risk." *PPP Quarterly: Public Private Partnerships* 9 (December): 4–5.

———. 2004. *Public Private Partnership Manual: National Treasury PPP Practice Notes Issued in Terms of the Public Finance Management Act*. Pretoria: National Treasury.

Government of United Kingdom, Her Majesty's Treasury. 2003. *PFI: Meeting the investment challenge*. London: Her Majesty's Treasury. http://www.hm-treasury. gov.uk/media//648B2/PFI_604.pdf.

———. 2004. *Standardisation of PFI contracts, Version 3*. London: Her Majesty's Treasury. http://www.hm-treasury.gov.uk/documents/public_private_partner ships/key_documents/standardised_contracts/ppp_keydocsstand_index.cfm.

Government of United States, Congressional Budget Office. 2004. "Estimating the Value of Subsidies for Federal Loans and Loan Guarantees." Washington, DC: Congressional Budget Office. http://www.cbo.gov/ftpdocs/57xx/doc57 51/08-19-CreditSubsidies.pdf.

Government of Victoria, Australia. 2001. *Partnerships Victoria Guidance Material: Risk Allocation and Contractual Issues*. Melbourne, Australia: Department of Treasury and Finance, Government of Victoria.

Graham, John R., and Campbell R. Harvey. 2001. "The Theory and Practice of Corporate Finance: Evidence from the Field. *Journal of Financial Economics* 60: 187–243.

Gray, Philip, and Timothy Irwin. 2003a. "Exchange-Rate Risk: Reviewing the Record for Private Infrastructure Contracts." *Public Policy for the Private Sector*. Note 162, World Bank, Washington, DC.

———. 2003b. "Exchange-Rate Risk: Allocating Exchange in Private Infrastructure Projects. *Public Policy for the Private Sector*. Note 266, World Bank, Washington, DC.

Gray, R. David, and John Schuster. 1998. The East Asian Financial Crisis—Fallout for Private Power Projects. *Public Policy for the Private Sector*. Note 146, World Bank, Washington, DC.

Guasch, J. Luis. 2004. *Granting and Renegotiating Infrastructure Concessions: Doing It Right*. Washington, DC: World Bank.

Haarmeyer, David, and Ashoka Mody. 1998. "Tapping the Private Sector: Approaches to Managing Risk in Water and Sanitation." Resource Mobilization and Cofinancing Discussion Paper 112. Project Finance and Guarantee Department, World Bank, Washington, DC.

Hahm, Junglim. 2003. "Private Participation in the Infrastructure Programme of the Republic of Korea." *Transport and Communications Bulletin for Asia and the Pacific* 72: 57–75. http://www.unescap.org/ttdw/Publications/TPTS_pubs/bulletin72/bulletin72_ch3.pdf.

Harris, Anthony C. 1998. "Credulity and Credibility in Infrastructure Funding." Paper presented at the Australian Capital Territory Department of Urban Services, Summer Seminar Series, Canberra, March 6.

Haywood, Richard Mowbray. 1969. *The Beginnings of Railway Development in Russia in the Reign of Nicholas I, 1835–1842.* Durham, NC: Duke University Press.

Helm, Dieter. 2004. *Energy, the State, and the Market: British Energy Policy since 1979.* Rev. ed. Oxford, U.K.: Oxford University Press.

Hemming, Richard, and Staff Team of the IMF (International Monetary Fund). 2006. *Public-Private Partnerships, Government Guarantees, and Fiscal Risk.* Washington, DC: International Monetary Fund.

Holbrook, Stewart H. 1947. *The Story of American Railroads.* New York: Crown.

Hoover, Calvin B. 1926. "The Sea Loan in Genoa in the Twelfth Century." *Quarterly Journal of Economics* 40 (3): 495–529.

Howard, Stanley E. 1918. "Some Aspects of French Railway War Finance." *Quarterly Journal of Economics* 32 (2): 309–32.

Hull, John C. 2003. *Options, Futures, and Other Derivatives.* 5th ed. Upper Saddle River, NJ: Prentice Hall.

IMF (International Monetary Fund). 2001a. *Code of Good Practices on Fiscal Transparency.* Washington, DC: IMF. http://www.imf.org/external/np/fad/trans/code.htm.

———. 2001b. *Government Finance Statistics Manual, 2001.* Washington, DC: IMF.

———. 2005. "Public Investment and Fiscal Policy—Summaries of the Pilot Country Studies." Washington, DC: IMF.

Innes, Robert. 1991. "Investment and Government Intervention in Credit Markets When There Is Asymmetric Information." *Journal of Public Economics.* Volume 46 (3): 347–81.

Institute of Chartered Accountants of England and Wales. 2003. *Accounting Standards 2003/2004.* London: Croner. CCH Group Limited.

International Accounting Standards Board. 2004. *International Financial Reporting Standards (IFRSs)—Including International Accounting Standards (IASs) and Interpretations as at 31 March 2004.* London: International Accounting Standards Board.

Irwin, Timothy C. 2003. "Public Money for Private Infrastructure: Deciding When to Offer Guarantees, Output-Based Subsidies, and Other Forms of Fiscal Support." Working Paper 10, World Bank, Washington, DC.

———. 2004. "Measuring and Valuing the Risks Created by Revenue and Exchange-Rate Guarantee in Korea." In *Developing Best Practice for Korea's PPI Market: With a Focus on PSC*, 257–73. Seoul: Private Infrastructure Investment Center of Korea.

Irwin, Timothy, Michael Klein, Guillermo E. Perry, and Mateen Thobani, eds. 1997. *Dealing with Public Risk in Private Infrastructure*. Washington, DC: World Bank.

Janda, Karel. 2005. "The Comparison of Credit Subsidies and Guarantees in Transition and Post-transition Economies." *Ekonomicky Casopis* [*Journal of Economics*] 53 (4): 383–98.

Jastrow, Morris. 2005 [1918]. *The War and the Bagdad Railway: The Story of Asia Minor and Its Relation to the Present Conflict*. Boston: Elibron.

Jeffreys, Richard. 2004. *Subjective Probability: The Real Thing*. New York: Cambridge University Press.

Jenkinson, Tim. 2003. "Private Finance." *Oxford Review of Economic Policy* 19 (2) 323–34.

Johnson, J. 1963. *The Economics of Indian Rail Transport*. Bombay: Allied Publishers.

Jones, E. Philip, and Scott P. Mason. 1980. "Valuation of Loan Guarantees." *Journal of Banking and Finance* 4 (1): 89–97.

Jorion, Philippe. 1988. "On Jump Processes in the Foreign Exchange and Stock Markets." *Review of Financial Studies* 1 (4): 427–45.

———. 1997. *Value at Risk: The New Benchmark for Controlling Market Risk*. Chicago: Irwin Professional Publishing.

Jorion, Philippe, and Richard J. Sweeney. 1996. "Mean Reversion in Real Exchange Rates: Evidence and Implications for Forecasting." *Journal of International Money and Finance* 15 (4): 535–50.

Juan, Ellis J. 1996. "Privatizing Airports: Options and Case Studies." *Public Policy for the Private Sector*. Note 82, World Bank, Washington, DC.

Kahneman, Daniel, and Don Lovallo. 1993. "Timid Choices and Bold Forecasts: A Cognitive Perspective on Risk Taking." *Management Science* 39 (1): 17–31.

Kahneman, Daniel, Paul Slovic, and Amos Tversky, eds. 1982. *Judgment under Uncertainty: Heuristics and Biases*. Cambridge, U.K.: Cambridge University Press.

Kahneman, Daniel, and Amos Tversky. 1979. "Prospect Theory: An Analysis of Decision under Risk." *Econometrica* 47 (2): 263–91.

———. 1982. "Intuitive Prediction: Biases and Corrective Procedures." In *Judgment under Uncertainty: Heuristics and Biases*, ed. Daniel Kahneman, Paul Slovic, and Amos Tversky, 414–22. Cambridge, U.K.: Cambridge University Press.

———. 1995. "Conflict Resolution: A Cognitive Perspective." In *Barriers to Conflict Resolution*, ed. Kenneth Arrow, Robert H. Mnookin, Lee Ross, Amos Tversky and Robert Wilson, 44–61. New York: W. W. Norton.

Karkar, Yaqub N. 1972. *Railway Development in the Ottoman Empire, 1856–1914.* Ann Arbor, MI: Vantage Press.

Kerf, Michel, with R. David Gray, Timothy Irwin, Céline Lévesque, and Robert R. Taylor, under the direction of Michael Klein. 1998. "Concessions for Infrastructure: A Guide to Their Design and Award." Technical Paper 399, Finance, Private Sector, and Infrastructure Network, World Bank, Washington, DC.

Kerr, Ian J. 1995. *Building the Railways of the Raj 1850–1900.* Delhi, India: Oxford University Press.

Klein, Michael. 1997. "The Risk Premium for Evaluating Public Projects." *Oxford Review of Economic Policy* 13 (4): 29–42.

Klein, Michael, Jae So, and Ben Shin. 1996. "Transaction Costs in Private Infrastructure Projects—Are They Too High?" *Public Policy for the Private Sector*. Note 95, World Bank, Washington, DC.

Knight, Frank H. 1921. *Risk, Uncertainty, and Profit.* Boston and New York: Houghton Mifflin.

Lachaume, Jean-François. 2002. *Droit administratif.* 13th ed. Paris: Presses Universitaires de France.

Leitch, David B. 1972. *Railways of New Zealand.* Newton Abbot, U.K.: David & Charles.

Levy, Brian, and Pablo T. Spiller. 1994. "The Institutional Foundations of Regulatory Commitment: A Comparative Analysis of Telecommunications Regulation." *Journal of Law, Economics, and Organization* 10 (2): 201–46.

Lewis, Christopher M., and Ashoka Mody. 1997. "The Management of Contingent Liabilities: A Risk Management Framework for National Governments." In *Dealing with Public Risk in Private Infrastructure*, ed. Timothy Irwin, Michael Klein, Guillermo E. Perry, and Mateen Thobani, 131–53. Washington, DC: World Bank.

Lewis, Colin M. 1983. *British Railways in Argentina 1857–1914: A Case Study of Foreign Investment.* Monograph 12. London: University of London Institute of Latin American Studies.

Lewis, Frank, and Mary MacKinnon. 1987. "Government Loan Guarantees and the Failure of the Canadian Northern Railway." *Journal of Economic History* 47 (1): 175–96.

Livy. 2006. *Hannibal's War.* Books 21–30. Trans. J. C. Yardley. Oxford, U.K.: Oxford University Press.

Lovei, Laszlo. 2000. "The Single-Buyer Model: A Dangerous Path toward Competitive Electricity Markets." *Public Policy for the Private Sector.* Note 225, World Bank, Washington, DC.

Luxemburg, Rosa. 1951. *The Accumulation of Capital.* Trans. by Agnes Schwarzchild. London: Routledge and Kegan Paul Ltd.

Machiavelli, Niccolò. 1992. *The Prince.* New York: Dover.

MacPherson, W. J. 1955. "Investment in Indian Railways, 1845–1875." *Economic History Review* 8 (2): 177–86.

Macquarie Infrastructure Group. 2001. "Macquarie Infrastructure Group Prospectus 2001." http://www.macquarie.com.au/au/mig/investor/prospectuses. htm.

March, James G., and Zur Shapira. 1987. "Management Perspectives on Risk and Risk-Taking." *Management Science* 33: 1404–8.

Marrison, Christopher. 2002. *The Fundamentals of Risk Measurement.* New York: McGraw-Hill.

Mas, Ignacio. 1997. "Managing Exchange Rate– and Interest Rate–Related Project Exposure: Are Guarantees Worth the Risk?" In *Dealing with Public Risk in Private Infrastructure,* ed. Timothy Irwin, Michael Klein, Guillermo E. Perry, and Mateen Thobani, 109–28. Washington, DC: World Bank.

Matsukawa, Tomoko, Robert Sheppard, and Joseph Wright. 2003. "Foreign Exchange Risk Mitigation for Power and Water Projects in Developing Countries." Energy and Mining Sector Board Paper 9, World Bank, Washington, DC.

McMurray, Jonathan S. 2001. *Distant Ties: Germany, the Ottoman Empire, and the Construction of the Baghdad Railway.* Westport, CT: Praeger.

Mellers, Barbara A., Alan Schwartz, and Alan D. J. Cooke. 1998. "Judgment and Decision Making". *Annual Review of Psychology* 49: 447–77.

Merton, Robert C. 1973. "Theory of Rational Option Pricing." *Bell Journal of Economics and Management Science* 4 (1): 141–83.

———. 1977. "An Analytic Derivation of the Cost of Deposit Insurance and Loan Guarantees: An Application of Modern Option Pricing Theory." *Journal of Banking and Finance* 1: 3–11.

Merton, Robert C., and Zvi Bodie. 1992. "On the Management of Financial Guarantees." *Financial Management* 21 (4): 87–109.

Modigliani, Franco, and Merton Miller. 1958. "The Cost of Capital, Corporation Finance, and the Theory of Investment." *American Economic Review* 48 (3): 261–97.

Mody, Ashoka. 2002. "Contingent Liabilities in Infrastructure: Lessons from the East Asian Financial Crisis." In *Government at Risk: Contingent Liabilities and Fiscal Risk,* ed. Hana Polackova Brixi and Allen Schick, 373–92. Washington, DC: World Bank.

Mody, Ashoka, and Dilip K. Patro. 1996. "Methods of Loan Guarantee Valuation and Accounting." In *Infrastructure Delivery: Private Initiative and the Public Good*, ed. Ashoka Mody. 191–220. Washington, DC: World Bank.

Morgan, Willis D. 1927. "The History and Economics of Suretyship." *Cornell Law Quarterly* 12: 153–71.

Moss, David A. 2002. *When All Else Fails: Government as the Ultimate Risk Manager*. Cambridge, MA: Harvard University Press.

Mueller, Dennis C. 2003. *Public Choice III*. Cambridge, U.K.: Cambridge University Press.

Munro, J. Forbes. 1987. "Shipping Subsidies and Railway Guarantees: William Mackinnon, Eastern Africa, and the Indian Ocean 1860–93." *Journal of African History* 28 (2): 209–30.

National Accounts Classification Committee, U.K. Office for National Statistics. 2004. "National Accounts Sector Classification of Network Rail." U.K. Office for National Statistics, London.

National Economic Research Associates. 2004. "Managing Guarantees and Long-Term Purchase and Subsidy Commitments in Public-Private Partnerships." Report for the World Bank, Washington, DC.

Nevitt, Peter K., and Frank J. Fabozzi. 2000. *Project Finance*. 7th ed. London: Euromoney Books.

Newbery, David M. 1999. *Privatization, Restructuring, and Regulation of Network Utilities*. Cambridge, MA: the MIT Press.

O'Donovan, James, and John Phillips. 2003. *The Modern Contract of Guarantee*. London: Sweet & Maxwell.

Olson, Mancur. 1965. *The Logic of Collective Action*. Cambridge, MA: Harvard University Press.

Petrie, Murray. 2002. "Accounting and Financial Accountability to Capture Risk." In *Government at Risk: Contingent Liabilities and Fiscal Risk*, ed. Hana Polackova Brixi and Allen Schick, 59–78. Washington, DC: World Bank.

Phaup, Marvin. 1993. "Recent Federal Efforts to Measure and Control Risk-Bearing." In *Government Risk-Bearing: Proceedings of a Conference Held at the Federal Reserve Bank of Cleveland, May 1991*, ed. Mark S. Sniderman, 167–76. Boston: Kluwer Academic Publishers.

Polybius. 1922. *The Histories, Volume II*. Trans. by W. R. Paton. Cambridge, MA: Harvard University Press.

Posner, Richard A. 2001. "Cost-Benefit Analysis: Definition, Justification, and Comment on Conference Papers." In *Cost-Benefit Analysis: Legal, Economic, and Philosophical Perspectives*, ed. Mathew D. Adler and Eric A. Posner, 317–42. Chicago: University of Chicago Press.

Pratley, Nils, and Frédéric Pons. 2004. "Deep in Debt." *Guardian*. April 7.

Prelec, Drazen. 1998. "The Probability Weighting Function." *Econometrica* 66 (3): 497–527.

Pressel, Wilhelm von. 1902. *Les chemins de fer en Turquie d'Asie: Projet d'un reseau complet.* 2nd ed. Zurich: Orell Füssli.

Project Finance Magazine. 2004. "Incheon Railroad Closes." November 1.

Quiggin, John. 2004. "Risk, PPPs, and the Public Sector Comparator." *Australian Accounting Review.* 14 (2): 51–61.

Rabin, Matthew. 2000. "Diminishing Marginal Utility of Wealth Cannot Explain Risk Aversion." In *Choices, Values, and Frames,* ed. Daniel Kahneman and Amos Tversky, 202–8. Cambridge, U.K.: Cambridge University Press and the Russell Sage Foundation.

Reverdy, Georges. 2004. *Les travaux publics en France, 1817–1847: Trente années glorieuses.* Paris: Presses de l'École Nationale des Ponts et Chaussées.

Rogoff, Kenneth. 1996. "The Purchasing Power Parity Puzzle." *Journal of Economic Literature* 34 (2): 647–68.

Rothschild, Michael, and Joseph E. Stiglitz. 1976. "Equilibrium in Competitive Insurance Markets: An Essay on the Economics of Imperfect Information." *Quarterly Journal of Economics.* Volume 90 (4): 629–49.

Rottenstreich, Yuval, and Amos Tversky. 1997. "Unpacking, Repacking, and Anchoring: Advances in Support Theory." *Psychological Review* 104 (2): 406–15

Ruster, Jeff. 1995. "Bankruptcies in the U.S. Utility Industry." World Bank, Washington, DC.

———. 1997. "A Retrospective on the Mexican Toll Road Program (1989–94)." *Public Policy for the Private Sector.* Note 125, World Bank, Washington, DC.

Schick, Allen. 2002a. "Budgeting for Fiscal Risk." In *Government at Risk: Contingent Liabilities and Fiscal Risk,* ed. Hana Polackova Brixi and Allen Schick, 79–98. Washington, DC: World Bank.

———. 2002b. "Conclusion: Toward a Code of Good Practice on Managing Fiscal Risk." In *Government at Risk: Contingent Liabilities and Fiscal Risk,* ed. Hana Polackova Brixi and Allen Schick, 461. Washington, DC: World Bank.

Scott, Graham C. 2001. *Public Sector Management in New Zealand: Lessons and Challenges.* Wellington: Australian National University.

Shafir, Eldar, Peter Diamond, and Amos Tversky. 1997. "Money Illusion." *Quarterly Journal of Economics* 112 (2): 341–74

Sharpe, William. 1964. "Capital Asset Prices: A Theory of Market Equilibrium under Conditions of Risk." *Journal of Finance* 19 (3): 425–42.

Shavell, Steven. 2004. *Foundations of Economic Analysis of Law.* Cambridge, MA: Harvard University Press.

Shiller, Robert J. 2002. "Bubbles, Human Judgment, and Expert Opinion." *Financial Analysts Journal* 58 (3): 18–26.

Shugart, Christopher. 1988. "Regulation-by-Contract and Municipal Services: The Problem of Contractual Incompleteness." PhD thesis, Harvard University, Cambridge, MA.

Siegel, Jeremy J., and Richard H. Thaler. 1997. "Anomalies: The Equity Premium Puzzle." *Journal of Economic Perspectives* 11 (1): 191–200.

Skamris, Mette K., and Bent Flyvbjerg. 1997. "Inaccuracy of Traffic Forecasts and Cost Estimates on Large Transport Projects." *Transport Policy* 4 (3): 141–46.

Smith, Warrick. 1997a. "Covering Political and Regulatory Risks: Issues and Options for Private Infrastructure Arrangements." In *Dealing with Public Risk in Private Infrastructure*, ed. Timothy Irwin, Michael Klein, Guillermo E. Perry, and Mateen Thobani, 45–85. Washington, DC: World Bank.

———. 1997b. "Utility Regulators—The Independence Debate." *Public Policy for the Private Sector*. Note 127, World Bank, Washington, DC.

———. 1997c. Utility Regulators—Roles and Responsibilities. *Public Policy for the Private Sector*. Note 128, World Bank, Washington, DC.

———. 1997d. Utility Regulators—Decisionmaking Structures, Resources, and Start-up Strategy. *Public Policy for the Private Sector*. Note 129, World Bank, Washington, DC.

Sniderman, Mark S. 1993. *Government Risk-Bearing: Proceedings of a Conference Held at the Federal Reserve Bank of Cleveland, May 1991*. Boston: Kluwer Academic Publishers.

Sosin, Howard B. 1980. "On the Valuation of Federal Loan Guarantees to Corporations." *Journal of Finance* 35 (5): 1209–21.

Staley, Eugene. 1935. *War and the Private Investor: A Study in the Relations of International Politics and International Private Investment*. Chicago: University of Chicago Press.

Standard and Poor's. 2003. "Research: Electricity Generating Authority of Thailand."

Stiglitz, Joseph. 1974. "Incentives and Risk-Sharing in Sharecropping." *Review of Economic Studies* 41 (2): 219–55.

———. 1989. "Markets, Market Failures, and Development." *American Economic Review* 79 (2): 197–203.

———. 1993. "Perspectives on the Role of Government Risk-Bearing within the Financial Sector." In *Government Risk-Bearing: Proceedings of a Conference Held at the Federal Reserve Bank of Cleveland, May 1991*, ed. Mark S. Sniderman, 109–30. Boston: Kluwer Academic Publishers.

Stiglitz, Joseph, and Andrew Weiss. 1981. "Credit Rationing with Imperfect Information." *American Economic Review* 71 (10): 393–410.

Suetonius. 1914. "The Life of Claudius." In *The Lives of the Twelve Caesars*, trans. J. C. Rolfe, Loeb Classical Library.

Summerhill, William R. 1998. "Market Intervention in a Backward Economy: Railway Subsidy in Brazil, 1854–1913. *Economic History Review* 51 (3): 542–68.

———. 2003. *Order against Progress: Government, Foreign Investment, and Railroads in Brazil, 1854–1913*. Stanford, CA: Stanford University Press.

Sunstein, Cass. 2001. "Cognition and Cost-Benefit Analysis." In *Cost-Benefit Analysis: Legal, Economic, and Philosophical Perspectives*, ed. Mathew D. Adler and Eric A. Posner, 223–67. Chicago: University of Chicago Press.

Surowiecki, James. 2004. *The Wisdom of the Crowds: Why the Many Are Smarter Than the Few and How Collective Wisdom Shapes Business, Economies, Societies, and Nations*. New York: Doubleday.

Taylor, Alan M., and Mark P. Taylor. 2004. "The Purchasing Power Parity Debate." *Journal of Economic Perspectives* 18 (4): 135–58.

Taylor, Mark P. 1995. "The Economics of Exchange Rates." *Journal of Economic Literature* 33 (1): 13–47.

Tetlock, Philip E. 2002. "Theory-Driven Reasoning about Plausible Pasts and Probable Futures in World Politics." In *Heuristics and Biases: The Psychology of Intuitive Judgment*, ed. Thomas Gilovich, Dale Griffin, and Daniel Kahneman, 749–62. Cambridge, U.K: Cambridge University Press.

Thévenez, René, with Fernand Manesse. 1909. *Législation des chemins de fer et des tramways*. Paris: H. Dunod et E. Pinat.

Thorner, Daniel. 1977 [1950]. *Investment in Empire: British Railway and Steam Shipping Enterprise in India, 1825–1849*. New York: Arno Press.

Timmins, Nicholas. 2004. "Past Proves There's No Place for Panic." *Financial Times*, U.K. ed., July 9, 22.

Tirole, Jean. 2006. *The Theory of Corporate Finance*. Princeton, NJ: Princeton University Press.

Towe, Christopher M. 1993. "Government Contingent Liabilities and Measurement of Fiscal Impact." In *How to Measure the Fiscal Deficit: Analytical and Methodological Issues*, ed. Bléjer, Mario I., and Adrienne Cheasty, 363–89. Washington, DC: International Monetary Fund.

Trujillo, Lourdes, Emile Quinet, and Antonio Estache. 2002. "Dealing with Demand Forecasting Games in Transport Privatization." *Transport Policy* 9 (4): 325–34.

Tversky, Amos, and Craig R. Fox. 1995. "Weighing Risk and Uncertainty." *Psychological Review* 102 (2): 269–83.

Tversky, Amos, and Daniel Kahneman. 1992. Advances in Prospect Theory: Cumulative Representation of Uncertainty. *Journal of Risk and Uncertainty* 5 (4): 297–323.

Tversky, Amos, and Derek J. Koehler. 1994. "Support Theory: A Nonextensional Representation of Subjective Probability." *Psychological Review* 101: 547–67.

Veenendaal, Augustus J. 1995. "State versus Private Enterprise in Railway Building in the Netherlands, 1838–1938." *Business and Economic History* 24 (1): 186–93.

Vernon, Ray. 1971. *Sovereignty at Bay: The Multinational Spread of U.S. Enterprises.* New York: Basic Books.

Ville, Simon P. 1990. *Transport and the Development of the European Economy, 1750–1918.* New York: St. Martin's Press.

Walker, Charles. 1969. *Thomas Brassey: Railway Builder.* London: Frederick Muller.

Weinstein, Neil D. 1989. "Optimistic Biases about Personal Risks." *Science* 246 (4935): 1232–33.

Westwood, J. N. 1964. *A History of Russian Railways.* London: George Allen & Unwin.

———. 1974. *Railways of India.* London: David & Charles.

White, Gerald I., Ashwinpaul C. Sondhi, and Dov Fried. 1998. *Analysis and Use of Financial Statements.* 2nd ed. New York: John Wiley & Sons.

Whitman, Marina von Neumann. 1965. *Government Risk-Sharing in Foreign Investment.* Princeton, NJ: Princeton University Press.

Williamson, Oliver E. 1989. "Transaction Cost Economics." In *Handbook of Industrial Organization*, vol. 1, ed. Richard Schmalensee and Robert Willig, 135–82. Amsterdam: North-Holland.

Woods, H. Charles. 1917. "The Baghdad Railway and Its Tributaries." *Geographical Journal* 50 (1): 32–56.

World Bank. 2004a. *Averting an Infrastructure Crisis: A Framework for Policy and Action.* 2nd ed. Washington, DC: World Bank.

———. 2004b. *World Development Report: A Better Investment Climate for Everyone.* New York: Oxford University Press.

———. 2005. *Uruguay: Improving the Efficacy of Public Expenditures.* Report 30943-UY. Washington, DC: World Bank.

Wright, Brian D. 1993. "Public Insurance of Private Risks: Theory and Evidence from Agriculture." In *Government Risk-Bearing: Proceedings of a Conference Held at the Federal Reserve Bank of Cleveland, May 1991*, ed. Mark S. Sniderman, 45–65. Boston: Kluwer Academic Publishers.

Wright, Winthrop R. 1974. *British-Owned Railways in Argentina: Their Effect on the Growth of Economic Nationalism, 1854–1948.* Latin American Monograph 34. Austin, TX: University of Texas Press.

Yin, Shihong, and Calum G. Turvey. 2003. "The Pricing of Revenue Assurance: Comment." *American Journal of Agricultural Economics* 85 (4): 1062–65.

Young, George. 1906. *Corps de droit Ottoman: Recueil des codes, lois, règlements, ordonnances et actes les plus importants du droit intérieur, et d'études sur le droit coutumier de l'Empire Ottoman.* Oxford, U.K.: Clarendon Press.

Zeckhauser, Richard J., and W. Kip Viscusi. 1990. "Risk within Reason." *Science* 248 (4955): 559–64.

Zhuravlyov, V. V. 1983. "Private Railway Companies in Russia in the Early Twentieth Century." *Journal of Transport History* 4 (1): 51–66.

Index